世界各国风筝赛会

KITE FESTIVALS AND
COMPETITIONS IN THE WORLD

主编 张崇高

北方妇女儿童出版社

图书在版编目(CIP)数据

世界各国风筝赛会 / 张崇高著. -- 长春 : 北方妇
女儿童出版社, 2019.5
　　ISBN 978-7-5585-3585-7

　Ⅰ.①世… Ⅱ.①张… Ⅲ.①放风筝 – 运动会 – 介绍
– 世界 Ⅳ.①G898.171

　　中国版本图书馆 CIP 数据核字(2019)第 069577 号

出 版 人　刘　刚
责任编辑　张晓峰
封面设计　梁文道　程　静　秦杰杰
开　　本　710×1000mm　1/16
印　　张　28
字　　数　150 千字
印　　刷　廊坊市国彩印刷有限公司
版　　次　2019 年 5 月第 1 版
印　　次　2021 年 1 月第 2 次印刷

出　　版　北方妇女儿童出版社
发　　行　北方妇女儿童出版社
地　　址　长春市龙腾国际出版大厦
电　　话　编辑部:0431-81629613
　　　　　发行科:0431-81629633

定　　价　80.00 元

《世界各国风筝赛会》编辑委员会

序 言 PREFACE

刘北剑

由国际风筝联合会文化促进委员会编写的《世界各国风筝赛会》一书，全面系统地介绍了各国风筝赛会、中国各地风筝赛会，有代表性的风筝文化展馆、放飞场等场所设施，中外风筝之"最"，以潍坊为代表的中外风筝文化交流活动等。本书资料翔实，文风朴实，可读性强，值得阅读和收藏。

风筝的故乡在中国，潍坊是中国风筝的重要发祥地。据史料记载，世界上第一只木鸢风筝，是在 2400 多年前的春秋战国时期，能工巧匠鲁班在潍坊境内扎制并放飞成功的，"飞三日而不败"。2000 多年来，风筝文化不仅在中国大地传承发扬，而且漂洋过海，传到世界各地。

改革开放以来，在中国国家体育总局、国际风筝联合会、中国风筝协会共同推动下，中国的风筝运动和风筝产业，从内容到形式均得到了很大的提升和发展。潍坊市通过举办一年一度的国际风筝会，不仅促进了改革开放，提高了潍坊知名度和美誉度，而且有力地传承弘扬了风筝文化，普及提高了风筝运动水平，成为著名的世界风筝之都和国际风筝联合会总部所在地。中国各地的风筝文化传承，在最近 40 年来，也有了长足发展进步，涌现出一批有影响力的品牌赛会。在国外，多年来高水平的风筝运动以欧美发达国家为代表，以高端赛事和创新风筝为标志，使风筝运动不断向高层次迈进，不断满足人们对美好生活的追求。

风筝代表着希望，也是友谊和平的象征。如何推动风筝越飞越高，越飞越好，并赋予其更多的内涵和作用，值得风筝界同仁思考。立足于推动发展这样一项意义深远的美丽事业，我谨提出以下建议：

加强交流，互相学习。他山之石，可以攻玉。风筝界同仁要以开阔的视野，走向全国，走向世界，走向未来，"请进来走出去"，向国内外先进地区的同仁学习，学他人之长，补己之短。

突出赛事，打造品牌。风筝赛会对于促进风筝运动健康发展，具有重要的促进作用。各地举办的风筝赛会，要进一步增强文化技术内涵，加强赛事的规范化、国际化；在促进传统风筝运动发展的同时，不断创新拓展风筝运动的内容与形式，提升赛会品牌价值和内生动力，从而使风筝运动充满生机与活力。

整合资源，合作共赢。各地在打造特色品牌赛事过程中，要坚持开放办赛的思路，寻求与高端的赛事组织合作，寻求与有责任感、有竞争力的开发商、承办组织合作，寻求经济效益与社会效益的有机统一，大力协同，合作共赢。

加强研发，做强产业。风筝产业与风筝运动密切相关。在生活日益富足的今天，风筝产业发展前景更加广阔。要重视风筝研发的科技投入，加强风筝人才的培养，注册风筝的商标、专利，依法保护风筝知识产权；加强风筝产业全产业链的研究，搞好风筝产业基地建设，大力扶持风筝龙头企业，促进风筝产业高质量发展。

重视宣传，营造氛围。风筝赛会活动对于促进全民健身活动具有重要作用。各地风筝组织要充分认识做好宣传工作的重要性，切实增强与媒体打交道的自觉性和协同能力，既注重传统媒体，又注意融合运用新媒体，提高宣传实效，扩大风筝运动的社会影响力和社会认知度。

（作者系国家体育总局社会体育指导中心原副主任，国际风筝联合会副主席兼文化促进委员会主任，中国风筝协会主席）

Preface

Liu Beijian

The book titled Kite Competitions and Festivals in the World, compiled by the Cultural Promotion Committee of the International Kite Federation provides a comprehensive and systematic introduction to the kite competitions and festivals of various countries and the kite competitions and kite festivals around China, representative kite culture exhibition halls, flying fields and other facilities, top kites in China and overseas, and the Chinese and foreign kite cultural exchange activities represented by Weifang. The book is informative, simple and readable, and worth reading and collection.

The hometown of kites is China, and Weifang is an important birthplace of Chinese kites. According to historical records, the world's first wooden kite was made during the Spring and Autumn Period and the Warring States period more than 2,400 years ago. It was successfully made by the skilled craftsman Luban in Weifang and according to the record the kite had been flying for three days. Over the past 2,000 years' history, the kite culture has not only been carried forward in China, but also been spread across the sea and to all parts of the world.

Since the reform and opening up, under the joint promotion of the General Administration of Sport of China, the International Kite Federation and the China Kite Flying Association, the kite sport and kite industry in China have been greatly improved and developed from content to form. The success holding of the annual Weifang International Kite Festival not only promoted the opening, but also enhanced the popularity and reputation of Weifang. It also effectively passed on the kite culture, popularized the level of kite sports, and Weifang has become the famous capital of kite in the world and headquarter of International Kite Federation. The inheritance of kite culture throughout China has also made great progress in the past 40 years, and a number of influential brand competitions and festivals have emerged.

In foreign countries, represented by developed countries in Europe and America, high-level kite sports, with high-end events and innovative kites as symbols, have facilitated the kite sport to move towards a high level, and have been constantly satisfying people's pursuit of a better life.

Kites represent hope and it is a symbol of friendship and peace. It is worth thinking about how to promote the kite flying higher and higher, flying better and better, and to give it more connotation and role by the colleagues in the kite field. Based on the promotion of such a far-reaching and beautiful cause, I would like to make the following recommendations:

Strengthen exchanges. There is an old Chinese saying that one can learn from each other to make himself improve. The colleagues of the kite filed should have an open mind to go to the whole country, go to the world, and go to the future with a broad vision. We should learn from colleagues in advanced regions at home and abroad, learn the strengths of others, and make up for ourselves.

Highlight competition events and build famous brands. The kite competitions and festivals play an important role in promoting the healthy development of kite sports. The kite competitions and festivals held in various places should further enhance the cultural and technical connotation, strengthen the standardization and internationalization of the competitions, and promote the development of traditional kite sports, constantly innovate and expand the content and form of kite sports, and enhance the brand value and endogenous power of the competition, making the kite sport full of vitality.

Integrate resources and achieve win-win situation. In the process of creating a distinctive brand event, all localities must adhere to the idea of building an opening competition, seek cooperation with high-end events, and seek cooperation with responsible and competitive sponsors and undertaken parties to seek the unification of economic and social benefits, and carry out vigorous cooperation and achieve a win-win situation.

Strengthen R&D and strengthen the industry. The kite industry is closely related to kite sports. Nowadays, with the growing affluence of life, the development of the kite industry is becoming more and more promising. It is necessary to attach importance to the scientific and technological input of kite research and development, strengthen the training of kite talents, register the trademarks and patents of kites, protect the intellectual property rights of kites according to law, strengthen the research of the whole industry chain of the kite industry, do a good job in the construction of kite industry bases, vigorously support kite leading enterprises, and promote the kite industry to develop with high quality. Attach importance to propaganda and create an atmosphere of kite promotion. Kite competitions and festivals play an important role in promoting national fitness. All local kite organizations should fully understand the importance of propaganda, and effectively communicate with the media. They should not only pay attention to traditional media, but also to the integration of new media, improve the effectiveness of publicity, and expand the social influence of kite sports.

(The author of the preface is the former deputy director of the Leisure Sports Center of the General Administration of Sport of China, vice president of the International Kite Federation and director of the Cultural Promotion Association, and chairman of the China Kite Flying Association)

鲁班

风筝之始祖

目录
CONTENTS

第二章 中国风筝赛会
Kite Competitions and Festivals in China

目录

CONTENTS

第三章 中外风筝场馆设施
China and Foreign Kite Venues and Facilities

第四章 中外风筝之最
Top Kites in China and Overseas

目录 CONTENTS

第五章 中外风筝文化交流
Kite Cutural Exchange at Home and Abroad

目录

CONTENTS

第一章 外国风筝赛会

FOREIGN KITE COMPETITIONS AND FESTIVALS

004-056

美　国

美国国际风筝节由全美风筝协会同各州风筝协会轮流举办，每年一届，具体时间不固定，一般以举办地的适宜时节确定时间。风筝节由各州向世界各国发邀请，每届都有几个或十几个国家和地区的风筝代表队参加。美国的风筝爱好者队伍庞大，年销售风筝 1.5 亿只以上，每年参加国际风筝会的人达几万人。地方举办风筝节时同时举办各类喜庆活动。全美风筝活动比较活跃的城市有纽约、波士顿、华盛顿、西雅图等。

（一）圣地亚哥风筝节

圣地亚哥风筝节历史悠久，已有近 70 年历史，每年春季，在圣迭戈各大海滩举办风筝节。风筝节期间有放风筝比赛、创作风筝、装饰风筝展等。风筝节的活动具体内容有四大部分。一是风筝制作区，凡到场的小朋友都可以免费领取一份制作和放飞风筝的材料，现场制作后即可自由放飞。二是自由放飞区，自由制作和自行带去的风筝可以在此区自由放飞，大人小孩同乐，热闹非凡。三是专业放飞区，在这一区放飞的风筝稍为大型和漂亮。四是风筝特技比赛区，属于风筝节上"阳春白雪"的内容。风筝特技比赛有单人、双人和四人表演。音乐响起时，风筝随着音乐的起伏舒缓变化，时而翻滚，时而停顿，不断变换姿势，不断变换图形或队形。

（二）华盛顿州风筝节

华盛顿州国际风筝节是一个为期一周的集风筝表演、观赏、竞技于一身的庆祝活动，举办地点西雅图，举办时间是每年8月份的第三个星期。每天都有丰富多彩的活动，

包括风筝制作，放飞技巧培训，各种文艺表演，游戏和比赛等，吸引着成千上万的众多游客，参与到这场风筝盛事。

（三）加州圣拉蒙市艺术风筝节

加利福尼亚州圣拉蒙市艺术风筝节已举办多年，每届为期一

周，成为当地一大盛事，通过风筝展览、展销、公园放飞风筝等，吸引着大批市民和游客前来参与。

United States

The American International Kite Festival is held by the American Kitefliers Association and the State Kite Fliers Associations by turns annually. The specific time is not fixed. Generally, the time is determined by the appropriate time of the venue. The invitations of the festival are sent from the states to the countries of the world. Each time there are several or more than a dozen of national and regional kite delegations. There are a great number of kite fans in the United States. More than 150 million kites are sold annually, and tens of thousands of people attend the International Kite Festival every year. Various festivals are held at the same time when the kite festival is held in the local area. The most active cities of kite events in the United States are New York, Boston, Washington, and Seattle, etc.

(1) San Diego Kite Festival

The San Diego Kite Festival has a long history of nearly 70 years. Every spring, the kite festival is held on the vast beaches of San Diego. During the kite festival, there are kite-flying competitions, kite creation, and decorative kites expo, etc. There are four major sections of the kite festival. The first section is the kite making area. All the children present can receive a set of kite materials for free. They can make their kites and then fly them. The second section is the free flying zone. The kites that are produced for free on site or brought by the fliers can fly in this area. Adults and children are usually very happy and lively. The third section is the professional fly area. The kites fly in this area are larger and more beautiful. The fourth section is the kite stunt competition area, which is more professional on the kite festival. The kite stunt competition has single, double and four people performances. The kite flies up and down with the changing of the music, sometimes rolling, sometimes pauses, and constantly changing its postures, graphics or formations.

(2)Washington State International Kite Festival

The Washington State International Kite Festival is a one-week celebration event of kite show, watching and competition. It is held in Seattle in the third week of August each year. During the festival, there are a variety of activities, including kite making, flying skills training, various cultural performances, games and competitions every day, attracting thousands of tourists participating in this kite event.

(3)San Ramon Art Kite Festival in California

The San Ramon Art Kite Festival in California has been held for many years and has become a major event in the region. It attracts a large number of citizens and tourists through kite exhibitions, sales and flying in the parks.

法 国

法国风筝运动比较普及，许多城市都举办各种类型的风筝比赛、表演活动，如迪耶普国际风筝节，贝尔克国际风筝节，都是著名的国际性风筝赛会，有着较高的知名度和影响力。

（一）迪耶普国际风筝节

迪耶普国际风筝节创建于 1978 年，每两年举办一次。是欧洲规模最大，也是世界三大风筝节之一，每年 9 月在法国大西洋海滨古城迪耶普举行。吸引着 30 多个国家地区，数百名选手和数千名业余选手参加，近 50 万游客来迪耶普观看风筝大赛。

届时，在迪耶普靠海约 8 公顷的草坪上，来自世界各国的专业选手和风筝爱好者们，借着大西洋的秋风，尽情放飞五彩斑斓的风筝，展示不同国家和地区的文化风情。现场还有多个观摩风筝助阵表演，其中的动漫风筝声色并茂，十分有趣。

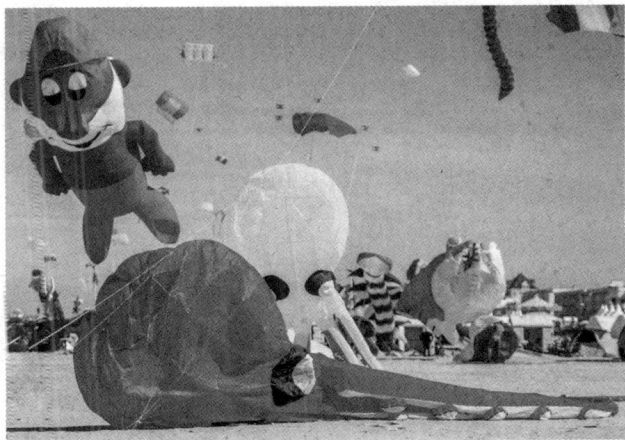

迪耶普国际风筝节最主要的特点就是它的国际化，每届比赛都邀请 30 多个国家地区的选手参加。对于各国的风筝爱好者来说，这是个展现各国不同风筝文化和相互学习交流的宝贵机会。

（二）贝尔克国际风筝节

　　贝尔克国际风筝节由贝尔克旅游局承办，地点设在贝尔克市，是世界上规模最大的风筝节之一，每一届风筝节都会吸引世界各地的风筝高手参赛。

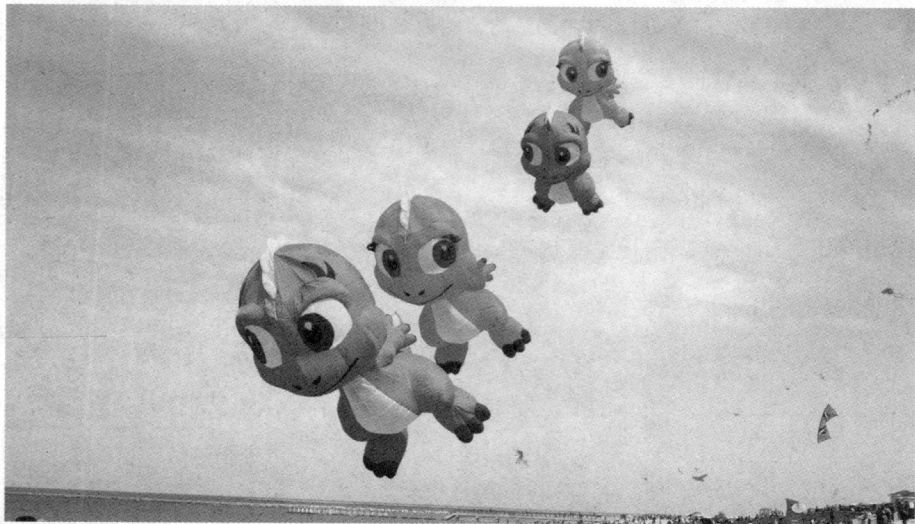

France

Kite sports are popular in France. Various types of kite competitions, performances and events were held in many cities, such as the Dieppe International Kite Festival and the Berck International Kite Festival, which are famous international kites and have a high reputation and influence.

(1)Dieppe International Kite Festival

The Dieppe International Kite Festival was created in 1978 and was held every two years. It is the largest in Europe and one of the three major kite festivals in the world. It is held in Dieppe, the ancient seaside city of Atlantic Ocean in France every September. It attracts more than hundreds of players and thousands of amateurs from over 30 countries and regions every year and nearly five hundred thousand tourists to Dieppe to watch the kite contest.

During that time, on the 8 hectares of grass on the seaside in Dieppe, professional players and kite enthusiasts from all over the world enjoy the colorful kites flying and show the cultural customs of different countries and regions in the autumn wind of the Atlantic Ocean. There are also a number of kite shows, and the anime kites are very interesting.

The main feature of the Dieppe International Kite Festival is its internationalization. In each competition, players from more than 30 countries and regions are invited to participate in the event. For kite enthusiasts from all over the world, this is a valuable opportunity to show the different kite cultures and have mutual learning and exchanges among different countries.

(2)Berck International Kite Festival

The Berck International Kite Festival is hosted by the Berck Tourism Bureau and is held in the city of Berck. It is one of the largest kite festivals in the world. The kite festival attracts many kites masters from all over the world.

英 国

20世纪初，英国大英航空协会曾多次举办风筝赛会，在第二次世界大战期间，英国曾用风筝载人监视德国潜艇的活动。20世纪40年代英国海军为防空，将风筝放于驱逐舰上。英国风筝玩赏协会设在伦敦。20世纪70年代，英国用玻璃钢、石墨碳纤维等轻型材料制作风筝，飞行效果非常好。如今，在英国举行的风筝节中，能看到各种超出人们想象的风筝动物造型，简直如同空中的"动物世界"。

（一）布里斯托尔国际风筝节

布里斯托尔国际风筝节是由马丁·莱斯特（Martin Lester）、约翰·佩顿（ John Peyton）和阿夫里尔·贝克（Avril Baker）三位好友共同发起的。在为当地某大会举办过一次成功的风筝展后，他们便有了筹办一个正式风筝节的想法。虽然首届风筝节的预算只有300英镑（约合人民币2854元），但如今它已成功举办30届，是当地最大的节日之一，吸引着数以千计的游客。

（二）朴茨茅斯国际风筝节

朴茨茅斯国际风筝节是全世界规模最大的风筝节之一，至今已成功举办了27届。国际风筝节内容琳琅满目，有风筝大赛，风筝展览，慈善风筝表演，少儿风筝学艺，风筝售卖，自由放飞等。风筝大赛每届吸引了来自英国、中国、法国、德国、澳大利亚、荷兰、瑞士、马来西亚、加拿大、美国、南非等数十个国家的数百名风筝高手参加，他们八仙过海，各显神通。

United Kingdom

At the beginning of the 20th century, the British Airways Association held many kite competitions. During the Second World War, the United Kingdom used kites to carry people to monitor German submarines. In the 1940s, the British Navy flew kites as air defense on the destroyers. The British Kite Tour Association is based in London. In the 1970s, the people in the United Kingdom made kites with light materials such as FRP and graphite carbon fiber etc, and the flight effect was very good. Nowadays, in the kite festival held in the UK, you can see all kinds of kite animals that are beyond people's imagination. It is like an animal world in the air.

(1)Bristol International Kite Festival

The Bristol International Kite Festival was launched by three friends, Martin Lester, John Peyton and Avril Baker. After a successful kite show for a local conference, they had the idea of organizing a formal kite festival. Although the budget for the first kite festival is only £300 (about RMB 2,854), it has been successfully held for 30 sessions and is one of the largest festivals in the region, attracting thousands of visitors.

(2)Portsmouth International Kite Festival

The Portsmouth International Kite Festival is one of the largest kite festivals in the world and has been successfully held for 27 sessions. There are a series of activities on the festival, including kite contests, kite exhibitions, charity kite performances, kite learning by children, kite sales, free flying etc. The kite festival attracts hundreds of kite masters from more than a dozen of countries including the United Kingdom, China, France, Germany, Australia, the Netherlands, Switzerland, Malaysia, Canada, the United States, and South Africa, etc. They show their kites and talents here.

澳大利亚

澳大利亚各种风筝赛事活动经常举办，吸引着当地市民和外国游客踊跃参加。

（一）悉尼邦迪海滩风筝节

一年一度的悉尼邦迪海滩风筝节，是澳大利亚新威尔斯悉尼春天最大的节日。举办点位于悉尼的邦迪海滩，每到这个时候来自世界各地的风筝爱好者都会聚集在此，届时不仅有风筝，还有各种娱乐活动和美食活动，至今已成功举办了 40 届。

邦迪海滩风筝节是以放飞风筝的形式迎接春天到来，是澳大利亚最大的放风筝盛事，每年都吸引数万当地民众、游客和海外风筝爱好者的参与和观看。每次放飞的风筝都千姿百态、五彩缤纷。来自澳大利亚风筝协会和海外风筝爱好者展示了他们手工制作的各种各样的风筝，展示了他们娴熟高超的风筝放飞技术。

（二）澳大利亚国际风筝节

澳大利亚国际风筝节是澳洲最大的风筝节，诞生于 1997 年，每年的 4 月中旬，在南澳大利亚首府阿德莱德举行，为期 3 天，游客很多。为期三天的节日里，来自各国的专业风筝高手一展风采。主办方通过观众的尖叫声来评判各款风筝的支持度。

Australia

Various kite events are held frequently in Australia, attracting lots of local citizens and foreign tourists.

(1)Festival of the Winds on the Bondi Beach of Sydney

The annual Festival of the Winds is the biggest festival in Sydney, New South Wales, Australia. The venue is held in Bondi Beach, Sydney. At that time, kite fans from all over the world gather here. There will be not only kites, but also various entertainment activities and food events. The event has been successfully held for 40 sessions.

The Bondi Beach Kite Festival is held in spring. It is the largest kite-flying event in Australia, attracting tens of thousands of locals, tourists and overseas kite fans every year. The kites are of different varieties and colors. The Australian Kiteflyers Society and overseas kite fans show various handcrafted kites and highly skilled kite flying technology.

(2)International Kite Festival in Australia

The International Kite Festival is the largest kite festival in Australia. It was initiated in 1997. It is held in Adelaide, the capital of South Australia, in mid-April every year. It lasts for three days and attracts a great number of tourists. During the three-day festival, professional kite players showed their talents. The organizers judged the supporting degree of each kite through the screams of the audience.

新西兰

新西兰风筝比赛和表演活动众多，各地经常举办此类活动，其中奥塔基国际风筝节和基督城风筝节都是比较有名的国际风筝盛会。

（一）奥塔基国际风筝节

奥塔基国际风筝节由奥塔基促进委员会主办，是新西兰规模最大、影响力最广泛、受众满意度最高的风筝节，也是国际风筝爱好者的年度狂欢盛事。每一届风筝节都有数万人参加，30多个独立方阵参加风筝放飞活动。近年来，主办方邀请中国、德国、澳大利亚、马来西亚等国家的风筝协会及爱好者都参加奥塔基风筝节，进一步拓展了该风筝节的国际化程度。

（二）基督城风筝节

新西兰基督城的夏天也有着一年一度的风筝节。由基督城市政府主办的风筝节已经举办13届，每年都吸引上万民众前来，New Brighton海滩上空色彩缤纷，形态各异的海洋生物，以及卡通，神马、老虎等都翱翔在蓝天白云里。

New Zealand

There are numerous kite competitions and performances in New Zealand, and such events are often held throughout the country, among which the Otaki Kite Festival and the Christchurch Kite Festival are the more famous international kite festivals.

(1) Otaki Kite Festival

Organized by the Otaki Promotion Committee, the Otaki Kite Festival is the largest, most influential and popular kite festival in New Zealand. And it is an annual carnival event for international kite enthusiasts. Tens of thousands of people participated in each kite festival, and more than 30 independent square arrays participated in kite flying activities. In recent years, the organizer invited kite associations and enthusiasts from China, Germany, Australia, Malaysia and other countries to participate in the festival to further expand the internationalization of the kite festival.

(2)Christchurch Kite Festival

There is also an annual kite festival in Christchurch, New Zealand in summer. The festival, hosted by the Christchurch City Government, attracting tens of thousands of people every year, has been held for 13 sessions. Colorful and diversified marine life, cartoons, horses and tigers kites fly in the blue sky and white clouds of New Brighton beach each year.

日 本

放风筝在日本是一项普及性较高的休闲娱乐活动，在不少中小学校也都开设有风筝扎制技艺的课程。每年日本全国各地，都有级别不同的风筝比赛和表演活动。据日本书中记载，风筝是在公元794年从中国传入。日本风筝骨架与中国类似，多用竹条或柏木等，面料多用和纸（似中国宣纸），彩绘也与中国类似。在日本，风筝不仅是求喜庆、庆丰收，也有为占卜的目的，有的地方更是将放风筝作为男女青年联姻的手段。日本风筝协会于1969年成立，该会会员大都是制作放飞风筝的能手。每年一度的东京新春风筝会是最为壮观、最有影响的，吸引着无数国内外高手前去参赛。

（一）日本滨松风筝节

日本滨松风筝节比赛，起源于16世纪，每年5月3日、4日和5日，在静冈县滨松市举办的"滨松风筝节"都会上演"放风筝比赛"，比赛在可望见远州滩的日本三大沙丘之一的"中田岛沙丘"进行，人们相互拉扯风筝，通过摩擦风筝线展开强弱之争，看看谁的风筝最坚固。5毫米粗麻线制的风筝绳纠缠在一起，利用摩擦割断对手绳线的畅快淋漓感，是比赛的魅力所在。

（二）日本春日部风筝节

日本春日部风筝节至今已有174年的历史，每年的5月3日和5月5日举行。在春日部风筝节上放的风筝属于日本国内的最大级别，长15m，宽11m，重800kg，在每秒7m风速以上的前提下，至少需要100人才能将这个巨大的风筝放到天上。春日部市位于东京北面埼玉县的东部，距离东京约40km，人口不足24万，在日本算是靠近东京近郊的一个小城市。风筝节的放飞场位于春日部市庄和町的江户川河畔。

（三）日本白根巨型风筝会

日本新潟县白根大风筝比赛始于江户时代，拥有300多年的历史。在新潟县南区中口川举行的巨型风筝比赛，人们在河两岸放飞起了每一只巨型风筝，每只风筝都足有24张榻榻米之大。当两只风筝的风筝线互相交缠在

一起后，双方就开始互相拉拽，先把对方的风筝线摩擦断的一方获胜。在空中悠然飘舞的两只巨型风筝的激烈的攻防战显得魄力十足。进入到互相对抗的阶段，观众也可以加入其中。游客和当地居民融为一体，共同分享胜利的喜悦，这也是在其他活动中不能体验到的独特魅力。

风筝大赛的第一天，将在市内举行风筝游行活动，以展示此次参加比赛的所有巨型风筝。届时还举办烟火大会，使人们既可以感受到盛大节日的欢乐气氛，又能体验到日本的传统文化。

Japan

Flying kite is a popular leisure activity in Japan, and many schools have courses of kite-making skills. Every year, there are different levels of kite competitions and performances throughout Japan. According to the recording of Japanese books, kites were introduced from China in 794 AD. The skeleton of Japanese kite is similar to that of China. It uses bamboo or cypress wood etc, and the fabric is mostly washi, a kind of Japan paper (like Chinese art paper). The painting is similar to that of China, too. In Japan, kites are not only for praying for joyfulness and celebration of good harvest, but also for the purpose of divination. In some places, kite flying is used as a means of allied marriage between young men and women. The Japan Kite Association was established in 1969. Most of its members are experts in making and flying kites. The annual Tokyo Spring Kite Festival is the most spectacular and influential festival, which attracts many domestic and foreign experts.

(1)Hamamatsu Kite Festival in Japan

The Hamamatsu Kite Festival in Japan originated in the 16th century. On May 3rd, 4th and 5th every year, the Hamamatsu Kite Festival is held in Hamamatsu, Shizuoka. There is kite flying competition on the festival. The competition is held on the Nakatajima Dunes, one of Japan's three major dunes. On the island, people can see the Enshuu-nada. People pull the threads of kites and fight against each other by cutting the kite string the opponent to see whose kite is the strongest. The kite string with 5mm diameter is entangled together, and they cut off each other by friction. The charm of the competition lies in the process of cutting off your competitors' string.

(2)Japanese Kasuga Kite Festival

The Kasuga Kite Festival in Japan has 174 years' history and is held every year from May 3 to May 5. One of the kites at the Kasuga festival is the largest in Japan. It is 15 meters long, 11 meters wide and weighs 800kg. At a speed of 7m per second or more, at least 100 people are need to put this huge kite into the sky. Kasuga is located in the eastern part of Saitama to the north of Tokyo. It is about 40km from Tokyo and has a population of less than 240,000. It is a small city near suburbs of Tokyo in Japan. The flying field of the kite festival is located on the banks of the Edo-gawa River of Kasuga.

(3)Giant Kite Festival in Shirane, Japan

The Giant Kite Festival in Shirane, Niigata, Japan began in the Edo period and has a history of more than 300 years. In the giant kite competition held in the southern district of Niigata, people fly giant kites on both sides of the river. Each kite has a size of more than 24 tatami mats. When the lines of the two kites are intertwined with each other, the two sides begin to pull the lines, and the party that first cuts the other's kite line wins. The fierce offensive and defensive battles of the two giant kites in the air seemed to be full of power. When entering the stage of confrontation, the audience can also join the event. Visitors and local residents play together to share the joy of victory, which is also a unique charm that cannot be experienced in other activities.

On the first day of the kite competition, a kite parade will be held in the city to show all the giant kites that will participate in the competition. A fireworks display will be held at that time, during which one will not only feel the joyful atmosphere of the grand festival, but also experience the traditional culture of Japan.

俄 罗 斯

俄罗斯风筝节活动较多，每年在全国许多地方都举办丰富多彩的风筝放飞表演活动。

（一）彩色天空风筝节

彩色天空风筝节，是为庆祝秋天的到来而举办的盛会，每年举办两次，至今已有 15 年的历史，举办地点在莫斯科察里津诺公园。精彩的风筝特技表演，每年都吸引众多市民和游客参与。

（二）哈巴罗夫斯克风筝节

哈巴罗夫斯克风筝节，在每年 5 月底的周末举行，为期两天，举办地点选在阿穆尔河畔的风景区，吸引不计其数的当地百姓、远东其他地区慕名而来的观光客以及亚太地区外国代表竞相参与和观看。

Russia

There are many kite festival events in Russia. And a variety of kite flying performances are held every year in many parts of the country.

(1)Colourful Sky Kite Festival

It is a grand gathering held in celebration of the coming of autumn. It is held twice a year and has a history of 15 years. It is held in the Tsaritsyno Park in Moscow. Wonderful kite stunts attract many citizens and visitors every year.

(2)Habarovsk Kite Festival

The Habarovsk Kite Festival is held on the weekend at the end of May annually, and lasts for two days. It is held in a scenic area along the Amur River, attracting countless local people, tourists from other parts of the Far East and foreign representatives from the Asia-Pacific region.

韩 国

韩国放风筝有着悠久的历史传承，成为民间一项重要的风俗。每年正月十五这一天是放风筝的节日，举办风筝比赛会，是送厄消灾的吉祥日。首尔、平昌、义城等多地均有开展风筝放飞表演比赛等活动，韩国风协等组织机构经常组织全国性和国际性的风筝比赛。

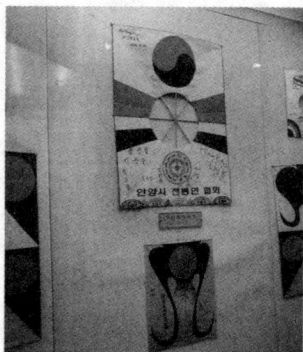

韩国风筝相传是佛教徒传入的，风筝的材料与中国类似，多以竹条、柏木和高丽纸制作。受中国文化的影响，绘画内容都具有浓郁的中国文化色彩，像太极八卦图、十二生肖、中国花鸟等。

在古代，韩国人民把"送厄迎福"等字样写在风筝尾部，然后把它放掉。取"去厄消灾"之意。近几年还兴起一种"打斗风筝"，风筝线为特制的，在放飞时，以相互割断对方线为胜。风筝的结构虽较简单，但做工认真，很能体现出韩国精神。

镜浦台沙滩风筝节
Gyeongpodae Beach Kite Festival

韩国义城国际风筝节
Korea Uiseong-gun International
Kite Festival

Republic of Korea

Kite flying has a long history and has become an important custom of the people in the Republic of Korea. On the 15th day of the first lunar month, it is a festival of flying kites. Kite competition will be held. And it is an auspicious day for sending disasters. In Seoul, Pyeongchang, and Uisong, there are many activities such as kite flying shows and competitions. Organizations such as the Korea Kite Association often organize national and international kite competitions.

It is said that the Korean kite is introduced in by Buddhists. The material of kite is similar to that of China, and the kite is usually made of bamboo, cypress and Korean paper. Influenced by Chinese culture, the painting content has a strong Chinese cultural characteristic. The typical paintings are the Supreme Ultimate and the Eight Diagrams, twelve zodiac, Chinese flowers and birds, etc.

In ancient times, the Korean people wrote the words "sending off disasters and greeting the blessings" to the tail of the kite and then let the kite fly away, the action of which means sending off the disaster. In recent years, the fighting kite has become more and more popular. The kite line is specially made. The kite will win through cutting the line of each other when flying. Although the structure of the kite is relatively simple, the manual work is careful, which can reflect the spirit of Korea.

印 度

放飞风筝在印度民间有着广泛的群众性，每年在不同城市都举办各种风筝展示展览和放飞表演活动，风筝爱好者和市民、游客参与的热情很高。放风筝也成为印度人最常见的休闲方式之一。印度的风筝节最著名的是玛克桑格拉提风筝节，每年1月14日丰收节前举办，以庆祝冬季的结束，迎接美好季节的来临。 风筝节吸引了来自中国、英国、德国、希腊、马来西亚等国家的众多风筝爱好者参与，大放异彩。1月14日风筝节最后一天，又是丰收节，人们放飞几百万只风筝，形成一道空中奇观。

India

Flying kites is very popular in the folk of India. Every year, various kite exhibitions and kite flying performances are held in different cities. The kite enthusiasts, citizens and tourists like the events very much. Flying kites has also become one of the most common leisure means for Indians. The most famous kite festival in India is the Makar Sankranti International Kite Festival, which is held every year before the harvest festival on January 14th to celebrate the end of the winter and welcome the coming of the beautiful season. The kite festival attracts many kite enthusiasts from China, UK, Germany, Greece, Malaysia and other countries. The last day of the festival, 14th Jan, was also the harvest festival. People fly millions of kites to form an aerial spectacle.

加 拿 大

加拿大各地每年都举行风筝放飞表演和比赛，规模档次不一的风筝节，吸引着当地市民和外地游客广泛参与。

（一）多伦多风筝节

多伦多风筝节由多伦多集贤会主办，每年9月中旬在士嘉堡美丽径公园举行，已举行了近20年，是加拿大最大型的风筝盛事，主要是进行

各种风筝的放飞表演。一年一度的多伦多风筝节，吸引着数万人参与。

（二）温哥华环太平洋风筝节

温哥华环太平洋风筝节每年6月举行，至今已举办了43届，来自加拿大各地的风筝爱好者和国外风筝高手共同放飞各自制作的风筝，展示风筝的独特设计和放飞风筝的技巧。

Canada

Kite flying demonstrations and competitions are held every year throughout Canada. The kite festivals of different scales attract lots of local citizens and foreign visitors.

(1) Toronto Kite Festival

Hosted by the Mandarin Club of Toronto, the Toronto Kite Festival is held in Milliken District Park of Scarborough in mid-September annually. It has been held for nearly 20 sessions and is the largest kite event in Canada, mainly for the flying show of various kites. The annual Toronto Kite Festival attracts tens of thousands of people.

(2) Vancouver Pacific Rim Kite Festival

The Vancouver Pacific Rim Kite Festival is held every June and has been held for 43 sessions. Kite fans from all over Canada and foreign kite masters fly their kites to show the unique design of kites and the skills of flying.

马来西亚

马来西亚在每年4月份稻田收割之后都会举行风筝放飞活动，以示庆丰收，向稻神致敬。马来西亚人喜欢鹰、猫、鱼、青蛙、孔雀等风筝，更喜欢月亮风筝，也称"月筝"，其形状有新月形，半月形和满月形等，别具特色。对马来西亚人民来说，放风筝是为了敬神，因此风筝的制作与放飞都应严肃认真，不得马虎从事。马来西亚人也把风筝作为装饰品，常把美丽精致的风筝悬挂在家中美化房间。

月亮风筝（马来西亚）
Moon Kite (Malaysia)

自1995年开始举办的柔佛州巴西古当国际风筝节，每年吸引数万名世界各地游客到访。这项类似嘉年华会的活动，不仅颠覆了多数人对风筝的认知，也为现场的游客们找回童年时的快乐回忆。马来西亚旅游局希望借此吸引更多游客赴该国旅游，让游客享受追风的乐趣，体验飞翔的快乐。

Malaysia

There is a kite-flying activity in Malaysia after the harvest of rice in April annually to show a good harvest and pay tribute to God of Rice. Malaysians like kites with a shape of hawks, cats, fish, frogs, peacocks, etc. They prefer moon kites, with a shape of a crescent, half moon or full moon. For the Malaysian people, flying kites is worship of the gods, so the production and flying of kites should be serious and careful. Malaysians also use kites as decorations, and they often hang beautiful and delicate kites at home to beautify the room.

The Pasir Gudang International Festival in Johore, initiated in 1995, attracts tens of thousands of visitors from around the world every year. This event is something like carnival, and it not only changes the majority of people's knowledge of kites, but also helps visitors to find happy memories of childhood. The Malaysia Tourism Promotion Board hopes to attract more tourists and let the tourists enjoy the fun of the kite and experience the joy of flying.

新加坡

风筝放飞表演活动在新加坡很受欢迎，每年在各地都组织各种形式的风筝展览展示、风筝比赛和表演活动，吸引着大量市民和游客参加。

新加坡风筝飞"乐"（Fun Flying）活动，是本地最大型的风筝节之一，由新加坡公用事业局主办，在滨海堤坝已经成功举办了8届。新加坡风筝协会负责邀请各国的风筝发烧友，帮助普及本地风筝运动。每一届风筝节，除了邀请中国、美国、日本、菲律宾、马来西亚、印度尼西亚、瑞典和德国等的风筝高手呈献各种精彩的特技表演外，市民和游客还可现场索取免费风筝，体验放风筝的乐趣，或参加一系列的相关活动，譬如制作风筝等。

Singapore

The kite-flying performance is very popular in Singapore. Every year, various forms of kite exhibitions, kite competitions and performances are organized, attracting a large number of citizens and tourists.

The Singapore Fun Flying is one of the largest local kite festivals. It is hosted by PUB Singapore and has been successfully held for 8 sessions in the Marina Barrage. The Singapore Kite Fliers Association is responsible for inviting kite fans from all over the world to popularize the local kite sport. In each kite festival, in addition to inviting kites masters from China, the United States, Japan, the Philippines, Malaysia, Indonesia, Sweden and Germany to present a variety of exciting stunts, citizens and tourists can also ask for free kites and have fun of kite flying, and participate in a series of related activities, such as making kites in the festival.

德 国

德国的风筝运动拥有广泛的爱好者，每年全国各地都举办丰富多彩的风筝节，吸引着本地市民和广大游客踊跃参与。德国的运动风筝和创新风筝在国际上有着重要影响。

（一）柏林风筝节

柏林风筝节已连续成功举办 7 届，每年都吸引着来自世界各地的游客前来观看这场风筝盛宴。活动举办地是一处军事遗址，曾经也被用作过机场，现如今被改造成一个占地面积约 355 公顷的公园，它也是世界上最大的市中心公园之一。

（二）库克斯风筝节

在德国北部海港城市库克斯，已连续成功举办了 17 届风筝节。每一届风筝节，都有上百个颜色各异、样式新颖的风筝出现在城市上空 ，如七星瓢虫、蜜蜂这种昆虫造型的，还有德国人喜欢的狗熊造型等风筝。不过最吸引眼球的还是来自中国的蜈蚣风筝，腾空而起的巨龙风筝给当地增添了一道靓丽的风景。

Germany

There is a wide range of enthusiasts for kite sport in Germany. Every year, a variety of kite festivals are held throughout the country, attracting local citizens and tourists. Sports kites and innovative kites of Germany have an important international influence.

(1)Berlin Kite Festival

The Berlin Kite Festival has been successfully held for 7 consecutive years, attracting visitors from all over the world to witness this kite event every year. The event is held on a military ruins site that was once used as an airport, and is now converted into a park of approximately 355 hectares. It is also one of the largest downtown parks in the world.

(2) Cux Kite Festival

In the northern port city Cux of Germany, the kite festival has been successfully held for 17 consecutive years. At each kite festival, there are hundreds of kites of different colors and styles appearing in the sky above the city, such as the seven-star locusts, bees, insects, as well as the bear kite which the Germans like. However, the most eye-catching one is the kite from China. The dragon-head and centipede-body kite from China added beautiful scenery to the festival.

丹 麦

丹麦每年都举行国际风筝节，已经举办了
33 届。该风筝节由德国人沃尔福冈于 1985 年
创办，后来演变发展为国际活动，目前官方活
动为 3 天，持续两个星期，期间，除放飞表演
外，各种派对、拍卖等活动也陆续登场。

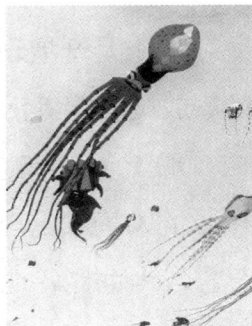

参加放飞的风筝体积几乎都相当庞大，巨
大的八爪鱼，可爱的卡通造型，色彩缤纷的风筝让游客大饱眼福。

这项活动在每年 6 月于丹麦日德兰半岛西岸的凡岛（Fanoe）
举行。6 月份的凡岛风大天晴，整个西岸就是一望无垠的沙
滩。就是这样的地形和气候，造就了凡岛国际风筝节（Fanoe
International Kite Fliers Meeting），每年都吸引挪威、日本、
马来西亚等不同国家地区的数千名风筝高手远道而来。

Denmark

The Kite Flying Festival is held annually in Denmark and has been held
for 33 sessions. The kite festival was founded in 1985 by the German
Wolfgang, and later it evolved into an international event. Currently the
official event lasts for three days. During two weeks' time cover this
period, there will be kite flying show, various parties and auctions.

The kites for the flying are almost quite large, such as huge octopus and
cute cartoons. These colorful kites greatly satisfy the tourists.

The event takes place every June in Fanoe, on the west coast of the Jutland
Peninsula in Denmark. In June, the wind of Fanoe Island is fine for flying
kites, and the entire west bank is a vast beach. It is such appropriate
terrain and climate that have created the Fanoe International Kite Fliers
Meeting, attracting thousands of kite masters from different countries
such as Norway, Japan and Malaysia etc every year.

瑞 士

瑞士是开展现代风筝运动比较普及的国家，每年各地都举办风筝放飞表演等活动。

瑞士于 1985 年在苏黎世湖首次举办了国际风筝会，期间还开展了风筝放飞理论和技术研究讨论会。还出版了《瑞士风筝》杂志，为世界各地的风筝爱好者提供了一个交流的平台。

瑞士高山风筝节，由当地一家主题俱乐部主办，每年一届，至今已成功举办了 23 届，每一届都有来自英国、比利时、丹麦、挪威等欧洲的大批风筝高手参加，在国际上有较高的知名度和影响力。在海拔2332米的高山上放飞风筝难度很大，挑战性强。各种风筝在雪山之巅轻舞飞扬，成为当地一道独特的风景线。

Switzerland

Switzerland is a country where modern kite sports are popular, and kite flying shows are held every year in many places.

The International Kite Festival was firstly hosted along the lakeside of Lake Zurich in Switzerland in 1985, during which time the Kite Flying Theory and Technology Research Seminar was held. Also the Swiss Kite magazine was published, which provided a platform for exchange among kite enthusiasts around the world.

The Swiss High Mountain Kite Festival is hosted by a local theme club. It has been held annually and has been successfully held for 23 sessions. On each festival, a large number of kite masters from Europe, including the United Kingdom, Belgium, Denmark, Norway and other countries participate in it. It has a high popularity and influence internationally. It is very difficult and challenging to fly a kite on a mountain at an altitude of 2,332 meters. All kinds of kites flew in the snow-capped mountains and became a unique landscape.

南 非

南非风筝放飞和表演活动近年来不断发展，比较有影响的是开普敦的国际风筝节活动。

（一）开普敦国际风筝节

开普敦国际风筝节每届为期2天，至今已成功举办24届，每一届都吸引数百名来自世界各地的风筝爱好者参加，而活动收入用于向贫困人群提供心理健康服务。

（二）首届中国 - 南非风筝节

首届中国—南非风筝节于2018年10月27日在开普敦举行，为2018年"欢乐春节嘉年华"系列活动拉开了序幕。2018年恰逢中南建交20周年，此次活动更增添了政治意义。

本届风筝节在开普敦的绿点公园举行。在8000平方米的绿色草坪上，来自世界风筝都中国潍坊的代表团和南非风筝协会的风筝专家们放飞了一个个具有中南文化元素的风筝，吸引了不少开普敦市民驻足观看，赢得了阵阵掌声。

South Africa

In South Africa, kite flying and performance activities have continued to develop in recent years, and one of the most influential event is the Cape Town Kite Festival.

(1)Cape Town Kite Festival

The Cape Town Kite Festival lasts for 2 days and has been successfully held for 24 sessions. The festival attracts hundreds of kite enthusiasts from all over the world, and the income of the event is used for providing mental health services to the poor.

(2)First China-South Africa Kite Festival

The first China-South Africa Kite Festival was held in Cape Town on October 27, 2018, and kicked off the 2018 Happy Spring Festival Carnival series events. It is the 20th anniversary of the establishment of diplomatic relations between China and South Africa in 2018, so political significance has been added to the event.

The kite festival was held at Green Point Park in Cape Town. On the 8,000 square meter green lawn, the delegation from Weifang, the capital of kite in the world, and the kite experts from the South African Kite Fliers Association flew kites with elements of China and South Africa cultural elements, attracted many Cape Town citizens and visitors.

印度尼西亚

印度尼西亚各类风筝文化活动比较普及，全国各地每年都举办各种风筝放飞表演和风筝比赛活动。

（一）雅加达国际风筝节

雅加达国际风筝节至今已成功举办了 24 届。每年的雅加达国际风筝节，在雅加达最大的海滩主题公园安佐尔举行，吸引了当地风筝爱好者和国际上众多的风筝高手参加。

（二）庞岸达兰国际风筝节

庞岸达兰国际风筝节在印度尼西亚西爪哇省的庞岸达兰（Pangandaran）县南部海滩举行，来自印尼及全球多个国家的成百上千只风筝在蓝天上一展风采。国际风筝节涵盖多个项目的竞赛，包括传统风筝类、现代风筝类、平面风

筝类、立体风筝类、六角风筝类等。风筝节期间还将举办风筝展览、风筝制作比赛、风筝绘画比赛、文艺表演等活动，另外风筝爱好者还可以欣赏到主办方准备的夜间风筝秀。

（三）巴厘岛风筝节

巴厘岛风筝节每年七八月间风季开始时举行，是巴厘岛省重大节日亮点之一，独特的文化场景与之前的巴厘岛艺术节交相辉映。通常会在沙努尔以北的 Padanggalak 东海岸举行，具体日期根据有利的天气条件确定。风筝节汇聚了岛上数百支竞赛风筝队伍放飞传统风筝，除此之外还有国际团队放飞表演造型各异的现代风筝。

Indonesia

Various kite cultural activities in Indonesia are relatively popular, and many kite flying performances and kite competitions are held every year throughout the country.

(1) Jakarta International Kite Festival

The Jakarta International Kite Festival has been successfully held for 24 sessions. The annual Jakarta International Kite Festival, held in Ancol, Jakarta's largest beach theme park, attracts local kite enthusiasts and many international kite masters.

(2) Pangandaran International Kite Festival

The Pangandaran International Kite Festival is held in the southern beaches of Pangandaran, West Java, Indonesia. Hundreds and thousands of kites from Indonesia and many countries around the world fly in the blue sky. The International Kite Festival covers many competitions, including traditional kites, modern kites, plane kites, three-dimensional kites, and hexagonal kite competitions, etc. During the kite festival, kite exhibitions, kite making competitions, kite painting competitions, cultural performances and other activities are held. In addition, kite fans can also enjoy the night kite show prepared by the organizers.

(3) Bali Kite Festival

The Bali Kite Festival is held at the beginning of the wind season in July and August. It is one of the highlights of major festivals in Bali. The unique cultural scene complements the Bali Art Festival. It is usually held on the east coast of Padanggalak, north of Sanur, and the time is depending on the time of favorable weather conditions. Hundreds of competitive kites teams on the island fly traditional kites on this kite festival. In addition, many international teams fly various modern kites of different shapes on the festival.

越 南

越南风筝节起源于唐朝的中国，这也是越南人喜欢过的一种民族节日。目前越南比较有影响的是巴地头顿国际风筝节，已成功举办了9届，每年都邀请20多个国家和地区的风筝艺人参加风筝节。风筝节期间举行多项活动，如哨子风筝、空气动力学风筝表演以及体育风筝比赛等。

Vietnam

The Vietnam Kite Festival was originated from China in the Tang Dynasty. This is also a national festival enjoyed by Vietnamese people. At present, Vietnam is more influential in the Ba Ria - Vung Tau International Kite Festival, which has been successfully held for 9 sessions. Every year, kite artists from more than 20 countries and regions are invited to participate in the kite festival. A number of events are held during the festival, such as whistle kites and aerodynamic kite performance and sports kite competitions, etc.

泰　国

放风筝在泰国有悠久的历史，泰国人一直都把它作为一种象征，它将满载着人们的梦幻和寄托以及精湛的手工艺一起飞向天堂。放风筝的季节一般是每年 2 月至 5 月，曼谷的王家田广场和帕玛尼场所是传统的放风筝中心，喜欢放风筝的人都会自然而然地到那里去集会。不仅于此，泰国人还把放风筝发展成为一项体育运动，专门组成了各自的风筝队，定出详细的比赛规则，并由泰皇赞助的体育协会定期举行风筝比赛。

据记载，泰国人自古以来就陶醉于放风筝的乐趣中。在一些著名的庙寺中，可看到不少描述古代风土人情的壁画，其中就有放风筝的篇章。放风筝几乎在泰国历史的每一个朝代都十分盛行，在大城王朝时期，甚至颁布法令禁止在皇宫上空放风筝。在一些史书上甚至还有把风筝作为交通工具和战争武器的记载。

泰国著名的风筝节是曼谷风筝节。每年 3 月，曼谷的王家田广场和帕玛尼场所是传统的放风筝中心。飞翔的风筝既有平面的也有立体的，各种造型应有尽有。最壮观的要数 12 只巨型章鱼比翼齐飞的场面了，这些章鱼风筝分别来自法国、意大利、美国和新西兰 4 个国家，其中有的制作成本高达 8 千美元。

Thailand

The flying of kite has a long history in Thailand, and the Thai people have always seen it as a symbol. The kite flies to heaven with people's dreams and best wishes and exquisite craftsmanship. The season of flying kites is generally from February to May each year. The Sanam Luang Square and the Parmani in Bangkok are traditional kite-flying centers. Those who like flying kites will gather there. Not only that, the Thai people also developed kite flying into a sport. They formed their own kite teams and set detailed rules of the game. The sports association sponsored by the Thai emperor held kite competitions regularly.

According to records, Thai people have been enchanted by the fun of flying kites since ancient times. In some famous temples, you can see a lot of murals depicting ancient customs, including chapters of kite flying. The kite flying was very popular in almost every dynasty in the history of Thailand. During the Ayutthaya Dynasty, a decree was issued prohibiting the flying of kites over the imperial palace. In some history books, there are even records of kites as vehicles and weapons of war.

The famous kite festival in Thailand is the Bangkok Kite Festival. Every March, Sanam Luang Square and the Parmani in Bangkok are traditional kite-flying centers. There are both flat and three-dimensional kites with all kinds of shapes. The most spectacular scene is the flying of 12 giant octopus from the four countries of France, Italy, the United States and New Zealand. One of the kite costs as much as $8,000.

荷 兰

荷兰的风筝运动拥有众多的爱好者和较高的竞技水平，有一定国际影响的是荷兰国际风筝节，在席凡宁根海滩举办，至今已举办 42 届。每一届国际风筝节，吸引着国内外众多风筝爱好者参与，众多造型各异的风筝扮靓天空。

Netherlands

There is a large number of enthusiasts for sport kite and a high level of competitions of in the Netherlands. The Netherlands International Kite Festival, held in Scheveningen Beach, has some international influence and has been held for 42 sessions. The festival attracts many kite enthusiasts from home and abroad. Many different styles of kites fly up the sky.

葡萄牙

葡萄牙国际风筝节举办地在该国首都里斯本以南30多公里的小城阿尔科谢蒂，国际风筝节是葡萄牙唯一的专业风筝节，每届都会有来自葡萄牙、英国、法国、德国、巴西、美国、西班牙、意大利等国的专业团队参加，其中不乏欧洲乃至世界的顶级选手。

该风筝节不做任何竞技排名，只是为了向公众展示放风筝这一传统娱乐活动给人们带来的乐趣。同时，为让孩子们快乐地参与风筝节，节会还组织孩子们参与制作、放飞风筝，让他们亲身体验这一活动的乐趣。

Portugal

Portugal International Kite Festival is held in the small city of Alcochete, more than 30 kilometers south of Lisbon. The International Kite Festival is the only professional kite festival in Portugal. Professional teams from Portugal, UK, France, Germany, Brazil, the United States, Spain, Italy and many other countries take part in the festival, including top players from Europe and in the world.

There is no rank in the competition of the kite festival. It is just aimed to show the public the fun of kite flying as a traditional entertainment. At the same time, children can participate in the production and flying of kites during the festival, so that they can experience the fun of this activity.

挪 威

　　挪威的风筝运动与滑雪运动是紧密联系在一起的，比较著名的是挪威国际风筝滑雪大赛，每一届都吸引着 30 多个国家的数百名运动员参加，赛程 100 公里，共 5 圈。参赛者可自由选择使用单板或双板。在皑皑白雪和蓝天之上，上演着速度与激情的艺术盛宴，令观众大饱眼福。

Norway

Kite sports and skiing are closely linked together in Norway. The more famous is the Norwegian International Kite Ski Competition, which attracts hundreds of athletes from more than 30 countries each time. The race is 100 kilometers, with a total of 5 laps. Participants are free to choose either a single or double board. On the snow and under the blue sky, the athletes show their talents of speed and passion here.

智　利

　　智利风筝节定在每年的 11 月 1 日举行。在首都圣地亚哥附近的部落里，玛雅人做的风筝多为圆形，彩绘民族图案，风筝上面插有小旗，色彩鲜艳。当地放风筝有两种含义：一为怀念前人，二为青年男女挑选意中人。

Chile

The Chile Kite Festival is scheduled to take place on November 1 of each year. In the tribes near the capital Santiago, the kites made by the Mayans are mostly round and painted ethnic patterns, with small flags on the kites and the kites are colorful. There are two meanings for kite flying by local people: one is to cherish the memory of the predecessors, and the other is to choose the person one is in love with by the young people.

科威特

　　科威特有影响的风筝节是 Alfarisi 国际风筝节。每年的 2 月 22 日前后，为纪念科威特国家成立及解放，人们在 Alfarisi 国际风筝节期间放飞风筝，表达自由，祈求和平。

Kuwait

The influential kite festival in Kuwait is the Alfarisi International Kite Festival. Every year around February 22, in order to commemorate the establishment and liberation of the Kuwaiti, people flew kites during the Alfarisi International Kite Festival, expressing freedom and praying for peace.

意大利

意大利每两年举行一次风筝会，日期为国庆节 6 月 2 日。放飞风筝全是经过结构形式改进以后，能适应空气动力性能的要求，运用新材料制作的。由于风筝花样的创新，愈来愈受到各国风筝爱好者的青睐，参加国和人数逐年增多。近 20 年来，意大利的风筝冲浪运动也发展很快，涌现出一批风筝冲浪高手。

Italy

Kite festival is held in Italy once every two years. The date is its National Day, June 2nd. The flying kites are all made of new materials after being improved in structural form and adapting to the requirements of aerodynamic performance. Due to the innovation of kite patterns, it has become more and more popular among kite enthusiasts in various countries. The number of participating countries and people has increased year by year. In the past 20 years, the kite surfing in Italy has also developed rapidly, and a number of excellent kite surfers have emerged.

斯里兰卡

斯里兰卡国际风筝节始办于 2015 年，每年举行一次，在首都科伦坡海边的加尔菲斯草地广场举行，是当地风筝爱好者的年度狂欢盛事。每届都吸引本国几万名民众参与，国内外 3000 多名选手报名参加。

Sri Lanka

The Sri Lanka International Kite Festival was initiated in 2015 and is held once a year at the Garphys Meadows Square in the capital of Colombo. It is an annual carnival event for local kite enthusiasts. The festival attracts tens of thousands of people from the country and 3,000 fliers from home and abroad.

比利时

比利时风筝节创办于 1995 年，每年 8 月的第一个周末在克诺克海斯特的海滨沙滩上举行，是欧洲的风筝爱好者的一大盛事。

克诺克-海斯特 (Knokke-Heist) 是位于比利时西佛兰德省部的一座城市，距首都布鲁塞尔约 110 公里，这里不仅有著名的海滨浴场，还建有 70 多家艺术及古玩展馆，是一座文化氛围浓郁的旅游城市，每年夏季都吸引大批游客。每年由比利时风筝协会组织的国际风筝节吸引了大批主要来自欧洲的风筝爱好者来到海滨小城，放飞他们亲手创作的风筝。

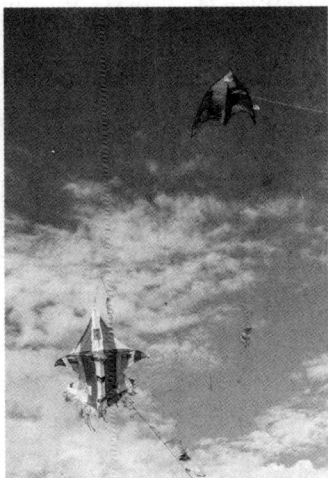

Belgian

Founded in 1995, the Belgian Kite Festival is held on the beachfront of Knokke-Heist on the first weekend of August and is a major event for kite enthusiasts in Europe.

Knokke-Heist is a city in the West Flanders province of Belgium, about 110 km from the capital Brussels. There are not only famous bathing beaches, but also more than 70 art and antique exhibition galleries. It is a tourist city with a strong cultural atmosphere, attracting a large number of tourists every summer. Each year, the international kite festival organized by the Belgian Kite Fliers Association attracts a large number of kite enthusiasts mainly from Europe to the seaside town to fly their kites.

哥伦比亚

　　每年8月进入风季，人们开始进入户外开展各种运动，哥伦比亚各地会举办各种形式的风筝节，其中历史名镇莱瓦镇举办的国际风筝节历史悠久，规模最大，影响最广。为期3天的风筝节，本地市民和特邀风筝选手齐聚小镇，放飞造型不一、多姿多彩的风筝，扮靓了古镇天空。每天9时至晚上7时，每隔半小时至一小时，就有一轮风筝放飞表演，分成儿童少年组和成人组进行放飞。放飞的风筝一般分成两类，一类是艺术风筝，一类是普通风筝。评价风筝放飞效果，一般要看技巧，垂直放飞等环节的处理。风筝节已成为当地一个盛大节日。

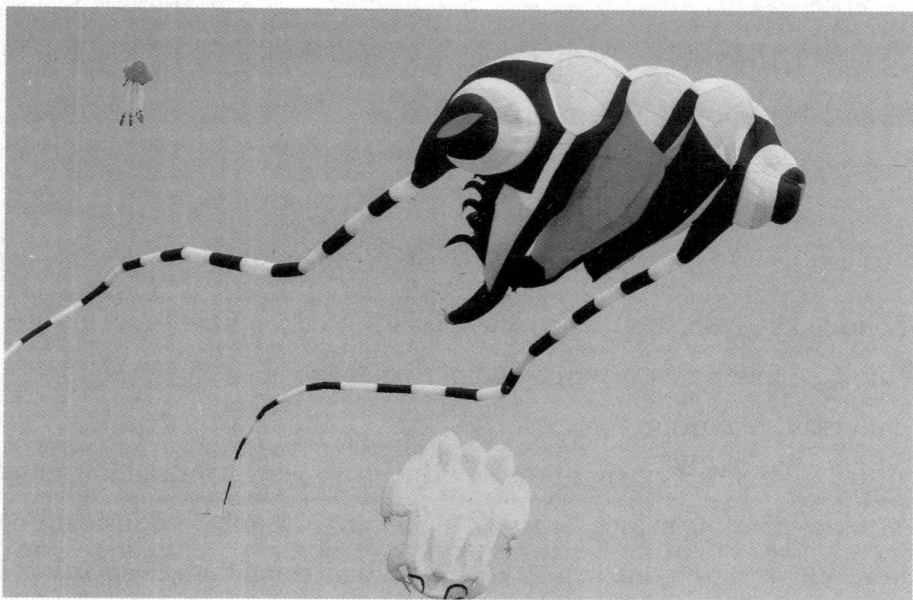

Colombia

Every year, the wind season begins in August, and people begin to have outdoors sports. Various types of kite festivals are held throughout Colombia. The International Kite-flying Festival held in the historic town of Leyva has a long history, the largest scale and the most extensive influence. During the three-day kite festival, local citizens and kite fliers gathered in the town. They flew colorful kites with different shapes, which dressed up the sky of the ancient town. Every day from 9:00 am to 7:00 pm, there was a kite-flying performance every half an hour to an hour, which is divided into children's groups and adults' groups. The kites are generally divided into two categories, one is art kite and the other is ordinary kite. To evaluate the effect of kite flying, it is generally necessary to judge the techniques and vertical flying effects, etc. The kite festival has become a grand festival in the local area.

西班牙

西班牙风筝节活动比较活跃，该国的巴伦西亚国际风筝节，富埃特文图拉特国际风筝节等已分别举办多届，在欧洲有着重要影响。该国的创新风筝，风筝冲浪也有较高知名度。

2018 年 11 月 8-11 日，西班牙小岛富埃特文图拉特举办第 31 届国际风筝节，吸引了来自意大利、法国、瑞士、英国、荷兰、西班牙和比利时等多个国家的 200

多名风筝参赛者，展示并放飞表演了 450 只精品风筝。风筝节活动专门选在冬季举行，更好地展示了当地全年气候的美妙多变。包括开幕式在内的诸多活动项目，都选择在海滩进行，不仅让风筝选手有更好的发挥，也让包括孩子在内的游客有了近距离接触风筝的机会。

Spain

The Spanish Kite Festival is active. The International Kite Festival of Valencia and Fuerteventura has been held for many times respectively and have important influence in Europe. The innovative kites and kite surfing are also well known.

From November 8th to 11th, 2018, the 31st International Kite Festival was held on the island of Fuerteventura, Spain, attracting more than 200 fliers from Italy, France, Switzerland, the United Kingdom, the Netherlands, Spain and Belgium, etc. 450 boutique kites were flown and showed on the festival. The kite festival is specially held in the winter to better show the wonderful changes in the local climate throughout the year. Many activities, including the opening ceremony, were held on the beach, which not only made the kite players fly better, but also allowed visitors including children to have close contact with kites.

第二章 中国风筝赛会

KITE COMPETITIONS AND FESTIVALS IN CHINA

060-146

潍坊国际风筝会

潍坊国际风筝会，是沐浴改革开放的春风，在国内最早冠以"国际"字眼的综合性、国际性重大地方节会。为了加快发展，促进对外开放和旅游事业发展，1984年4月1日-3日，潍坊市举办了第一届潍坊国际风筝会，邀请了11个国家、地区的17支风筝代表队来潍坊放飞表演，并取得了圆满成功。从此，潍坊国际风筝会每年举办一届，每年4月第三个星期六为开幕日，由国家体育总局、国际风筝联合会、潍坊市人民政府等联合主办，至今已成功举办了35届。

1988年4月1日，在第五届潍坊国际风筝会期间，经各国风协代表会议竞选，潍坊市被一致推举为"世界风筝都"。

1989年4月1日，经中国国务院批准，国际风筝联合会在潍坊成立，并将总部设在潍坊，创会的理事国和地区共16个。现有会员国、地区67个。国际风筝联合会的成立，标志着世界风筝事业有了领导核心，标志着潍坊成为世界风筝文化传播中心。多年来，国际风筝联合会在与潍坊市主办国际风筝会，促进风筝文化传播、风筝运动普及与提高、风筝产业发展等方面，发挥了十分重要的作用。

潍坊国际风筝会是集风筝、文化、旅游、招商四大版块于一体的综合性、国际性盛会，是改革开放以来在全国创办最早、坚持时间最长、经济

和社会效益最好、为数不多的重大节会，并在全国率先创造了"风筝牵线，文化搭台，经贸唱戏"的办会宗旨，一种形式（风筝会）四种结合（文化、体育、旅游、经济），以及"政府主办，市场运作，社会参与"的办会方式，为外地众多节会所效仿和借鉴，并催生和带动了潍坊市会展节庆活动的开展，取得了突出的成效。

经过多年努力，潍坊国际风筝会打造了全球规模最大的"万人风筝放飞表演"、"世界风筝锦标赛"、"潍坊风筝大赛"等品牌赛事，成功地举办了一届又一届风筝会开幕式大型文艺演出，创新培育了"世界风筝小姐大赛"、"狂欢大巡游"等一批特色文体活动。设计建设了体现潍坊风筝文化特色的世界风筝博物馆、世界风筝都纪念广场、潍坊富华会展中心、浮烟山国际风筝放飞场、市民文化艺术活动中心、北海路迎宾大道等一大批硬件设施，使这座城市的风筝内涵和特色更加浓郁，被称为"长着翅膀的城市"。

潍坊国际风筝会的成功举办，对于促进潍坊市的对外开放，增进与各国、地区友谊，扩大交流与合作，提升潍坊市的知名度和美誉度，促进风筝健身运动，推动城市建设，招商引资，风筝文化产业和旅游等各业发展起到了重要的"助推器"作用。风筝和风筝会成为潍坊走向世界的一张亮丽名片，成为潍坊最有价值、最有代表性、最有影响力的城市品牌，成为潍坊对外开放的窗口，合作发展的平台，全市人民热切期盼的一个盛大节日，受到中外来宾的高度评价。潍坊国际风筝会先后获得"中国10大品牌节庆""改革开放40年中国10佳品牌节会"等诸多殊荣。

一座著名城市必有一个著名节庆，一个著名节庆必将促进一座著名城市的发展。放飞风筝，传递友谊，收获荣誉。从潍坊飞向世界，将民俗做成产业。潍坊国际风筝会，不仅打造了一座"世界风筝都"，更是将中国传统风筝文化传向了世界。

Weifang International Kite Festival

With the development of reform and opening up, Weifang International Kite Festival is the first comprehensive and international major local festival named with the wording of International. In order to accelerate development and promote the opening up and tourism, Weifang held the first Weifang International Kite Festival from April 1st to 3rd, 1984, and invited 17 kites delegations from 11 countries and regions to Weifang. They flew kites in Weifang and the event showed a complete success. Since then, the Weifang International Kite Festival has been held annually, and the opening ceremony is on the third Saturday of April. The festival has been jointly hosted by the General Administration of Sport of China, the International Kite Federation, and the Weifang Municipal People's Government. Up until now, it has been successfully held for 35 sessions.

On April 1, 1988, during the 5th Weifang International Kite Festival, Weifang was unanimously elected as the Capital of Kite in the world through the election on the meeting of the delegates of kite fliers associations from the world.

On April 1, 1989, with the approval of the State Council of China, the International Kite Federation was established in Weifang. And its headquarters is located in Weifang. There were 16 initial council members and regions. Nowadays, there are 67 existing member states and regions. The establishment of the International Kite Federation marks the establishment of core of leadership in the world's kite cause and marks that Weifang had become the world's kite culture communication center. Over the years, the International Kite Federation has played an important role in hosting the International Kite Festival together with Weifang Municipal Government, promoting the spread of kite culture, the popularization and improvement of kite sports, and the development of the kite industry, etc.

Weifang International Kite Festival is a comprehensive and international event that integrates kites, culture, tourism and investment. It is one of the few festivals which is earliest initiated in the country since the reform and opening up, experienced longest years, and has the best economic and social benefits. The festival has initiated the tenet of "Kite, culture, economy and trade develop together", and the organization form of combining four aspects of culture, sports, tourism and economy through Weifang International Kite Festival, and set the mode of organization through the way of hosting the festival by the government, having market operation and social participation. The above mode has been used by many other festivals in other places, and has promoted the development of exhibition and festival activities in Weifang and has achieved outstanding results.

After years of hard work by the organizers, Weifang International Kite Festival has created the world's largest Ten Thousand People Kite Flying Performance, World Kite Championship, Weifang Kite Competition and other competitions, successfully held large-scale cultural performance on the opening ceremony of the festival, initiated special cultural and sports activities such as World Miss Kite Contest and Carnival Parade. A large number of hardware facilities with Weifang kite cultural characteristics have been designed and built. Such as the World Kite Museum, the World Kite Memorial Plaza, the Weifang Fuhua Convention and Exhibition Center, the Fuyan Mountain International Kite Flying Field, the Citizen Culture and Art Activity Center, and the Beihai Road Greeting Avenue, etc, make the city's kite content and features more remarkable. Weifang is known as the City with Wings.

The success of the Weifang International Kite Festival will greatly promote the opening up of Weifang, enhance the friendship with other countries and regions, expand exchanges and cooperation, enhance the popularity and reputation of Weifang, promote kite fitness, promote urban construction, introducing investment, and kite culture and tourism industry, etc. Kite and the Weifang International Kite Festival will become a bright business card of Weifang to the world. They will become the most valuable, representative and influential city brand in Weifang and will become a window for Weifang to open to the outside world, a platform for cooperation and development. The festival has become an event enjoyed by the local peopl and is highly praised by Chinese and foreign guests. Weifang International Kite Festival has won many awards such as China's Top 10 Brand Festivals and China's Top 10 Brand Festivals in the 40 Years of Reform and Opening up.

A famous city should have a famous festival, and a famous festival will surely promote the development of a famous city. Flying kites, passing on friendships and harvesting honors are what happened in the city of Weifang. Kites have flown from Weifang to the world. And the folk custom has been made into an industry. The Weifang International Kite Festival not only created a capital of kite in the world, but also spread the traditional Chinese kite culture to the world.

世界风筝锦标赛

世界风筝锦标赛是当代全球风筝领域层次最高、规模最大、影响最大的顶级国际风筝赛事。

2005 年，经中国国家体育总局批准，首届世界风筝锦标赛在第 22 届潍坊国际风筝会期间成功举办，标志着世界风筝运动迈向更高水平，进一步提升了潍坊国际风筝会的档次和影响力。从此，世界风筝锦标赛落户潍坊，伴随着潍坊国际风筝会每年在潍坊举办，吸引了大批优秀中外风筝选手参与。到 2018 年，世界风筝锦标赛已成功举办了 14 届，在国内外产生了重要影响。经过多年打造，该项赛事已成为著名国际风筝比赛品牌，成为潍坊国际风筝会的重要赛事支撑。

World Kite Championship

The World Kite Championship is the top international kite event with the highest level, largest scale and influence in the global kite field.

In 2005, with the approval of the General Administration of Sport of China, the first World Kite Championship was successfully held during the 22nd Weifang International Kite Festival, marking the world's kite sport developed to a higher level, and further enhanced the influence of the Weifang International Kite Festival. Since then, the World Kite Championship has been held annually in Weifang during the Weifang International Kite Festival, attracting a large number of outstanding Chinese and foreign kite fliers. By 2018, the World Kite Championship has been successfully held for 14 sessions, which has had an important impact at home and abroad. After years of development, the event has become a famous international kite competition and has become an important event during the Weifang International Kite Festival.

潍坊滨海国际风筝冲浪公开赛

　　创办于 2009 年的中国潍坊滨海国际风筝冲浪邀请赛（2011年改为公开赛），是目前世界水平最高、规模最大的风筝冲浪顶级赛事之一。2010 年山东潍坊滨海正式被确定为中国国际风筝冲浪基地。目前，滨海区已成功举办了八届世界顶尖水平的国际风筝冲浪赛事，每一届都吸引了国内外众多风筝冲浪爱好者前来参赛，赛事知名度和影响力逐年提高。

　　2018 年 9 月 1 日，世界风筝水翼板锦标赛暨第十届中国潍坊滨海国际风筝冲浪公开赛在潍坊滨海旅游度假区欢乐海开赛。本届赛事由国际帆联风筝帆板协会、中国帆船帆板运动协会、潍坊滨海经济技术开发区管委会主办，潍坊滨海旅游集团承办。本次赛事有来自 25 个国家和地区的 70 名职业风筝冲浪选手参赛，世界职业排名前 30 位的选手基本都报名参加，其中很多曾获得世界冠军头衔。比赛项目包括风筝冲浪水翼板男子组、风筝冲浪水翼板女子组、风筝冲浪水翼板大师组、风筝冲浪水翼板青年组 4 项比赛，赛事奖金达到 60000 欧元，国际比赛等级分为 200 分。世界风筝冲浪高手云集潍坊滨海，在为期 5 天的比赛时间里展开激烈角逐，极大地推动了风筝冲浪运动的开展和普及，打造了潍坊滨海一块含金量极高的金字招牌，助力加快品质滨海、活力滨海建设。

Weifang Binhai International Kitesurfing Open Tournament

Founded in 2009, China Weifang Binhai International Kitesurfing Invitational Tournament (changed name in 2011) is one of the world's highest level and largest scale kite surfing top events. In 2010, Weifang Binhai was officially identified as the China International Kitesurfing Base. At present, Binhai has successfully hosted eight world-class international kite surfing events. The event attracted many kitesurfers from home and abroad. The popularity and influence of the event have been increased year by year.

On September 1, 2018, the World Kite Foilboard Championships and the 10th Weifang Binhai International Kitesurfing Open Tournament were held at the Joy Sea of Weifang Binhai Tourism Resort. The event was hosted by the Kite-surfing Association of International Sailing Federation, China Sailing Boat and Sailboard Association, Management Committee of the Weifang Binhai Economic and Technological Development Zone, and undertaken by Weifang Binhai Tourism Group. 70 professional kite-surfing players from 25 countries and regions participated in the competition. Almost all the top 30 players in the world registered and took part in the competition, many of whom had won the title of world championship. The competition covers four fields, men's kite surfing foilboard ,women's kite surfing foilboard, master kite surfing foilboard and youth kite surfing foilboard. The prizes are 60,000 euros and the international competition level is 200 scores. The world's kitesurfing masters gathered in Weifang Binhai, and launched a fierce competition during the five-day competition period, which greatly promoted the development and popularization of kite surfing, and make Weifang Binhai famous around the world, helping to speed up the development and coastal construction of Binhai.

寒亭区杨家埠风筝年画艺术节

近年来，以潍坊市寒亭区"杨家埠风筝年画艺术节"为代表的民风民俗节庆活动，以其独特的形式和内涵、浓郁的乡土气息、高雅的民间艺术、优质的民俗服务，正不断地吸引着来自欧美、日韩等全球数十个国家和地区的众多游客。

寒亭区的民间艺术源远流长，形成了以杨家埠风筝年画为代表的独特地方民间艺术。杨家埠是中国3大木板年画产地之一，以杨家埠风筝为代表的潍坊风筝驰名中外。2002年杨家埠被山东省政府命名为"历史文化名村"，有"中国民俗风情第一村"的美誉。风筝和年画这两朵姐妹艺术之花又于2006年被正式列入国家首批"非物质文化遗产名录"。杨家埠风筝以造型优美、色彩艳丽、想象丰富、取材广泛而自成一家。其构图质朴简洁，形象鲜明生动，品类繁多，富有神韵和艺术魅力，深受人们的喜爱。杨家埠风筝现已漂洋过海，遍布全球、成为外国人最喜爱的"中国民间艺术名品"。杨家埠木板年画具有浓郁的乡土气息和淳朴鲜明的艺术风格，题材广泛，内容丰富，以象征、寓意、夸张等表现手法展现了人们企盼幸福、吉祥、美好生活的强烈愿望。

Yangjiabu Kite and New Year Pictures Festival in Hanting District

In recent years, the folk customs events represented by the Yangjiabu Kite and New Year Pictures Festival in Hanting District of Weifang, attracted many tourists from dozens of countries and regions in Europe, America, Japan and South Korea with its unique form and connotation, rich local flavor, elegant folk art, and high-quality folk services.

The folk art in Hanting District has a long history and has formed a unique local folk art represented by Yangjiabu kite and new year painting. Yangjiabu is one of the three major wooden board paintings bases in China. The Weifang kites represented by Yangjiabu kites are well-known both at home and abroad. In 2002, Yangjiabu was named by the Shandong Provincial Government as "Historical and Cultural Village" and it has the reputation of "No. One Village of Chinese folk Customs". The kites and New Year pictures were officially listed in the first batch of national "Intangible Cultural Heritage" in 2006. Yangjiabu kites are unique for their beautiful style, colorful painting, extensive imagination etc. The composition of its picture is simple and brief, the image is vivid, and the varieties are wide. It is full of artistic charm, and is deeply loved by people. The Yangjiabu kite has now crossed the ocean and been spread to all over the world, becoming the favorite famous Chinese folk art and it is enjoyed by foreigners. Yangjiabu wooden board new year paintings have a strong local flavor and simple and distinct artistic style. The subject of the painting is wide and the content is rich. The symbolic, implied and exaggerated expressions show the strong desire of people to hope for happiness, auspiciousness and a better life.

青岛国际风筝会

青岛国际风筝会创办于1997年。青岛飞翔旅行社总经理台兰德（现飞翔国际旅行社董事长）在崂山区政府、崂山区旅游局等领导的大力支持下，经过考察潍坊等地的国际风筝会，结合青岛实际，于1997年4月23日在青岛崂山石老人风景区举办了第一届青岛国际风筝会，来自美、英、法、港、澳、台等18个国家和地区21支代表队130余名专业风筝选手参加了此次风筝会，从此拉开了一年一度青岛国际风筝会的序幕。飞翔国际旅行社作为唯一承办单位，承揽了历年青岛风筝会的举办权，从发出邀请、组织食宿接待、放飞比赛，到交通保障，做了大量艰苦细致而卓有成效的工作。每届风筝会飞翔国际旅行社都自筹资金，加大投入，确保了风筝会圆满成功，到目前，已接待了上万名世界各地的风筝选手、爱好者来青参会。

Qingdao International Kite Festival

The Qingdao International Kite Festival was founded in 1997. With the support of the leaders of Laoshan District Government and Laoshan District Tourism Bureau, the general manager of Qingdao Feixiang Travel Agency, Tai Lande (now the chairman of Feixiang International Travel Agency), after investigating the international kite festivals in Weifang and other places, combined with the actual situation in Qingdao, held the first Qingdao International Kite Festival in Stone Elderly Scenic Area of Laoshan Mountain, in Qingdao on April 23rd, 1997. More than 130 professional kite fliers of 21 teams from 18 countries including the United States, Britain, France, and Hong Kong, Macao ,Taiwan, districts participated in the festival. It was the open of the annual Qingdao International Kite Festival. As the sole organizer, Feixiang International Travel Agency has undertaken the right to host the Qingdao Kite Festival over the years. They have done a lot of hard and meticulous and fruitful work from issuing invitations, organizing accommodation and reception, flying competitions to transportation and security. The travel agency has raised funds and increased investment to ensure the success of the kite festival. Up to now, it has attracted tens of thousands of kite players and enthusiasts from all over the world.

阳江风筝节

阳江风筝有 1400 多年的历史。早在宋代，阳江已有重阳放风筝的习俗。《阳江县志》载："重九日，结伴携酒选胜登高，士人赋诗，儿童放纸鸢较高下。"到了清代，场面更为壮观。清人林葆莹诗云："浮屠七级北山坳，纸鹞参差万影交。"可见当时之盛况。

阳江有"纸鹞城"、"中国风筝之乡"的美称。从 1992 年开始，每年农历九月初九重阳节，阳江都在南国风筝竞技场举办不同层次的风筝比赛。至今阳江市已成功举办了 20 多届风筝节和风筝邀请赛，弘扬了风筝文化，促进了对外交流和全民健身运动，扩大了阳江市的知名度和美誉度。阳江市风筝代表队多次在国内外风筝比赛中获佳绩。

2018 年 9 月 16 日，漠阳风筝文化节隆重开幕，其中，重头戏的活动是两项风筝大赛——2018 年阳江国际风筝邀请赛和 2018 年阳江市风筝大赛同时举行，来自世界各地的放飞队和风筝爱好者集结南国风筝场，在蓝天白云下同场竞技，为广大市民带来一场视觉盛宴。

阳江市风筝协会在阳江市委，市政府和市文广新局的大力支持下，与时俱进，勇于开拓，在传承弘扬风筝文化，培养风筝人才，组织承办各种风筝活动，探索市场化运作机制等方面，率先突破，取得了突出成效，为全国各级风筝协会改革发展树立了标杆。

Yangjiang Kite Festival

The Yangjiang kite has a history of more than 1,400 years. As early as the Song Dynasty, Yangjiang had the custom of flying kites in Double Ninth Festival. It is recorded in the annals of Yangjiang County during the Double Ninth Festival., people carried wine and climbed the hills together with friends and family members, the scholars made poems, the children flew the kites and had competitions. In the Qing Dynasty, the scene is even more spectacular. Lin Baoying wrote in the poem that many kites were flying in the north mountain where there was seven-floor pagoda. From the poem we can see that kites were very popular at that time.

Yangjiang has the reputation of City of Kite and Hometown of Chinese Kite. From 1992, every year on the September 9th of the Lunar Year, Yangjiang held different levels of kite competitions in the South Kite Arena. Up to now, Yangjiang has successfully held more than 20 Kite Festivals and Kite Invitational Tournaments, which has promoted the kite culture, foreign exchanges and national fitness, and expanded the reputation of Yangjiang. The Yangjiang Kite Team has achieved good results in many domestic and international kite competitions.

On September 16th, 2018, the Moyang Kite Culture Festival was grandly opened. The major events were two kite contests - the Yangjiang International Kite Invitational Tournament in 2018 and the Yangjiang

Kite Competition in 2018. The kite flying teams from all over the world and kite fans gathered in the South Kite Field and competed under the blue sky, which attracted lots of citizens.

Under the strong support of the Yangjiang Municipal Committee, the Municipal Government and the Municipal Cultural, Broadcasting, TV and News Bureau, Yangjiang Kite Association keeps pace with the times and makes innovations, inherits and promotes kite culture, trains kite talents, organizes various kite events, and explores market-oriented operations. In terms of mechanisms and other aspects, it has taken the lead in breaking through and achieved outstanding results, and has set a benchmark for the reform and development of kite associations at all levels across the country.

WEIFANG1996

南通如东风筝节

南通市如东县特有的哨口板鹞风筝，是中国四大风筝门派之一。哨口板鹞风筝工艺考究，制作精良，通过哨口发出低、中、高三种音效，声音能够传到很远的地方，享有"空中交响乐"的美名。如东国际风筝节，作为如东传统赛事、特色赛事，已经成功举办19届，成为交流提升风筝技艺、传承弘扬传统风筝文化的重要平台，推动文化体育事业繁荣发展、宣传推介如东的有效载体。2015年如东县被国家体育总局命名为"中国风筝之乡"。

2018年9月28日至29日，如东第19届国际风筝会、国际风筝邀请赛暨江苏省风筝精英赛在如东县小洋口国家级风筝放飞场举行。邀请了全国各地的52支代表队，特邀老挝、孟加拉国、纳米比亚、印度等4支留学生代表队，近300名选手参加比赛。本次比赛由国家体育总局社会体育指导中心、江苏省社会体育管理中心支持，中国风筝协会主办，江苏省风筝协会、南通市体育局、如东县人民政府承办，江苏省如东小洋口旅游度假区协办。

本次比赛设竞技风筝赛和特色风筝表演赛等2大类14个项目，竞技风筝赛设双线双人运动风筝芭蕾赛、双线团体运动风筝芭蕾赛、四线团体运动风筝芭蕾赛、打斗风筝个人赛等4项；特色风筝表演赛设板鹞类、龙串类、串类最长、最大风筝、软体造型（挂件）、滚地龙等比赛项目。五彩斑斓的风筝自由地在空中摇曳，演绎了一场空中"筝"奇斗艳的秋日盛会，令观众大饱眼福。

Nantong Rudong Kite Festival

The unique whistle board kite in Rudong, Nantong is one of the four major kite schools in China. The whistle board kite is crafted and well-made. It can make low, medium and high sound through the whistle. The sound can be transmitted far away and it enjoys the reputation of symphony in the air. As a traditional and featured event in Rudong, Rudong International Kite Festival has been successfully held for 19 sessions. It has become an important platform for exchange and promotion of kite skills, inheriting and promoting traditional kite culture, promoting the prosperity and development of culture and sports undertakings, and promoting the county of Rudong. In 2015, Rudong was named "Hometown of Chinese Kite" by the General Administration of Sport of China.

From September 28th to 29th, 2018, Rudong 19th International Kite Festival, International Kite Invitational Tournament and Jiangsu Kite Classic Competition were held at the Xiao Yang Kou National Kite Flying Field in Rudong. 52 teams from all over the country, and 4 teams of foreign students from Laos, Bangladesh, Namibia and India were invited to take part in the competition. Nearly 300 fliers participated in the competition. The competition was supported by the Leisure Sports Center of the General Administration of Sport of China and National Sports General Administration Social Sports Guidance Center, hosted by China Kite Association, undertaken by the Jiangsu Provincial Kite Association, Nantong Sports Bureau, Rudong People's Government, and co-organized by Jiangsu Rudong Xiao Yang Kou Tourism Resort.

In this competition, there were 14 categories of sports kites and featured kite competitions. The competitive kite competition consisted of dual-line double sports kite ballet, dual-line group sports kite ballet, quad-line group sports kite ballet, and fighting kite. There were 4 competitions in the special kite exhibition competitions, such as board kite, dragon string, longest string, largest kite, inflation (pendant) and rolling kite. The colorful kites flew in the air at the festival were very beautiful.

北京国际风筝节

北京国际风筝节至今已成功举办5届，是北京市体育总会主办、单项协会承办的北京市十大群众性国际品牌赛事活动之一。

2018年北京国际风筝节国际风筝邀请赛暨京津冀风筝联谊赛在位于丰台区永定河西岸的北京园博园举行。赛事以"蓝天中飘飞梦想，奔跑中传递友谊"为主题，包括开幕式、国际风筝邀请赛、京津冀风筝联谊赛、传统特色风筝展示和风筝制作放飞活动五个部分。其中，国际风筝邀请赛设置软体类、盘旋类等5个比赛项目，京津冀风筝联谊赛设置龙类、板子类等4个传统风筝比赛项目。随着这一品牌赛事的国际影响力不断提升，参与规模也逐步扩大，内容不断丰富。国际风筝邀请赛首次在国际风筝节期间举办，吸引了来自美国、英国、德国等31个国家，港台地区，以及特邀的山西、上海、山东等10个省区市的10支队伍和北京的4支队伍近200名风筝爱好者参加邀请赛；为贯彻中央和北京市关于京津冀协同发展的要求，为加强三地体育的交流，国际风筝节期间同时举办京津冀风筝联谊赛，三地的22支队伍共100余名风筝爱好者参与联谊赛；为传承风筝文化，风筝节期间新增了传统特色风筝展，邀请了 10 个省地市和北京的共 30 名传统风筝制作大师参加特色风筝展评，由专家评出优秀的传统风筝作品。风筝节期间，邀请了驻京使领馆、外资机构代表，外国专家以及"一带一路"国家驻京外籍学生代表共 200 余人参与风筝制作、体验放飞活动。国内外风筝大师、爱好者共聚一堂，通过比赛切磋风筝技艺，通过展示制作和放飞表演等交流活动，学习借鉴各国风筝文化，达到了加强民间风筝交流，推动了解各国民俗，增进各国人民友谊的目的，也有力地促进了各国之间的文明互鉴。

Beijing International Kite Festival

The Beijing International Kite Festival has been successfully held for five sessions. It is one of the top ten mass international events hosted by the Beijing Sports Association and undertaken by Single Association.

The 2018 Beijing International Kite Festival, International Kite Invitational Tournament and the Beijing-Tianjin-Hebei Kite Festival Friendship Tournament were held in Beijing Garden Expo Park on the west bank of Yongding River in Fengtai District. The theme of the event was "Flying Dreams in the Blue Sky and Passing Friendship in Running". The event covered the opening ceremony, the International Kite Invitational Tournament, the Beijing-Tianjin-Hebei Kite Festival Friendship Tournament, the traditional feature kite show and the kite production and fly activities. The International Kite Invitational Tournament had five competitions, such as inflation and hovering kites, etc, and the Beijing-Tianjin-Hebei Kite Festival Friendship Tournament had four traditional kite competitions, including dragons and boards kites, etc. As the international influence of this event continues to increase, the scale of participation has gradually expanded and the content has been continuously enriched. The International Kite Invitational Tournament was held for the first time during the International Kite Festival, attracting 10 teams from the United States, Britain, Germany totally 31 countries, Hong Kong and Taiwan districts, as well as nearly 200 kite enthusiasts from 10 teams of 10 domestic provinces, autonomous regions including Shanxi, Shanghai and Shandong, etc, 4 teams from Beijing participated in the invitational tournament; in order to implement the requirements of the Beijing-Tianjin-Hebei coordinated development of the Central and Beijing Municipalities. strengthen the exchange of sports between the three places, the Beijing-Tianjin-Hebei Kite Friendship Tournament was held during the International Kite Festival. A total of more than 100 kite enthusiasts from 22 teams participated in the competition. In order to inherit the kite culture, a traditional kite exhibition was held during the kite festival, and 30 traditional kite makers from 10 provinces and cities and Beijing were invited to participate in the expo. The kite exhibition was judged by experts and the expert chose outstanding traditional kites. During the Kite Festival, more than 200 people from the embassies and consulates in Beijing, representatives of foreign-funded institutions, foreign experts, and foreign students from the Belt and Road Initiative countries in Beijing were invited to participate in kite production and experience the kite flying. During the event, the domestic and overseas kite masters and enthusiasts gathered together to learn kite skills through competitions, learn about the kite culture of various countries through exchange activities such as production and flying performances, and achieved the purpose of strengthening the exchange of folk kites, promoting understanding of various national customs, and enhancing friendship among people of all countries. It also strongly promoted mutual understanding between civilizations among countries.

贵阳白云国际风筝节

贵州白云国际风筝节是一个以风筝为媒介，集风筝竞赛、大型综艺晚会、热气球飞行表演、舞龙舞狮竞赛、民间绝技绝活展演、市民狂欢游等为一体的大型主题文化体育活动。始创于1992年，每年4月30日至5月7日在贵阳举办一届。前七届是地方性活动，1999年后渐渐发展为国际性的体育盛会。节日期间，除风筝比赛，还有精彩纷呈的文艺演出、精品花卉展等活动。风筝盛会吸引了

来自美国、法国、哥伦比亚、泰国等国家和全国各省及港、澳、台等地的风筝代表队参赛。

2018年贵阳白云第12届风筝系列活动于4月30日至5月3日举行，蓝天、白云、纸鸢，让来宾们感悟中国风筝文化的博大精深和异域风筝的奇异魅力。来自国内外50余支参赛队300余名运动员共同竞技蓝天，手牵银线，畅游白云蓝天，放飞梦想，弘扬了风筝文化，打造了风筝品牌。

Guiyang Baiyun International Kite Festival

The Guizhou Baiyun International Kite Festival is a large-scale theme cultural and sports event that integrates kite competition, grand show, hot air balloon flight show, dragon and lion dance competition, folk stunt performance show, and citizen carnival, etc. Founded in 1992, it is held in Guiyang from April 30th to May 7th. The first seven sessions were local events and gradually developed into an international sports event after 1999. During the festival, in addition to the kite competition, there are also a variety of cultural performances, fine flower exhibitions and other activities. The kite event attracts teams from the United States, France, Colombia, Thailand and other countries, as well as teams from domestic provinces and Hong Kong, Macao and Taiwan, etc.

In 2018, the 12th Kite Series of Baiyun Guiyang was held from April 30th to May 3rd. The blue sky, white clouds and beautiful kites made the guests feel the profound charm of Chinese kite culture and the charm of exotic kites. More than 300 fliers from more than 50 teams from home and abroad competed under the blue sky, which promoted the kite culture and built the kite brand.

深圳大梅沙国际风筝赛

深圳大梅沙拥有珠三角地区规模最大、条件最好的放飞场地，沙滩面积18万平方米，也是中国风筝运动发展最前沿的城市之一。

深圳大梅沙国际风筝赛是一年一度的滨海风筝盛典，它不仅是一场风筝赛事，而且还是一场风筝嘉年华。自2006年至今已连续举办了12届，每年吸引20多个国家地区的300多名专业选手、1000多名业余选手及众多游客前来参与，已经打造成为蜚声海内外的重要品牌赛事。

2017年10月27日至29日，第十二届深圳（大梅沙）国际风筝赛，在盐田区大梅沙海滨公园举行。本届风筝大赛以"风之舞"为主题，由盐田区人民政府、深圳市文体旅游局主办，盐田区文化体育局、深圳市风筝协会承办，大梅沙海滨公园管理处、深圳市民俗摄影学会协办。本届赛事共设9个组别，来自美国、德国、日本、韩国等国家和地区30支风筝代表队、超过上百名的选手齐聚深圳，共享飞行乐趣。赛事分为特色风筝比赛、国际风筝大师进校园、万人放飞三部分。比赛中，世界各地的风筝达人们积极参与了运动风筝双线团体芭蕾赛、六角风筝个人赛、优秀传统风筝、夜光

风筝等 9 个类别的竞技角逐。除了高水平的国际风筝赛，大梅沙海滨公园内还升起了各种造型独特的风筝，包括京剧人物、三叶虫等超大软体风筝，以及小黄人、海绵宝宝、蜘蛛人、哆啦 A 梦等吸引小朋友的造型风筝。而"大师进校园"活动，让小朋友们与国外风筝大师"零距离"接触，通过现场教学互动，让小朋友加深了对风筝文化的认知。最充满欢乐和爱心的要数"万人放飞区"的义卖风筝募集善款活动了，义卖所得将全部用于公益项目。晚间还组织了美轮美奂的夜光风筝表演赛，吸引了众多市民和游客前来观赏。

深圳市风筝协会会长于灏表示，吸引国内外最优秀的风筝选手参赛，让深圳市民观看到世界最前沿的风筝设计一直是深圳市风筝协会追寻的目标。

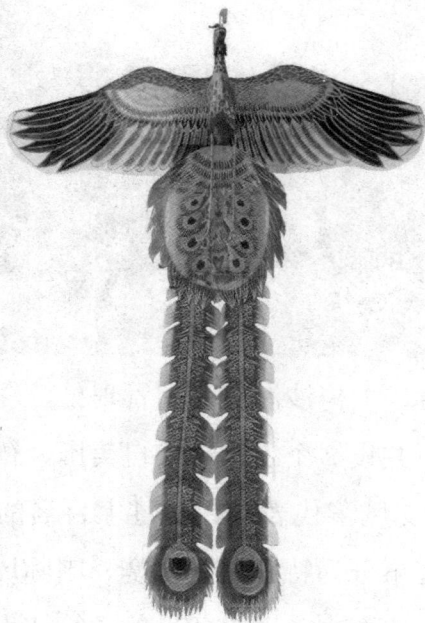

Shenzhen Dameisha International Kite Competition

Shenzhen Dameisha has the largest and best conditions in the Pearl River Delta Region, with a beach area of 180,000 square meters. It is also one of the most advanced cities in China's kite sports development.

The Shenzhen Dameisha International Kite Competition is an annual coastal kite event. It is not only a kite competition, but also a kite carnival. Since 2006, it has been held for 12 sessions. It attracts more than 300 professional players, more than 1,000 amateurs and many tourists from more than 20 countries and regions every year. It has become an important event at home and abroad.

From October 27th to 29th, 2017, the 12th Shenzhen (Dameisha) International Kite Competition was held in Waterfront Park of Dameisha in Yantian District. With the theme of Dance in the Wind, the event was hosted by Yantian District People's Government, Shenzhen Municipal Bureau of Culture and Sports, undertaken by Yantian District Cultural and Sports Bureau, Shenzhen Kite Association, co-organized by Dameisha Waterfront Park Management Office and Shenzhen Folk Photography Association. There were 9 groups in this competition. Hundreds of fliers from 30 kite teams from the United States, Germany, Japan, South Korea and other countries and regions gathered in Shenzhen to share the fun of flying. The competition was divided into three parts: the characteristic kite competition, the international kite masters entering the campus, and the masses kite flying. During the competition, kite fliers from all over the world actively participated in the competition of 9 categories including sports kite dual-line group ballet competition, hexagonal kite individual competition, excellent traditional kite and luminous kite. In addition to the holding of high-level international kite competition, a variety of unique kites, including Peking Opera characters, trilobites and other large inflation kites, as well as Minions, SpongeBob, Spiderman, and Doraemon were flown in the sky of Dameisha Waterfront Park. These kites attracted lots of children. The "Masters Enter the Campus" activity allows children to have "zero distance" contact with foreign kite masters, and through the interactive teaching on-site, children can deepen their understanding of kite culture. The most joyful and loving events are the selling kites to raise funds in the flying zone. The charity proceeds will be used for public welfare projects. In the evening, a beautiful night light kite exhibition was organized, which attracted many citizens and tourists.

Yu Hao, president of the Shenzhen Kite Association, said that it has always been the goal of the Shenzhen Kite Association to attract the best kite players from home and abroad and let the Shenzhen citizens witness the world's foremost kite design.

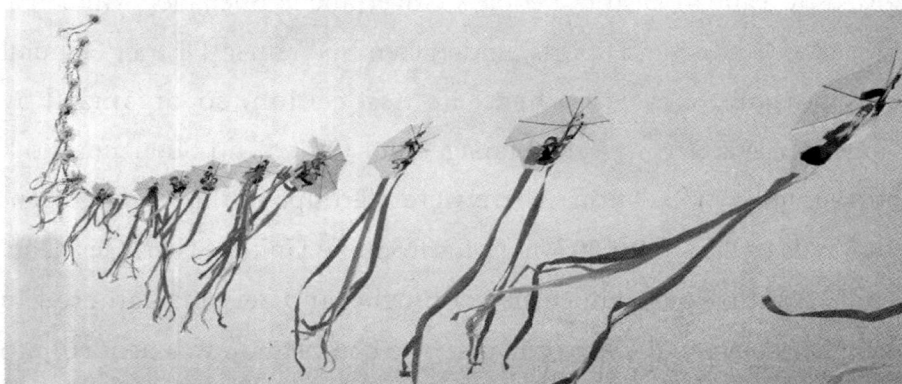

梧州国际风筝邀请赛

梧州国际风筝邀请赛，由梧州市总工会、梧州市体育局、广东风筝协会共同承办，举办地点在梧州国家体育训练基地，已连续成功举办六届。举办特点，一是与每年一届的梧州宝石节活动紧密结合，并作为宝石节的重要活动内容。二是与全民健身活动紧密结合，每届都有基层众多单位和干部职工报名参与，形成了梧州新的品牌，有着广泛的社会影响。三是放飞表演与竞赛有机结合，每届举办期间，既安排群众性的自由放飞活动，又邀请国内外高水平放飞团队，按照国际国内风筝比赛规则、规程进行正规比赛，每年都创新赛事组织，提升赛事水平，有力地促进了风筝运动的普及和提高。

2018 年 10 月 28、29 日第十五届梧州宝石节"活力梧州 放飞梦想"风筝邀请赛在梧州国家体育训练基地成功举办，160 多支国内外风筝团队、600 多名运动员共聚一堂，切磋风筝技艺。本届比赛竞争激烈、观赏性强、盛况空前，吸引了现场观众累计达 5 万人次。

Wuzhou International Kite Invitational Tournament

The Wuzhou International Kite Invitational Tournament was jointly undertaken by the Wuzhou Federation of Trade Unions, the Wuzhou Sports Bureau and the Guangdong Kite Association. It is held in the Wuzhou National Sports Training Base and has been successfully held for 6 consecutive sessions. The event is closely combined with the annual Wuzhou Gem Festival and it is an important activity of the Gem Festival. It is closely integrated with the national fitness activities. A number of people participated in the event. It has formed a new brand of the city and has a wide range of social influences. And the flying performances and competitions are combined together. During each session, there are not only free-flying activities, but also regular competitions in accordance with international and domestic kite competition rules and regulations among high-level flying teams from at home and abroad. There are innovations in the organization every year, and the level of the event has effectively improved, which promoted the popularization and improvement of the kite sport.

On October 28 and 29, 2018, the Kite Invitational Tournament with the theme of "Energetic Wuzhou, Flying Dreams" on the fifteenth Wuzhou Gem Festival was successfully held in the Wuzhou National Sports Training Base. More than 160 domestic and international kite teams and 600 fliers gathered here. The competition was fiercely competitive, attracting about a total of 50,000 visitors.

台湾新北市北海岸国际风筝节

新北市北海岸国际风筝节，已成功举办了 19 届。每届风筝节秉持国际风筝文化、技艺交流的宗旨，邀请德国、美国、澳大利亚、新加坡、马来西亚、印尼、日本以及大陆等各地风筝好手，还有中华特技风筝推广协会、8+ 特技风筝队、OA 特技风筝队、台北市风筝推广协会、三马风筝队、社子特技风筝队、云林县风筝委员会、彰化炫风风筝队、阿鲁米卡通风筝队、西盛风筝队、澎湖风筝协会等中国台湾本地 20 多支队伍，逾 100 位国内外风筝好手与会，展现精湛的风筝放飞技巧和最新创作的艺术风筝作品。届时，各具特色的造型风筝、软体风筝、特技风筝等千筝万鸢齐飞上天，将北海岸的天空点缀的美丽辉煌，让民众体验一场集观赏性、娱乐性、参与性于一体的风筝盛宴。

International Kite Festival in North Coast of Xinbei, Taiwan

The North Coast International Kite Festival in Xinbei has been successfully held for 19 sessions. The aim of international kite festival was culture and skill exchange. More than 100 kites fliers from Germany, the United States, Australia, Singapore, Malaysia, Indonesia, Japan and the mainland, as well as many local kite teams, including China Stunt Kite Promotion Association, 8+ Stunt Kite Team, OA Stunt Kite Team, Taipei Kite Promotion Association, Sanma Kite Team, Shezi Stunt Kite Team, Yunlin County Kite Committee, Zhanghua Xuanfeng Kite Team, Arumi Cartoon Kite Team, Xisheng Kite Team, Wuhu Kite Association, etc., with a total of more than 20 local teams took part in the festival. The local and international kite players showed their exquisite kite flying skills and the latest kite created. At that time, different kinds of kites, including inflation kites, stunt kites etc flew in the sky, and made the North Coast a very beautiful place, which enabled the visitors to experience a wonderful kite event.

岱山岛国际风筝节

岱山立足打造"中国风筝岛"品牌，不断探索"政府主办，市场运作，社会参与"的发展模式，推动"体育+"向纵深化发展。以传承风筝文化、做大文化产业、推动全域旅游、撬动县域经济发展为目标，办成"北有潍坊，南有岱山"的国家级风筝盛会。从 2010 年起，岱山开始举办全国风筝锦标赛、国际运动风筝邀请赛，良好的放飞条件、规范的竞赛流程、浓厚的海洋文化与旅游紧密结合，每年均有50支以上国内外队伍参赛，运动员、裁判员和工作人员人数达 500 余人，吸引国内外万余名风筝爱好者前来放飞表演。

2018 年 10 月 12 日至 14 日，中国·岱山岛国际风筝节在舟山岱山举行。70 会支国内外风筝代表队参赛，本地组成了上万人的放飞队伍，在美丽的岱山鹿栏晴沙放飞场进行了风筝放飞表演和比赛。同时，为丰富风筝节活动内容，主办方首次举办了风筝产品展销会，吸引了国内外20多家风筝企业前来参展，寻找商机。主办方还安排了包括"风之走廊"观赏区、"风筝秀"表演区、特色美食区和沙滩体育娱乐休闲区等在内的休闲互动板块，让观众在观看各类风筝赛事的同时，体验各具特色的休闲娱乐活动，促进旅游消费。

Daishan Island International Kite Festival

Based on the establishment of the brand of China Kite Island, Daishan has continuously explored the development model integrating government sponsorship, market operation and social participation and promoted the development of "sports+" policy. With the goal of inheriting kite culture, expanding the cultural industry, promoting global tourism, and invigorating the county's economic development, it has held a national-level kite event with a saying that "Weifang in the north and Daishan in the south". Since 2010, Daishan has held the National Kite Championship and the International Sports Kite Invitational Tournament. The good flying conditions, standardized competition process, and strong marine culture and tourism are closely combined together. Each year, more than 50 domestic and foreign teams participated in the event. The number of athletes, referees and staff has reached more than 500. The event attracts more than 10,000 kite enthusiasts from home and abroad annually.

From October 12 to 14, 2018, the China · Daishan Island International Kite Festival was held in Daishan, Zhoushan. More than 70 domestic and international kite teams participated in the competition. There were more than ten thousand people participating kite flying performances. And competitions were held in the beautiful Lulan Qingsha flying field of Daishan. At the same time, in order to enrich the content of the kite festival, the organizer held the first kite product fair, attracting more than 20 kite companies from home and abroad to participate in the exhibition and look for business opportunities. The organizers also arranged a leisure interactive section including the "wind corridor" viewing area, the "kite show" performance area, the special food area and the beach sports entertainment and leisure area, allowing the audience to experience various kinds of leisure events while watching the kite events. The unique leisure and entertainment activities promoted tourism consumption.

大庆连环湖雪地风筝锦标赛

近年来，大庆市杜尔伯特县通过举办雪地风筝赛等冰雪活动，将雪地风筝赛由表演项目晋升为冬季旅游主打项目，做足冰雪文化、冰雪艺术、冰雪体育和冰雪旅游基本功，提升了冬季旅游品牌影响力和旅游目的地号召力，将雪地风筝打造成为一个有代表性的区域名片。赛事活动每年吸引一大批来自全国各地的风筝爱好者前来观风筝表演、赏北国雪景、体验雪地温泉，享受冰雪世界带来的刺激与乐趣。杜尔伯特县先后被授予"中国雪地风筝之乡"，"省级雪地风筝训练基地"等称号。

中国大庆第三届连环湖雪地风筝锦标赛暨杜尔伯特首届冰雪那达慕，于 2018 年 1 月 27 日在连环湖温泉景区火热开赛。来自北京、上海、江苏、山东、宁夏、辽宁、吉林、湖南、山西等 26 省市的 36 支代表队 153 人参加比赛。风筝比赛共分为 2 个大项 9 个小项，其中雪地风筝竞技赛分为 5 公里速度赛、9 公里三角绕标赛、15 公里穿越耐力赛；传统风筝表演赛分为龙串类风筝赛、串类最多风筝赛、滚地龙风筝赛、软体造型（挂件）风筝赛、双线运动风筝团体芭蕾赛、四线运动风筝团体芭蕾赛。首届冰雪那达慕将风靡全球的雪地风筝极限运动与蒙古族的民族体育文化活动有机融合，让游客在观赏极限刺激雪地风筝的同时，还可以参与博克、射箭、投掷布鲁等民族体育活动，观赏到安代舞、威风锣鼓、东北大秧歌等北方特点的歌舞，沐浴到雪地温泉和蒙医药特色温泉，体验到民俗冬捕渔猎活动。

Daqing Lianhuan Lake Snowfield Kite Championship

In recent years, Dulbert in Daqing has organized snow and ice events such as the snowfield kite competition. The performance project has been upgraded to the main project in winter tourism. The culture, art, sports and tourism of ice and snow have been integrated together. It has enhanced the influence of winter tourism brands and the appeal of tourist destinations, and has made snow-field kites a representative regional name card. The event attracts a large number of kite enthusiasts from all over the country to watch kite performances, enjoy the snow scene of northern country, experience the springs in snow fields, and enjoy the excitement and fun brought by the ice and snow world. Durbert has been awarded the title of China's Snowfield Kite Town and Provincial Snow-filed Kite Training Base.

The 3rd Lianhua Lake Snow-field Kite Championship in Daqing, China and the first Ice Snow Nadam in Dulbert were opened on January 27, 2018 in the hot springs scenic area of Lianhuan Lake. 158 people from 36 delegations of 26 provinces and municipalities including Beijing, Shanghai, Jiangsu, Shandong, Ningxia, Liaoning, Jilin, Hunan, and Shanxi, etc participated in the competition. The kite competition is divided into 2 major items and 9 sub items, of which the snow-field kite competition is divided into 5 km speed race, 9 km triangle round competition, 15 km endurance race; traditional kite exhibition competition is divided into dragon string kite, top stringed kite, the rolling dragon kite, the inflation (pendant), dual-line sports kite group ballet, and the quad-line sports kite group ballet competition. The first ice and snow Nadam integrated the extreme sports of the snow-field kites that are popular around the world with the Mongolian national sports and cultural activites, allowing visitors to watch the extreme stimulating snow-field kites while participating in national sports such as Boke, archery and throwing Bulu, etc. The visitors had the chance to witness the songs and dances with North China characteristic, such as the Andai Dance, imposing percussion, Northeastern Yangko, etc., and experience bathing in the hot springs and Mongolian medicine hot springs, and the folk fishing and hunting activities in winter.

天津风筝文化艺术节

天津是中国风筝的主要产地之一。天津风筝以"魏记"生产的风筝最为精美、著名。"魏记"风筝发展到今天已有 100 余年的历史，国家级非物质文化遗产项目"风筝魏"的发展经久不衰，在魏元泰第二代传人魏慎行，第三代传人魏永昌、魏永珍，第四代传人魏国秋的继承和不断创新下，风筝魏的风筝品种已经达到了 1000 多个品种。近年来，为了传承天津传统风筝文化，天津市西青区创办了风筝文化节。风筝节举办地点在世界精武文化中心精武门·中华武林园的霍元甲纪念馆万人广场，活动内容主要包括，"风筝魏"等老字号现场展示，风筝制作技巧，放飞巨型风筝，还举办了亲子风筝 DIY 活动，让市民体验亲手制作风筝的乐趣。此外，市民和游客除了观看风筝放飞表演，还可到霍元甲纪念馆里近距离观赏"风筝博览展"。

Tianjin Kite Culture and Art Festival

Tianjin is one of the main production bases of Chinese kites. Tianjin kites are featured with the beautiful and famous kites produced by Wei Ji. The Wei Ji kite has more than 100 years of history. The development of the national intangible cultural heritage project "Kite Wei" has been enduring for a long time. Under the inheritance and constant innovation of the second generation of Wei Yuantai named Wei Shenxing, the third generation Wei Yongchang and Wei Yongzhen, the four generations Wei Guoqiu, the varieties of Wei's kites have reached more than 1,000. In recent years, in order to inherit the traditional kite culture in Tianjin, the Xiqing District of Tianjin has established the Kite Culture Festival. The Kite Festival is held at the Huo Yuanjia Memorial Hall Square of Chinese Wulin Garden of the World Jingwu Cultural Center Jingwumen. The activities include the live show of time-honored brand such as "Kite Wei", kite making skills demonstration, flying of giant kites, and parent-child kite DIY event, which allows the public to experience the fun of making kites by hand. In addition to watch the kite flying show, the citizens and tourists can watch the Kite Expo at the Huo Yuanjia Memorial Hall.

万山国际风筝节

铜仁市万山国际风筝节始创于 2016 年，是在学习借鉴潍坊国际风筝会的基础上，与国际风筝联合会、国家体育总局社会体育指导中心、潍坊国际风筝会办公室等联合打造的国际性风筝盛会。每届风筝节万山都邀请到 20 多个国家和地区的国外高水平风筝放飞队，以及国内 20 多支、100 多人的专业风筝放飞队参加，并组织开展饮食文化艺术节、风筝知识大赛、爱我万山放飞梦想等多项系列活动。2017 年，创新举办了全国首届盘鹰风筝大赛。

铜仁市万山区有着独特的区位优势，航空、高铁等现代化立体交通网络非常便捷，同时拥有适合风筝放飞的气候条件和足够开阔的比赛场地。风筝节以"风筝牵手，文化搭台，经贸唱戏"为主旨，充分展示了铜仁市的时尚、活力、开放，为广大市民提供了一场视觉盛宴。通过风筝节进一步塑造和提升铜仁城市形象，扩大对外交流，更好地带动铜仁文化、体育、旅游和经贸发展。

Wanshan International Kite Festival

Founded in 2016, Tongren Wanshan International Kite Festival is an international kite event, which is co-organized with the International Kite Federation, the Leisure Sports Center of the General Administration of Sport of China, and the Weifang International Kite Festival Office, was held on the base of learning the Weifang International Kite Festival. Foreign high-level kite flying teams from more than 20 countries and regions, as well as more than 100 fliers from more than 20 domestic professional kite flying teams participated in the event. On this event, a series of activities, such as food culture and art festivals, kite knowledge contests, Love Wanshan and Fly Dreams were held. In 2017, the first national eagle kite competition was initiated.

Wanshan District of Tongren has a unique advantage in location. The modern three-dimensional transportation network such as aviation and high-speed rail is very convenient. At the same time, it has the climatic conditions suitable for kite flying and the open field of competition. The kite festival is based on the theme that kite links the culture, economy and trade. It fully demonstrates the fashion, vitality and openness of Tongren and makes the general public enjoy the event very much. Through the kite festival, the image of Tongren is further shaped and enhanced, foreign exchanges are expanded, and culture, sports, tourism and economic and trade development of Tongren are promoted.

南昌湾里区风筝文化节

为弘扬中华民族传统文化，丰富湾里旅游活动内涵，让更多人认识湾里、走进湾里，全面展现大美湾里"筝筝日上"的图景，开创"大美湾里"新境界，南昌市湾里区于2016年创办风筝文化节，由国家体育总局社会体育指导中心支持，江西省体育总会主办，湾里区教科体局、湾里区旅发委、梅岭旅游公司协办，幸福街道办事处承办。

"大美湾里·筝筝日上"2018江西省第三届大型风筝文化节于11月3日至4日在南昌市湾里区岭秀湖广场盛大举行。国内外风筝高手齐聚湾里，奉献了一场精美的"天空盛宴"。47支海内外风筝队伍、百名风筝高手、数百只大型风筝同场竞技，角逐龙串、软板串、硬板串、软翅串、硬翅串、串类最长、最大风筝、软体风筝、最佳空中效果、运动风筝（技巧风筝）、新奇特风筝、盘旋风筝等12个专业奖项。风筝节期间，同时举办风筝文化展、露天帐篷电影、家庭风筝DIY、老年追风合唱团、情侣风筝放飞等精彩绝伦的活动，全景展示风筝这一传统文化，全面展现大美湾里"筝筝日上"的图景。此次湾里风筝文化节还增设了"筝智能"活动，机器人表演秀、人工智能对弈、VR体验展纷纷亮相，为大众带来了一场丰富多彩、别开生面的科技展。

Wanli District Kite Culture Festival in Nanchang

In order to promote the traditional culture of the Chinese nation, enrich the tourism activities in the Wanli, let more people know about Wanli and come to Wanli, fully display the picture of Wanli, and create a new Wanli, Wanli District of Nanchang established the Kite Culture Festival in 2016. The event was supported by the Leisure Sports Center of the General Administration of Sport of China, Hosted by the Jiangxi Provincial Sports Federation, co-organized by the Wanli District Education, Science and Sports Bureau, the Wanli District Tourism Development Committee, and the Meiling Tourism Company, undertaken by the Happiness Street Office.

With the theme of "Beautiful Wanli, Be More and More Prosperous", the third large-scale Kite Culture Festival in Jiangxi Province was held from November 3rd to 4th 2018 at Lingxiu Lake Square, Wanli District, Nanchang. The kite masters at home and abroad gathered in Wanli and put on a wonderful show in the sky. 47 kite teams at home and abroad, 100 kites masters, hundreds of large kites competed in the field. They competed for 12 professional kites awards, including dragon strings, soft board strings, hard board strings, soft-winged strings, hard-winged strings, longest string, largest kites, inflation, best air effects, sports kites (kite skill), new and fancy kites, and hovering kites. During the kite festival, the Kite Culture Exhibition, open-air tent movie, kite DIY by families, Performance by Chasing-wind Choir, kite flying by the couples and other exciting activities were held during the event, which displayed traditional culture of kites in a panoramic view, and fully displayed the beautiful kites in Wanli. The Kite Intelligence event was a special activity at the Wanli Kite Culture Festival. The robot show, the artificial intelligence chess game, and the VR experience show were held at the festival, bringing a colorful and unique technology exhibition to the public.

四川北川民族风筝节

北川民族风筝节已成功举办4届。北川是国际风筝联合会的放飞基地，近年来，多次成功承办或举办了各类大型活动，成功打造了北川民族文化节品牌，助推了全域旅游健康持续发展。

每一届北川民族风筝节，都吸引来自国内外的数十支风筝代表队前来参赛表演，与羌乡儿女一起放风筝、游羌城，畅享春的欢乐。第35届潍坊国际风筝会选拔赛暨北川第四届民族风筝节于2018年3月24日在北川羌族自治县国家级航空飞行示范营地开幕。主会场设在北川羌族自治县国家级航空飞行示范营地，并在新生广场、巴拿恰周边、新县城中小学、体育中心等地设分会场。旨在展示北川国家航空飞行营地的风采，进一步打造北川民族文化体育旅游品牌。

Beichuan National Kite Festival in Sichuan

The Beichuan National Kite Festival has been successfully held for 4 sessions. Beichuan is the kite flying base of the International Kite Federation. In recent years, it has successfully undertaken or hosted various large-scale events and successfully built the brand of the Beichuan National Culture Festival, which has promoted the healthy and sustainable development of tourism in the whole region.

Each Beichuan National Kite Festival attracts dozens of kite teams from home and abroad to participate in the competition and performances. They flew kites and visited Qiangcheng to enjoy the joy in spring together with the local people. The qualification trials of 35th Weifang International Kite Festival and the Beichuan Fourth National Kite Festival were held on March 24, 2018 in the National Aviation Flight Demonstration Camp of Qiang Ethnic Minority Autonomous County of Beichuan. The main venue was located in the above place, and sub-venues were set up in Xinsheng Square, Banaqia, Primary and Secondary School of the new county, Sports Center and other places. The purpose is to show the view of the Beichuan National Aviation Flight Camp and further build the brand of Beichuan national culture, sports and tourism.

大明宫国家遗址公园风筝会

大明宫国际遗址公园风筝会自 2011 年创办，至今已成功举办 8 届。大明宫国家遗址公园掀起的风筝热潮已成为人们娱乐、放松、感受大自然的优选方式。这项风筝会活动由西安市旅游发展委员会、共青团西安市委、西安曲江新区管委会、西安曲江大明宫遗址区保护改造办公室、陕西省唐大明宫遗址文物保护基金会主办，由西安曲江大明宫国家遗址公园管理有限公司、西安教育电视台承办，旨在通过系列活动的举办，为广大游客市民带来非比寻常的踏春体验。

2018 年 4 月 3 日上午，第二届丝绸之路国际风筝节暨大明宫国家遗址公园第八届风筝会开幕，来自 15 个国家和地区的近百名风筝专家齐聚御道广场，助力春游、点亮大明宫底色，搭建全球风筝文化桥梁，为广大游客市民带来一场"筝"奇斗艳的春日盛会。

Kite Festival in National Heritage Park of Daming Palace

The Kite Festival in the National Heritage Park of Daming Palace was founded in 2011 and has been successfully held for 8 sessions. The kite boom in the National Heritage Park of Daming Palace has become the preferred way for people to entertain, relax and feel the beauty of nature. The kite event was hosted by Xi'an Tourism Development Committee, the Communist Youth League Committee in Xi'an, Management Committee of Qujiang New District in Xi'an, Qujiang Daming Palace Site Protection and Reconstruction Office in Xi'an, and Shaanxi Tang Dynasty Daming Palace Heritage Site Cultural Relics Protection Foundation, and was undertaken by Xi'an Qujiang Daming Palace National Heritage Park Management Co., Ltd. and Xi'an Education TV Station, with the aim to provide an extraordinary outing experience in spring for the tourists and local citizens through a series of events.

On the morning of April 3, 2018, the 2nd Silk Road International Kite Festival and the 8th Kite Festival of Daming Palace National Heritage Park were opened. Nearly 100 kite experts from 15 countries and regions gathered in Yudao Square to dress up the Daming Palace and made the spring tour more beautiful. A global kite culture bridge was built. And the event brought a classic spring with kites to the masses and tourists.

厦门国际风筝节

厦门国际风筝节，已成功举办 11 届。经过多年的持续努力，打造成了以风筝为载体展示城市魅力的城市嘉年华活动。

2018 年 11 月 3 日，第 11 届厦门国际风筝节在观音山梦幻海岸黄金沙滩开幕。本届风筝节是 2018 厦门国际海洋周的配套活动之一，共邀请境内外的 16 支风筝队、59 名风筝竞技高手，为市民带来特技风筝表演和大型软体风筝放飞展示。这些风筝队中，既有厦门国际风筝节的老朋友——来自上海的特技风筝队、马来西亚 kkf 风筝队、马六甲风筝队，又有首次来厦的湖北炜辉特技运动风筝队、日本风筝协会队、A2SKA。精彩的放飞表演吸引了大批的市民和游客前来观赏参与。

International Kite Festival in Xiamen

The Xiamen International Kite Festival has been successfully held for 11 sessions. After years of continuous efforts, it has become a city carnival event that uses the kite as a carrier to show the charm of the city.

On November 3, 2018, the 11th Xiamen International Kite Festival was opened on the Golden Beach of Guanyin Mountain of the Dream Coast. The kite festival was one of the supporting activities of the 2018 Xiamen International Ocean Week. 16 kite teams and 59 kite athletes from home and abroad were invited to bring stunt kite performances and large-scale inflation kite flying demonstrations to the public. Among these kite teams, there are old friends of the Xiamen International Kite Festival. They were the stunt kite team from Shanghai, the kkf kite team from Malaysia, the Malacca kite team, and teams came for the first time, such as the Hubei Weihui Stunt Sports Kite Team and the Japan Kite Association team, A2SKA. The wonderful flying show attracted a large number of citizens and tourists to watch and participate in the flying.

保利国际风筝节

保利国际风筝节作为中国重要的风筝盛会之一，已成功举办了 8 届。每一届保利国际风筝节，都邀请来自美国、墨西哥、新西兰、马来西亚、泰国、乌克兰等国家地区的代表队，以及来自全国各个省份代表队积极参与。

第八届保利国际熊猫风筝节于 2018 年 3 月 18 日至 20 日在成都保利狮子湖隆重举行。风筝节主题是"熊猫人妖艳儿的飞"。本届风筝节聚集了来自全球多个国家地区的代表队，以及全国省份代表队的积极参加，各个代表队都带

来了代表各自最新成果的风筝精品力作，并成功在现场放飞。本届保利国际风筝节在观众人数上也创造了新的记录，累计观众人数达 25 万人次以上。

Baoli International Kite Festival

As one of the important kite festivals in China, Baoli International Kite Festival has been successfully held for 8 sessions. Teams from the United States, Mexico, New Zealand, Malaysia, Thailand, Ukraine and other countries and regions were invited to the Poly International Kite Festival invites. Representatives from various provinces across the country actively participated in the event.

The 8th Baoli International Panda Kite Festival was held in Lion Lake, Baoli, Chengdu from March 18th to 20th, 2018. The theme of the kite festival was "Panda gone". Representatives from many countries and regions around the world, as well as the national provincial teams actively participated in the festival. Each team brought a kite masterpiece representing their latest achievements and successfully flew them on the scene. The festival has also created a new record in the number of visitors, with a cumulative audience of more than 250,000.

武汉江岸区国际风筝节

江岸区国际风筝节，已成功举办8届。8年来，江岸区国际风筝节不断传承创新，引领江岸区国际风筝节品牌更上新台阶，丰富了辖区群众的精神文化生活，促进了全民健身，展现了"精美江岸、品质江岸"的魅力形象，使风筝节的社会影响力进一步扩大。

2018年10月27日，由武汉市体育局、武汉市旅游委、武汉市水务局指导，中共武汉市江岸区委、武汉市江岸区人民政府主办的"与军运同行"2018年江岸区第八届国际风筝节在汉口江滩三阳广场亲水平台盛大开幕，吸引了俄罗斯、土耳其、加纳、北京、广东等国家和地区的众多风筝爱好者参加。风筝节期间，高水平的国际风筝大赛，首次举行的大型夜光风筝暨风筝特技《空中芭蕾》表演，Mini风筝音乐节，非遗文化展等一系列丰富的活动，为本届风筝节注入了创新元素，得到了社会各界的广泛关注和国际友人的赞誉。

Jiang'an District International Kite Festival in Wuhan

The Jiang'an District International Kite Festival has been successfully held for 8 sessions. In the past 8 years, the festival has continued to inherit and made new innovation, leading the festival to a new level, and has enriched the spiritual and cultural life of the local people, and promoted the fitness of the whole nation and demonstrated the glamour image of Jiang'an, and further expanded the social influence of the kite festival.

On October 27, 2018, guided by Wuhan Sports Bureau, Wuhan Tourism Commission, Wuhan Water Affairs Bureau, hosted by Wuhan Jiang'an District Committee of Wuhan CPC Municipality, and Jiang'an District People's Government of Wuhan, with the theme of Peer with Military Sport, the 2018 Jiang'an District the 8th International Kite Festival were grandly opened in the Water Platform of Sanyang Square in Jiangtan, Hankou, attracted many kite enthusiasts from Russia, Turkey, Ghana, Beijing, Guangdong and other countries and regions. During the kite festival, the high-level international kite competition, the first large-scale luminous kite and kite stunt "air ballet" performance, the Mini Kite Festival, the intangible cultural heritage exhibition and a series of rich activities were held. The above activities added innovation into this kite festival. The event have received wide attention from all walks of life and won praise from international friends.

武汉木兰草原风筝节

　　武汉木兰草原风筝节创办于 2013 年，旨在扩大木兰文化旅游的品牌影响力，让世界了解黄陂、了解武汉，提高城市文化软实力，弘扬武汉城市精神、扩大城市影响力，同时打响武汉风筝国际赛事品牌，促进风筝运动，弘扬风筝文化，拉动旅游消费。

　　2018 年 4 月 14 日，中国·武汉木兰草原国际风筝邀请赛开幕式于木兰草原风景区举办，国家体育总局社体中心，中国风筝协会及友好城市、港澳台地区代表队代表等出席本次开幕式。22 个国家和地区的 47 支队伍、近 200 位风筝爱好者欢聚草原，与武汉千名风筝爱好者同台竞技、交流学习。本届国际风筝邀请赛，设有特技风筝表演区、传统风筝区、大型软体风筝区以及风筝 DIY 区四个主区域，除主体赛事外，还有风筝校园爱心巡礼、国际风筝展演、万人签名墙、万人放飞、六角风筝打斗表演赛、亲子 DIY 风筝制作、风筝文化摄影比赛、观众互动风筝赛等丰富多样的周边活动。

　　本次邀请赛特别引进了近年兴起的一项时尚休闲运动——室内风筝。有别于常见的户外风筝放飞，室内风筝是在封闭无风的场馆内，依靠放飞者熟练的操控，融合音乐、舞蹈、灯光进行的风筝放飞和表演。为增进国内外室内风筝爱好者的交流学习，本次邀请赛在黄陂体育馆举办了首届武汉室内风筝展演和对抗赛，室内风筝放飞表演和比赛，进行了大胆尝试和探索，对武汉乃至全国室内风筝运动发展起到了示范和推动作用。

Wuhan Mulan Grassland Kite Festival

The Wuhan Mulan Grassland Kite Festival was founded in 2013 with the aim to expand the influence of Mulan Cultural Tourism, let the world know about Huangpi and Wuhan, improve the soft power of urban culture, promote the urban spirit of Wuhan, expand the influence of the city, make the Wuhan Kite International Competition more and more famous, promote kite sports and culture and stimulate the development of tourism.

On April 14, 2018, the opening ceremony of the China Mulan Prairie International Kite Invitational Tournament was held in Mulan Grassland Scenic Area. The Leisure Sports Center of the General Administration of Sport of China, the China Kite Association and the sister cities, representatives from Hong Kong, Macao and Taiwan delegations attended the opening ceremony. 47 teams from 22 countries and regions and nearly 200 kite enthusiasts gathered in the grasslands to compete and exchange with thousands of kite enthusiasts in Wuhan. There were four main featured areas in this event: stunt kite performance area, traditional kite area, large inflation kite area and kite DIY area. In addition to the main event, there were love tour of kite on campus, international kite show, and signature wall, 10,000 people kite flying, hexagonal kite fighting competition, parent-child kite DIY, kite culture photography competition, and interactive kite competition participated by audiences, etc.

This invitational event has specially introduced a fashion and leisure sport that has emerged in recent years - indoor kites. Different from the common outdoor kite flying, the indoor kite flying and performances is played in the closed windless venue, the skilled manipulative control is required, the music, dance and lighting are integrated into the flying and performance. In order to promote the exchanges and learning of indoor kite enthusiasts at home and abroad, the first Wuhan indoor kite show and competition, the indoor kite flying show and competition were held in Huangpi Gymnasium, and bold attempts and explorations were made to develop indoor kite sports. The above events have played a demonstration and promotion role in kite sport in Wuhan and even the whole country.

廊坊·第什里风筝节

第什里风筝文化传承已久，距今已有 500 余年历史，形成了集北京、天津流派于一身，独具特色的代表性风筝——宫廷风筝。第什里风筝运动氛围浓厚，已举办大规模赛事 10 多次。2018 年 5 月 11 日 -12 日举办了第四届中国廊坊·第什里风筝节暨全国风筝锦标赛（北方赛区）。此次大赛以"什里芳华，艺生相伴"为主题，以传承风筝文化、做大文化产业、搞活乡村旅游、带动群众致富、实现乡村振兴为目标，办出了超越往届的新特色，有来自全国的 31 支代表队，180 余名运动员

参加，赛事活动包括传统风筝赛、竞技风筝赛和特色风筝表演赛等 3 个大项，15 个子项。从 2016 年起，廊坊市委、市政府高度重视第什里景区建设，举全市之力重点打造第什里风筝小镇，成为廊坊一张代表性名片。

Dishili Kite Festival in Langfang

The kite culture in Dishili has been inherited for a long time. It has been more than 500 years' history and has formed representative palace kite, which integrated the feature of Beijing and Tianjin kite. Dishili has a strong atmosphere in kite sport and has hosted more than 10 large-scale events. The 4th China Langfang · Dishili Kite Festival and National Kite Championship (Northern Competition Area) were held on May 11 to 12, 2018. With the theme of the Beauty of Dishili integrated with Arts of Kite, the competition aims to inherit the kite culture, expand the cultural industry, invigorate rural tourism, drive the masses to become rich, and achieve rural revitalization. The event had new characteristic compared with that of the prior events. more than 180 fliers of 31 teams from all over the country participated in the event. The competition covered 3 major items and 15 sub-items, such as traditional kite competition, fighting kite race and characteristic kite show. Since 2016, the Langfang Municipal Party Committee and the Municipal Government have attached great importance to the construction of the Dishili Scenic Area, and have given all the city's strength to build the Dishili Kite Town and it has become a representative business card of Langfang.

崇州风筝节

四川崇州市自古有制作和放飞风筝习俗，尤以金鸡乡为甚，以风筝制作技术精湛、种类繁多而闻名国内外，享有风筝之乡的美誉。为活跃群众文化生活，自1999年开始，举办崇州金鸡风筝节。此外，近年来在崇州市羊马嘉裕湿地公园举办的国际风筝邀请赛、四川省风筝比赛等赛事活动，产生了广泛影响，该地已成为成都近郊地区开展风筝户外活动的好去处。

一年一度的"崇州金鸡风筝节"是风筝的盛会，四川省风筝比赛、全国风筝精英赛经常在此举行。风筝节活动内容色彩纷呈，风筝类特色活动有：东西部风筝对抗赛，川西风筝精英赛，国内著名风筝放飞表演队表演，大型、超大型、微型、精品、收藏品风筝展览；文艺类活动有：兰花展，川剧、京剧表演，烙铁画、奇石、根艺、道明竹编展和大型文艺节目；群众参与性活动有：游览金鸡风筝之乡，群众性自由放飞希望活动，风筝制作表演，游客亲手制作风筝；

地方特色饮食文化活动有：品崇州名小吃查渣面、天主堂鸡片、王鸡肉、留客鸡、怀远三绝等。每年3月，春风和煦的崇州上空风筝飞舞，来自海内外的游客尽享放飞的乐趣。

Chongzhou Kite Festival

Chongzhou in Sichuan Province has the customs of flying kites since ancient times, especially in the town of Jinji. It is famous for its superb craftsmanship and a variety of kites, and enjoys the reputation of the hometown of kite. To promote the cultural life of the masses, since 1999, the Chongzhou Jinji Kite Festival has been held.In addition, in recent years, the International Kite Invitational Tournament and the Sichuan Kite Competition held in Yangmajiayu Wetland Park in Chongzhou have had wide influence. And the place has become a good place for kite outdoor activities in the suburbs of Chengdu.

The annual Chongzhou Jinji Kite Festival is a grand event for kites. Sichuan Kite Competition and the National Kite Classic Competition are usually held here. The activities of the festival cover East-West kite competition, West Sichuan Kite Classic Competition, kite flying performance by domestic famous kite teams, large, super large, miniature, boutique, collectible kite exhibition, orchid exhibition, Sichuan opera, Peking opera performance, iron painting, strange stone, root art, Daoming bamboo weaving exhibition and large-scale literary and artistic programs; visit the hometown of Jinji kites, free flying activities, kite production performance, hand-made kites by tourists; taste Chongzhou famous snacks Chazha Noodles, Tianzhutang chicken slice, king chicken, guests Chicken, three famous food of Huaiyuan, and so on. Every March, the tourists from home and abroad enjoy the fun of flying in the spring breeze of Chongzhou.

武隆仙女山国际风筝节

重庆武隆仙女山国际风筝节是中国西部规模盛大的国际性风筝主题盛会，自2013年创办以来，吸引着来自世界各地的顶级风筝选手及团队踊跃参加，架起了友谊和平的桥梁，为宣扬中国传统文化体育项目做出了积极贡献。

2018年武隆仙女山国际风筝节于4月29日在仙女山大草原举行，国际风筝表演赛精彩纷呈，各种动物风筝、卡通风筝、落地风筝等风筝元素与风车创意融合，七仙女主题风筝、多彩风车长廊、卡通情景风筝、蝴蝶蜻蜓海洋等不同风筝风车主题造型，给市民和游客带来了独特的视觉冲击和美的享受。

Wulong Fairy Mountain International Kite Festival

The Chongqing Wulong Fairy Mountain International Kite Festival is a grand international kite theme event in western China. Since its inception in 2013, it has attracted top-level kite players and teams from all over the world and built a bridge of friendship and peace, and has made positive contributions to the Chinese traditional culture and sports.

In 2018, the Wulong Fairy Mountain International Kite Festival was held on April 29th in the prairie of the Fairy Mountain. The international kite exhibition was very exciting. Various kites such as animal kites, cartoon kites and floor kites were merged with windmills. Kite and windmills with different themes, such as seven fairy kites and colorful windmills gallery, cartoon scene kites, butterflies, dragonflies and oceans, brought unique visual impact and beauty to the citizens and tourists.

双鱼岛国际风筝节

双鱼岛国际风筝节于2016年创办，由福建省社会体育指导中心主办，海西晨报社、厦门市风筝协会承办。在双鱼岛举办国际风筝节，旨在注入更多的文化活动内容到岛上，打造旅游度假、休闲娱乐和生态居住的圣地。举办双鱼岛国际风筝节以来，先后有来自芬兰、俄罗斯、马来西亚、加拿大、潍坊、中国香港、大连等境内外的近百支风筝团队前来参加，用风格各异的风筝在双鱼岛海梦湾蓝天碧海间画出一道道靓丽风景线，吸引了大批市民和游客登岛参与盛会，促进了文化旅游的发展。

Double-fish Island International Kite Festival

The Double-fish Island International Kite Festival was founded in 2016 and hosted by the Fujian Provincial Social Sports Guidance Center, undertaken by Haixi Morning News and Xiamen Kite Association. The holding of the International Kite Festival held in Double-fish Island is aimed to add more cultural activities into the island to create a good place for tourism, recreation and ecological living. Since the establishment of the festival, nearly 100 kite teams from Finland, Russia, Malaysia, Canada, Weifang, Hong Kong China, Dalian, etc. have come and participated in the kites events. A beautiful scenery of kites was drawn between the blue sky and the blue sea, attracting a large number of citizens and tourists to the island to participate in the grand event and promote cultural tourism.

太湖风筝节

每年一度在江苏宜兴周铁镇举办的太湖风筝节，至今已成功举办了21届。周铁镇位于太湖之滨，放飞风筝有着得天独厚的地理优势，是太湖流域风筝的发源地、传承地。该镇党委政府历来重视风筝活动的开展和风筝文化的发展，早在1990年3月，就在周铁镇成立了宜兴市风筝协会。目前，其会员已从成立时的30名发展到了全市各地上千人，自发的风筝爱好者超过万人。近年来，为更好地传承、弘扬和发展这一民间特色文体活动，该镇还投资1700多万元，在竺山湖湿地公园修建了6万㎡的太湖风筝广场，在周铁老街修建了太湖风筝博物馆。该镇把传统风筝制作技艺与太湖流域民俗文化相融合，如今，风筝已成为周铁镇一张响当当的名片。2013年，"周铁鹞笛（灯）风筝制作技艺"被评为"无锡市非物质文化遗产"。2016年，周铁镇被命名为"江苏省风筝放飞基地""无锡市特色文化之乡——风筝之乡"。2017年，该镇被命名为"无锡市第二批非物质文化遗产传承示范基地""中国风筝之乡"。

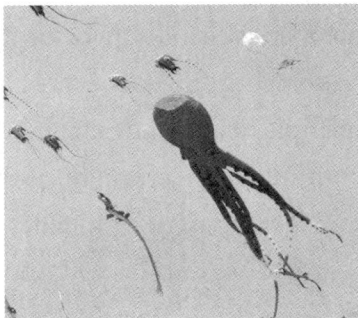

2018年10月20至22日，中国·宜兴第二十一届太湖风筝节暨2018年"东泽杯"国际风筝邀请赛、全国风筝精英赛（宜兴站）、江苏省风筝公开赛在宜兴周铁镇太湖风筝广场举行，来自国内外近300名参赛队员将齐聚周铁，同台竞技。在美丽的太湖湖畔，漫天飞舞的纸鸢"筝"奇斗艳，给广大市民和游客奉献了一场震撼人心、美轮美奂的视觉盛宴。

Taihu Kite Festival

The Taihu Kite Festival, held in Zhoutie Town, Yixing, Jiangsu, has been successfully held for 21 sessions. Located on the shore of Taihu Lake, Zhoutie Town has a unique geographical advantage and is the birthplace and inheritance of kites in the Taihu Lake Basin. The party committee government of the town has always attached importance to the development of kite activities and the development of kite culture. As early as March 1990, the Yixing Kite Association was established in Zhoutie Town. At present, its membership has grown from 30 at the time of its establishment to thousands of people across the city, and more than 10,000 spontaneous kite enthusiasts. In recent years, in order to better inherit, carry forward and develop this folk cultural and sports activities, the town has invested more than 17 million yuan to build Taihu Kite Square with a space of 60,000 m2 in the Wetland Park of Zhushan Lake and build a Taihu Lake Kite Museum along the Zhoutie Ancient Street. The town combines traditional kite making skills with folk culture in the Taihu Basin. Today, kites have become a namecard of Zhoutie. In 2013, "Zhoutie Yaodi (light) kite production skills" was listed "Wuxi Intangible Cultural Heritage". In 2016, Zhoutie was named as Jiangsu Province Kite Flying Base and Town of Characteristic Culture in Wuxi - Hometown of Kite. In 2017, the town was listed in "the second batch of intangible cultural heritage inheritance demonstration base in Wuxi" and the hometown of Chinese kites.

From October 20th to 22nd, 2018, China's 21st Taihu Kite Festival in Yixing, 2018 Dongze Cup International Kite Invitational Tournament, National Kite Classic Competition (Yixing Station), Jiangsu Kite Open Tournament in Taihu were held at the Kite Square in Zhoutie, Yixing, nearly 300 players from home and abroad gathered and competed in Zhoutie. On the shores of the beautiful Taihu Lake, the kite flying attracted lots of public and tourists.

慈溪长河镇风筝节

浙江省慈溪市长河镇人文荟萃，文化底蕴深厚。而其中源远流长，流派纷呈，以长河为代表的姚北风筝，其浓郁的乡土气息和淳朴鲜明的艺术风格，在民间艺术宝库中一枝独秀。长河镇历来就有制作和放飞风筝的传统，如今又是市级非物质文化遗产风筝制作基地。为进一步推动全民健身活动的深入开展，长河镇自 2013 年开始组织举办内容丰富多彩的风筝节，到目前，已成功举办了 6 届。长河镇在风筝节期间，注重在学校普及风筝文化，聘请了非物质文化遗产风筝制作传承人担任学校风筝课指导老师，专门给学生上风筝制作课，讲解风筝制作的技艺和放飞风筝的技巧。当地学校通过风筝节这个平台举办主题征文、风筝制作比赛、风筝绘画比赛，极大地激发了学生的学习热情，学生从中得到了充分锻炼。同时，长河镇还将非物质文化遗产风筝制作传承，向乡村、企业拓展，通过各种形式弘扬风筝文化。

Changhe Kite Festival in Cixi

The town of Changhe in Cixi, Zhejiang has a rich gathering of talents and profound cultural heritage. Among them, the Yaobei kites represented by the Changhe River have a long history. The kites are unique in the folk art due to their rich local flavor and simple and beautiful artistic style. Changhe has always had the tradition of making and flying kites, and now it is a city-level intangible cultural heritage kite production base. In order to further promote the in-depth development of national fitness activities, Changhe has organized a variety of kite festivals since 2013. Up to now, it has successfully held 6 sessions. During the Kite Festival, Changhe popularized kite culture in schools, and hired the intangible cultural heritage kite production inheritor to serve as the instructor for kite class in schools, had kite making classes for students, and explained the skills of kite making and the skills of flying kites. The local school organized the theme essay, kite making competition and kite painting competition through the platform of the kite festival, which greatly stimulated the students' enthusiasm for learning, and the students got full exercise from the events. At the same time, Changhe also expanded the heritage of intangible cultural heritage of kites to the countryside and enterprises, and promoted the kite culture through various forms.

大同风筝节

　　山西省大同市风筝节已连续成功举办了8届。在举办风筝节过程当中，大同市有关部门注重体育和文化的有效结合，让风筝体育项目更加生动化、多元化，吸引全民参与，促进文化体育发展。

　　2018年4月14日，大同市第十届职工文化博览会·风筝放飞活动暨大同市第八届风筝节开幕式在山西省大同县乌龙峡风景区举行。此次活动由大同市总工会、大同市体育局、大同市体育总会、大同市社体中心主办，桑干古道乌龙峡景区、大同市飞翔风筝俱乐部、大同市风筝协会承办，吸引了来自全国五省市的20多家风筝俱乐部和民间组织的风筝高手参加。

Datong Kite Festival

The Datong Kite Festival in Shanxi Province has been successfully held for 8 consecutive years. During the organization of the kite festival, the relevant departments of Datong attached great importance to the effective combination of sports and culture to make the kite sports project more vivid and diversified, attracting the participation of the people and promoting the development of culture and sports.

On April 14, 2018, the opening ceremony of the 10th Workers' Cultural Exposition, Kite Flying and Datong 8th Kite Festival was held in Wulong Canyon Scenic Area, in Datong, Shanxi. The event was hosted by Datong Municipal Federation of Trade Unions, Datong Municipal Sports Bureau, Datong Sports Association and Datong Leisure Sports Center, and was undertaken by the Sanggan Ancient Road Wulong Canyon Scenic Area, Datong Flying Kite Club, and Datong Kite Association. More than 20 kite clubs in five provinces and cities and kite masters from civil organizations participated in the event.

张家口康保草原国际风筝节

康保草原国际风筝节，创办于2013年。每年都邀请国内外风筝团队参赛，组织国际大型风筝放飞表演，组织运动风筝、盘鹰风筝进行竞技比赛。通过竞技表演来展示国际、国内风筝放飞技巧，是规模较大的草原国际风筝盛会。在举办风筝比赛和放飞表演的同时，还组织开展风筝展览展示，民族民间文艺表演等丰富多彩的活动，宣传推介康保旅游投资环境，打造城市名片，吸引市民和广大游客积极参与。

Zhangjiakou Kangbao Grassland International Kite Festival

The Kangbao Grassland International Kite Festival was founded in 2013. Every year, many domestic and foreign kite teams were invited to participate in the competition. International large-scale kite flying performances, sports kites and hawk kites competitions were organized. It is a large-scale grassland international kite event to show international and domestic kite flying skills through competitive performances While holding kite competitions and flying performances, a variety of activities such as kite exhibitions and national folklore performances were organized to promote the tourism and investment environment of Kangbao, and attracted citizens and tourists.

奉贤风筝节

位于杭州湾北岸的奉贤，自 1992 年起，每年在早春三月或是金秋十月都要举办风筝节，以风筝会友，切磋风筝放飞技艺，这已成为奉贤人民的一个传统节日。

风筝节举办期间，奉贤海湾的国际风筝放飞场早早被各式风筝所占领，人们手牵风筝线怡然自乐，蓝天白云间看纸鸢翩翩起舞，追云逐日。小小的风筝寄托着人类的飞天之梦，风筝已然穿越了时空，架起了一座无形的文化桥梁。各路风筝高手、各种形状、材质的风筝、各种高超的技艺齐聚一堂。这里不仅仅是专业选手的舞台，更是孩子们的天堂。大人和孩子可以参加亲子活动，与孩子一起亲手做风筝，深入直接的了解风筝，感受风筝的魅力。除了风筝表演和比赛外，主办方还安排举行形式多样的"东方对虾节"、"经贸洽谈会"、"商品交流会"、文艺表演等文化旅游经贸活动，以从而实现风筝牵线，促经贸合作的目的。

Fengxian Kite Festival

Fengxian, located on the north shore of Hangzhou Bay, has been holding a kite festival every year in March of the early spring or in autumn since 1992. It is a traditional festival for the Fengxian people to make friends and learn kite flying skills.

During the kite festival, the international kite flying field in Fengxian Bay was occupied by various kites. People enjoyed themselves from kite flying under the blue sky and white clouds. The little kites were entrusted with the flying dreams of human beings. The kites have already crossed the time and space and set up an invisible cultural bridge. Kite masters of all kinds, kites of various shapes and materials, and various superb skills gathered together. It is not only a stage for professional players, but also a paradise for children. Adults and children can participate in parent-child activities, make kites together and learn about kites in depth, and feel the charm of kites. In addition to kite performances and competitions, the organizers also arranged cultural tourism and economic activities such as the Oriental Prawn Festival, Trade Fairs, Commodity Exchanges and cultural performances to achieve the goal of promoting economic and trade cooperation at the same time.

平潭国际风筝冲浪节

平潭是中国风力条件最好的地区之一，也是中国风筝冲浪运动发展最好的地区之一，自2012年以来已举办多场国际性风筝冲浪大赛，优越的风力和沙滩条件已经被国际风筝冲浪界所认可，现在每天都有很多国内外风筝冲浪爱好者自发前来平潭展开他们的追风之旅。赛事的成功举办将进一步扩大平潭风筝冲浪的国际影响力，为平潭国际旅游岛建设助力添彩。

风筝冲浪比赛以其时尚新颖、场面宏大、贴近观众、精彩刺激的特点，已经成为国际海洋运动中最具吸引力的赛事。第七届平潭国际风筝冲浪节暨世界风筝水翼板金杯赛于2018年9月10日至15日在平潭龙王头海滨浴场举行。此次比赛由世界风筝冲浪协会、中国帆船帆板运动协会、福建省体育局、平潭综合实验区管理委员会主办。赛事共吸引到了来自意大利、美国等23个国家和地区百名风筝冲浪高手齐聚岚岛，一起逐浪前行。比赛分为"2018世界风筝水翼板锦标赛""风筝板国际公开赛""风筝板全国锦标赛"，设有总奖金5万美元，国际等级排名分200分。

Pingtan International Kitesurfing Festival

Pingtan is one of the regions with the best wind conditions and one of the best development areas for kite surfing in China. Since 2012, it has hosted many international kite surfing competitions. The superior wind and beach conditions have been recognized by international kites-surfing field. Nowadays, many kite-surfing players will come here for kite surfing. The successful holding of the event further expands the international influence of kite surfing in Pingtan and facilitate the construction of International Tourism Island in Pingtan.

The kite surfing competition has become the most attractive event in the international ocean sports with its novelty, grand scene, closing to the audience and exciting features. The 7th Pingtan International Kitesurfing Festival and World Kite Waterfoil Gold Cup Competition was held from September 10th to 15th, 2018 at the Pingtan Longwangtou Bathing Beach. The competition was hosted by the World Kitesurfing Association, the China Yachting Association, Fujian Provincial Sports Bureau, and the Management Committee of Pingtan Comprehensive Experimental Zone. The event attracted more than 100 kitesurfers from 23 countries and regions, including Italy and the United States, to gather in Landao Island. The competition covered 2018 World Kite Waterfoil Championship, Kite Surfing International Open Competition and Kite Surfing National Championship. The total prize was 50,000 US dollars and international ranking score was 200 points.

海南博鳌国际风筝冲浪节

为提升琼海旅游国际化水平，推动"体育+旅游"发展，打造博鳌独特的体育旅游品牌，近年来，琼海市政府支持推动风筝冲浪运动，全力打造博鳌风筝冲浪运动国际赛事训练基地，将风筝冲浪赛事打造成博鳌的又一张靓丽名片。

2018年中国博鳌国际风筝冲浪节于5月3日晚在海南博鳌亚洲湾开幕，本次国际风筝冲浪节以青奥会风筝冲浪资格赛暨世界风筝冲浪青年锦标赛为主项。在为期5天的比赛期间，来自32个国家和地区的100名运动员就2018年布宜诺斯艾利斯夏季青奥会风筝冲浪项目的参赛名额展开了激烈的争夺。根据2018年布宜诺斯艾利斯夏季青奥会规定，全球男、女选手各有12个参加风筝冲浪项目的名额，且每个国家和地区限定一名。在本次比赛之前，已先后举行了数场洲际资格赛，各大洲已经产生男、女各一名参赛选手，剩下的参赛名额将在此次资格赛上决出。两位中国小将在2018世界风筝冲浪青年锦标赛障碍追逐赛项目中斩获两枚奖牌，张浩然在男子组获得亚军，李科汶获得女子组季军。

本次风筝冲浪赛事层次高、水平高，是琼海有史以来最具规模最高水准的国际体育赛事之一。在本届风筝冲浪节开幕式上，琼海市还被授予"世界风筝冲浪协会国际赛事中心"。

Hainan Boao International Kitesurfing Festival

In order to promote the internationalization level of tourism in Qionghai, promote the development of sports and tourism, and build a unique sports tourism brand in Boao, in recent years, Qionghai Municipal Government has supported the promotion of kite surfing and made efforts to build a training base for Boao kite surfing international competition. The kite surfing event has created another beautiful business card for Boao.

In 2018, the China Boao International Kitesurfing Festival was held in Asia Bay in Boao, on the evening of May 3. The International Kitesurfing Festival was dominated by the Youth Olympics Kitesurfing Qualification Competition and World Kitesurfing Youth Championship. During the five-day competition, 100 athletes from 32 countries and regions competed fiercely for the qualification of the 2018 Buenos Aires Summer Youth Olympics kite surfing program. According to the 2018 Buenos Aires Summer Youth Olympic Games, there will be 12 male and 12 female players participating in the kite surfing program, and each country and region is limited to one player. Prior to this competition, several intercontinental qualifiers have been held. One male and one female contestant in each continent has been elected. The remaining quotas will be decided in this qualifying round. Two Chinese teenagers won two medals in the Obstacle Pursuit of 2018 World Kitesurfing Youth Championship. Zhang Haoran won the second place in the men's team and Li Kewen won the third prize in the women's team.

This kite surfing event has a high level and is one of the most high-profile international sports events in Qionghai's history. At the opening ceremony of this kite surfing festival, Qionghai was also awarded the title of International Event Center of the World Kitesurfing Association.

兴仁市放马坪露营风筝赛

第二届全国"兴仁放马坪"露营风筝赛，于 2018 年 11 月 3 日至 4 日在贵州省黔西南州布依族苗族自治州兴仁市放马坪高山草原景区举行。

兴仁放马坪景区位于云贵高原向广西丘陵过渡的斜坡地，这里有广袤无垠的天然草场，风轻草绿，地貌奇特，素有"高原塞外"之称。兴仁放马坪景区举办第二届全国露营风筝赛，把露营与风筝两个元素有机结合，让运动员和观众在放飞风筝、观赏风筝，领略塞外豪情，欣赏旖旎风光的同时，尽情体味以天为盖、以地为床、天人合一的浪漫，享受独特的绿色运动带来的愉悦，感受奇妙的露营生活赋予的雅韵。

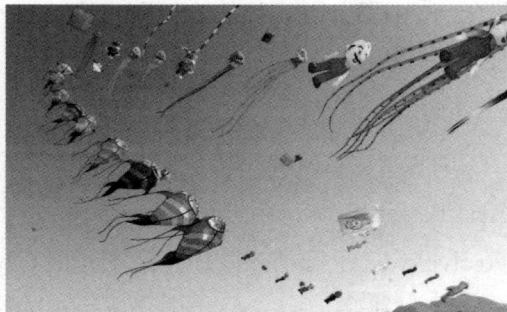

本届露营风筝赛有来自北京、上海、重庆、黑龙江、吉林、辽宁、河北、山东、山西、四川、江苏、湖北、贵州、中国香港、中国澳门等 15 个省市和地区的 30 支代表队、138 名风筝高手参赛。他们带来了 370 余件国内难得一见的传统风筝精品和大型、超大型软体风筝、"挂件"风筝等，将最美的风筝展现给最热情的观众。

赛事为突出露营比赛特色，特设龙串类风筝（中型以上）、软体章鱼风筝、软体三叶虫风筝、其它软体风筝、滚地龙风筝（中型直径 20 米以下）、滚地龙风筝（大型直径 20 米以上含 20 米）、软体造型（单只挂件）风筝、软体造型（多只挂件）风筝、串类最长风筝、串类最多风筝、夜光风筝赛（中型 6 平方米以下）、夜光风筝赛（大型6平方米以上含6平方米）、打斗风筝、双线运动风筝团体芭蕾赛、四线运动风筝团体芭蕾赛等15个竞赛项目，及地方特色风筝表演赛、传统风筝制作表演赛等2个表演项目。同时，开展了风筝文化进校园等活动。

本届露营风筝赛由国家体育总局社会体育指导中心大力支持，中国风筝协会、贵州省体育局、黔西南州人民政府主办，贵州省社会体育管理中心、黔西南州旅游发展委员会、黔西南州文体广电新闻出版局、兴仁市人民政府承办，兴仁市文体广电旅游局、黔西南州山地旅游开发有限公司协办，是该地区以风筝为媒重点打造的品牌赛事之一。本着"倡导绿色运动，回归自然，健康生活"的宗旨，赛事致力于倡导全民健身，推进文化体育旅游深度融合发展，深入推动兴仁市旅游业产业化、特色化进程，让两千多年的风筝文化在兴仁的高山草原得以传承弘扬，把广袤无垠的"高原塞外"打造成别具一格的风筝文化基地，彰显了兴仁山地旅游和高山草原旅游形象，进一步推动兴仁市山地旅游健康、快速发展。

Xingren Fangmaping Camping Kite Competition

The 2nd National Xingren Fangmaping Camping Kite Competition was held from November 3rd to 4th, 2018 in the Fangmaping Alpine Prairie Scenic Area of Xingren, Buyi and Miao Autonomous Prefecture, Southwest Guizhou.

The Fangmaping Scenic Area of Xingren is located on the slope of the transition from the Yunnan Plateau to Guizhou Hill. There is a vast and innocent natural pasture. The wind is light and grass is green here. The 2nd National Camping Kite Competition held in Xingren combined the two elements of camping and kite, which enabled the fliers and the audience enjoy the beautiful scenery and the fun brought by the kite sports and camping.

138 kite masters of 30 teams from 15 provinces, cities and regions including Beijing, Shanghai, Chongqing, Heilongjiang, Jilin, Liaoning, Hebei, Shandong, Shanxi, Sichuan, Jiangsu, Hubei, Guizhou, Hong Kong, and Macau participated in the competition. They brought more than 370 traditional kite boutiques and large-scale, inflation kites and hanging kites that are rare in China, showing the most beautiful kites to the most enthusiastic audience.

The event highlights the characteristics of the camping competition. There were competitions of dragon-string kites (over medium-sized), inflation octopus kites, inflation trilobita kites, and other inflation kites, rolling dragon kites (the medium size with diameter 20 meters or less), and rolling dragon kites (the large size with diameter 20 meters or more), inflation (single pendant) kite, inflation (multiple pendants) kite, longest string kite, kite with most strings, luminous kite (medium size below 6 square meters), luminous kite(large size with 6 square meters or more), kite fighting, dual-line sports kite group ballet, and quad-line sports kite group ballet, totally 15 competitions, as well as local featured kite exhibitions and traditional kite production exhibitions competitions. At the same time, other activities such as kite culture into the campus were launched.

The camping kite competition was strongly supported by the Leisure Sports Center of the General Administration of Sport of China, hosted by the China Kite Association, Guizhou Sports Bureau, and the People's Government of Southwest Guizhou, and undertaken by the Guizhou Provincial Social Sports Management Center, the Southwest Guizhou Tourism Development Committee, the Southwest Guizhou Culture, Sport, Broadcasting and Television Bureau and the People's Government of Xingren, co-organized by Xingren Culture, Sports, Broadcasting, Television and Tourism Bureau and the Southwest Guizhou Mountain Tourism Development Co., Ltd. It is one of the famous kite events in the region. Based on the tenet of advocating green sports, returning to nature, and enjoying healthy living, the competition is committed to advocating national fitness, promoting the in-depth development of culture, sports and tourism, and promoting the industrialization and specialization of tourism in Xingren, and promote the inherit of the kite culture with more than two thousand years' history in the alpine grasslands of Xingren, and making the vast plateau into a unique kite culture base, which shows the image of Xingren Mountain Tourism and Alpine Grassland Tourism, and further promoting the healthy and rapid development of mountain tourism in Xingren.

珠海香洲区风筝节

珠海香洲区风筝节，由珠海市香洲区文化体育旅游局主办，香洲区风筝协会承办，至今已成功举办了3届。2018年10月27日晚，第三届香洲区风筝节在珠海市香洲区开幕，主题为"日夜双景、耀动韵城"。今年风筝节与前两届不同的是选择在晚间举行，除了进行特技风筝表演、软体风筝放飞外，还特别增加了夜间夜光风筝表演。风筝表演队员们为市民带来了一场精彩绝伦的特技风筝表演，吸引了5000余名居民观赏。

Zhuhai Xiangzhou District Kite Festival

The Xianghai District Kite Festival in Zhuhai is hosted by the Cultural and Sports Tourism Bureau of Xiangzhou District, Zhuhai and undertaken by the Xiangzhou District Kite Association. It has been successfully held for three sessions. On the evening of October 27, 2018, the third Xiangzhou District Kite Festival was opened in Xiangzhou District, Zhuhai. The theme of the festival was Double Scenery in the Day and Night Shines in the City. This kite festival was different from the previous two festivals. It was chosen to be held in the evening. In addition to stunt kite performances and inflation kites flying, there were also luminous kite performances. The kite fliers brought a wonderful stunt kite show to the public, attracting more than 5,000 visitors.

西宁市高原风筝挑战赛

西宁市高原风筝赛已成功举办 10 届。2018 年 6 月 27 日，西宁市"丹噶尔杯"笫十届高原风筝挑战赛在石刻广场盛大开幕。此次挑战赛由西宁市体育局、湟源县人民政府主办，湟源县文化旅游体育局承办。来自全国 19 个参赛队的百名风筝选手及当地的风筝爱好者在日月山景区进行形式多样的风筝比赛。本次比赛项目主要包括：传统风筝赛、竞技风筝赛、特色风筝和夜光风筝表演。

在日月山景区，一支支精美的风筝飞上蓝天，既有巨大的龙形风筝、老鹰风筝，也有现代软体挂件风筝、小狗风筝、金鱼风筝等。其中哈尔滨队的滚地龙风筝直径达 43 米，在绿色的草地上随风舞动，成为此次比赛中最大的亮点。27 日晚上在县体育场举行夜光风筝表演，采用 LED 发光灯组成不同图案花样的风筝在高空中点亮整个丹噶尔古城。

西宁市高原风筝挑战赛的成功举办，不仅打造了群众体育活动精品赛事，而且推动了湟源文化、旅游、体育的深度融合，促进了湟源社会、经济的全面发展。

Xining Plateau Kite Challenge Competition

The Xining Plateau Kite Challenge Competition has been successfully held for 10 sessions. On June 27, 2018, the 10th Dange'er Cup Plateau Kite Challenge Competition was grandly opened in the Stone Carving Square of Xining. The competition was hosted by the Xining Sports Bureau and Huangyuan People's Government and undertaken by the Huangyuan Culture, Tourism and Sports Bureau. Hundreds of kite fliers and local kite enthusiasts from 19 teams across the country conducted a variety of kite competitions in the Sun and Moon Mountain Scenic Area. The competition covered traditional kite, competitive kites, featured kites and luminous kites.

In the Sun and Moon Mountain Scenic Area, beautiful kite flew up into the sky. They were huge dragon-shaped kite, eagle kite, modern inflation kite, little dog kite, golden fish kite, etc. Rolling Dragon Kite of Harbin Team with 43 meters in diameter danced with the wind on the green grass, becoming the biggest highlight in this competition. On the evening of the 27th, a luminous kite performance was held at the county stadium. The kites with different patterns of LED lights lighted the entire ancient city of Dange'er.

The successful holding of the Xining Plateau Kite Challenge Competition not only created a mass sports event, but also promoted the deep integration of culture, tourism and sports in Huangyuan, and promoted the comprehensive development of society and economy in Huangyuan.

山东省全民健身运动会风筝比赛暨风筝锦标赛

山东省全民健身运动会风筝比赛暨风筝锦标赛，由山东省体育局主办，山东省风筝协会会同有关市体育局承办，至今已举办八届全民健身运动会风筝比赛暨五届风筝锦标赛。

2018 年 10 月 14 日，山东省第八届全民健身运动会风筝比赛暨第五届风筝锦标赛，在滕州市上善公园山东省风筝放飞基地举行。全省 24 支代表队参加了传统风筝和运动风筝比赛及地方特色风筝与夜光风筝表演赛。

Kite Competition of Shandong National Fitness Sports Meeting and Kite Championship

The Kite Competition of Shandong National Fitness Sports Meeting and Kite Championship are hosted by the Shandong Sports Bureau, undertaken by the Shandong Kite Flying Association and the relevant Municipal Sports Bureau. So far, eight sessions of Kite Competition of Shandong National Fitness Sports Meeting and five sessions of Kite Championship have been held.

On October 14, 2018, the 8th Kite Competition of Shandong National Fitness Sports Meeting and 5th Kite Championship were held in the Shandong Kite Flying Base of Shangshan Park in Tengzhou. 24 teams from the province participated in the traditional kite and sport kite competition, and the local kite and luminious kite demonstration match.

全国风筝精英赛总决赛

为大力发展风筝运动，传承风筝文化，推动全民健身活动广泛开展，备受广大风筝爱好者关注的"2018年全国风筝精英赛总决赛"，于2018年11月27日在广东省河源市巴伐利亚庄园举行。

"2018年全国风筝精英赛总决赛"得到国家体育总局社会体育指导中心大力支持，由中国风筝协会、广东省体育总会主办，河源市体育局、河源市巴伐利亚庄园承办。来自北京、天津、上海、黑龙江、辽宁、河北、山东、山西、浙江、江苏、湖北、安徽、江西、广东、中国香港、中国澳门等16个省市和地区的30支代表队、171名运动员、395只中型以上各类风筝同场竞技，激烈角逐"龙串类"、"硬板串类"、"软板串类"、"硬翅串类"、"软翅串类"（以上为中型及以上）、"动态类"（风力机械传动）、"串类最长"、"串类最多"、"盘鹰类套路"、"打斗风筝个人"、"大型软体类"（面积25平方米及以上）、"软体造型"（挂件）、"滚地龙"、"广告宣传类"、"夜光风筝"、"双线团体芭蕾"、"四线团体芭蕾"等17个风筝"竞技项目"和一个"特色风筝表演"项目的各个奖项。

经过2天激烈而友好的角逐，17个风筝"竞技项目"和一个"特色风筝表演"项目的桂冠各归其主——天津市东丽区风筝队、江苏省风筝协会、浙江省农民体协、温州市风筝协会、上海江川北街风筝队、中国石油体协代表队、马鞍山诗城风筝运动俱乐部和江苏常熟阿庆嫂风筝队获得团体成绩前八名；地方特色风筝表演赛也评出了创新风筝奖、最佳人气奖、最佳造型奖、最佳工艺奖等各6名。

中国石油体协代表队、天津市东丽区风筝队、江苏省风筝协会、浙江省农民体协、武汉市风筝协会、太原市三晋风筝运动俱乐部、上海江川北街风筝队、马鞍山诗城风筝运动俱乐部、江西省九江市风筝协会和山东省德州市风筝办会等10支参赛队获得体育道德风尚奖。

Finals of National Kite Classic

In order to vigorously develop the kite sport, inherit the kite culture and promote the wide-ranging fitness activities of the whole nation, the 2018 Finals of National Kite Classic, which was highly concerned by the majority of kite enthusiasts, was held in the Bavarian Manor of Heyuan, Guangdong on November 27, 2018.

The 2018 Finals of National Kite Classic was strongly supported by the Leisure Sports Center of the General Administration of Sports of China. It was hosted by the China Kite Association and the Guangdong Provincial Sports Federation, and undertaken by the Heyuan Municipal Sports Bureau and the Bavarian Manor of Heyuan. 30 teams and 171 fliers from 16 provinces, cities and regions including Beijing, Tianjin, Shanghai, Heilongjiang, Liaoning, Hebei, Shandong, Shanxi, Zhejiang, Jiangsu, Hubei, Anhui, Jiangxi, Guangdong, Hong Kong, and Macau took part in the event. 395 more than medium-sized kites competed fiercely for Dragon Strings, Hard Plate Strings, Soft Board Strings, Hard-winged Strings, Soft-winged Strings (the above are medium size and above), Dynamic (wind power transmission), longest string, top number of strings, eagle routine, fighting kite individual, large inflation (with an area of 25 square meters or more), inflation shape (pendant), rolling dragon kite, advertising kite, luminous kite, dual line group ballet, quad-line group ballet, totally 17 kites competition and one awards for the Fetured Kite Show.

Tianjin Dongli District Kite Team, Jiangsu Kite Association, Zhejiang Farmers Sport Association, Wenzhou Kite Association, Shanghai Jiangchuan North Street Kite Team, China Petroleum Sports Association Team, Maanshan Shicheng Kite Sports Club and Jiangsu Changshu Aqingsao Kite Team won the top eight in group performance;The local featured kite exhibition also had 6 awards for each item of the innovative kite award, the best popularity award, the best style award and the best craft award.

China Petroleum Sports Association Team, Tianjin Dongli District Kite Team, Jiangsu Kite Association, Zhejiang Farmers Sport Association, Wuhan Kite Association, Taiyuan Sanjin Kite Sports Club, Shanghai Jiangchuan North Street Kite Team, Maanshan Shicheng Kite Sports Club, Jiujiang Kite Association of Jiangxi and the Dezhou Kite Association of Shandong Province, totally 10 teams won sports morality awards.

第三章 中外风筝场馆设施

CHINA AND FOREIGN KITE VENUES AND FACILITIES

150-206

美国国家航空航天博物馆

美国国家航空航天博物馆于 1976 年 7 月开馆，是史密森学会创建的众多博物馆之一，也是全世界首屈一指的有关飞行的专题博物馆。

博物馆的 24 个展厅共有 18000 平方米的展览面积。各展厅陈列飞行史上具有重要意义的各类飞机、火箭、导弹、宇宙飞船及著名飞行员、宇航员用过的器物。这些展品反映了美国乃至世界航空航天史的发展。展品绝大多数是珍贵的原物或备用的实物。每年吸引来自世界各地的 800 万游客，是美国最受欢迎的博物馆之一。

博物馆的正厅命名为"飞行里程碑"，形形色色的飞行器或悬吊在大厅天花板下，或停放在宽敞大厅的地面上。这里有最原始的飞行器：中国古代的风筝和火箭的模型。在现场导引牌的说明上写着"人类最早的飞行器是中国的风筝和火箭。"这里还有蒙特哥菲尔兄弟飞越巴黎上空的热气球复制品，以及莱特兄弟的"飞行者"1 号飞机。在莱特兄弟飞机的近旁，陈列着"阿波罗"11号登月舱。

在空间飞行器展行里，除美国展品外，还展出世界各国发射的卫星及航天器的复制品。有美国"阿波罗"和苏联"联盟"号飞船实现对接的模型。

National Air and Space Museum in USA

The National Air and Space Museum was opened in July 1976. It is one of the many museums created by the Smithsonian Institution and the world's premier museum for flying.

The 24 exhibition halls in the museum have a total exhibition area of 18,000 square meters. Various types of aircraft, rockets, missiles, spacecraft, and artifacts used by famous pilots and astronauts in the history of flight are displayed in each exhibition hall. These exhibits reflect the development of aerospace history in the United States and the world. The vast majority of exhibits are precious originals or spare objects. It attracts about 8 million visitors from all over the world annually and is one of the most popular museums in the United States.

The main hall of the museum is named Flight Milestone, and the various aircraft are suspended under the ceiling of the hall or parked on the floor of the spacious hall. There are the most primitive aircraft here: models of ancient Chinese kites and rockets; There is guide plate on which it mentioned that the earliest aircrafts are the kite from China and rocket. There are replicas of the hot air balloons flying over Paris by the Montgolfier brothers; and the Wright brothers' aircraft. Near the aircraft by Wright brothers, the Apollo 11 lunar module is on display.

In the spacecraft exhibition hall, in addition to the US exhibits, replicas of satellites and spacecraft launched by countries around the world were also exhibited. There is a model for the docking of the US "Apollo" and the Soviet "Alliance" spacecraft.

美国西雅图世界风筝博物馆

该博物馆被称作风筝的天堂，馆藏风筝1300多种。这些不同颜色、各式各样的风筝，吸引着当地市民和国内外游客，从四面八方前来参观，观赏风筝制作的电影或是参观风筝制作工作方，学习了解风筝的制作的技艺，风筝发展演变的历史，感受风筝的无穷魅力，受到风筝文化的教育熏陶，其乐无穷。

World Kite Museum, Seattle, USA

The museum is known as a paradise for kites with a collection of more than 1,300 kinds of kites. These kites of all kinds of colors and shapes attract local citizens and tourists from all over the world. It is a great joy to watch kite-making movies or visit kite-making workshops, learn about kite-making techniques and the history of kite development and evolution, feel the infinite charm of kite and the edification of kite culture.

日本风筝博物馆

日本风筝博物馆，是由茂出木心护于1977年在自己经营的"Taimeiken餐厅"楼上创立的，地点位于东京都中央区日本桥附近。馆内收藏了3000多只风筝，其中有日本最具代表性的江户锦画风筝，还有江户刺绣风筝、迷你风筝及其他国风筝，以及古老的放风筝道具、专做风筝的版画画作等。该博物馆虽为私人设立，却吸引不少西方游客到此寻宝。

日本的风筝最早是从中国传来，直到江户时代才开始流行，因为各地风俗民情不同而染上浓厚的地方色彩，从传统的日本风筝仿佛可欣赏到日本庶民的艺术文化。

茂出木心护是个标准的风筝迷，不管走到那个国家，风筝总是不离手，昭和四十年（一九六五年）时他在法国放日本传统风筝，成为各国风筝迷所熟知的风筝名人。

目前"日本风筝博物馆"已由第二代的茂出木雅章接手，馆内不仅收藏了数量可观的国内外代表性风筝，还不定期开办制作风筝的培训班，并有闻名世界的江户风筝老师父桥本祯三的工作室展示。同时，日本风筝博物馆也肩负起与其他国家地区风筝同仁开展业务交流的重任。

Japan Kite Museum

The Japan Kite Museum was founded in 1977 by Modegisingo on the floor above his Taimeiken restaurant that was near Nihonbashi, Chuo-ku District, Tokyo. The museum has a collection of more than 3,000 kites, including the most representative Japanese kites painted in Edo brocade kites, the Edo embroidered kites, mini kites and kites from other countries, as well as the ancient kite-flying props and printmaking paintings used to make kites. Although the museum is privately owned, it attracts many western tourists.

The Japanese kite was first introduced from China, and it was not popular until the Edo period. It has a strong local characteristic due to the different customs and conditions in different regions. The traditional Japanese kite seems to embody the art and culture of the Japanese common people.

Modegisingo is a big fan of kites. He takes a kite with him no matter where he goes. In the 40th year of the Showa era (1965), he flew a traditional Japanese kites in France and became a famous person of kite among kite fans around the world.

Presently the "Japan Kite Museum" has been taken over by the second generation of Modegimasaaki. The museum not only collects a large number of typical kites at home and abroad, but also runs training courses on kite making from time to time, and has a studio show of the world-famous Edo kite master, Hiroshi Hashimoto. At the same time, the Japan Kite Museum also shoulders the responsibility of conducting business exchanges with kite colleagues in other countries.

日本白根大风筝历史纪念馆

　　日本白根大风筝历史纪念馆坐落于新潟县白根市。在馆里，可以感受到传统的日本风筝的壮美。馆内陈设有和大风筝打斗时实际使用过的同样大的风筝、孩子们放的玩具风筝、世界各国的风筝等，共展示了世界以及日本的约 800 种风筝。风筝上的各种图案显示着日本民族的审美意识和民俗文化。馆内还为游客提供风筝制作的指导。能把自己亲手制作的风筝作为旅行纪念品，将不虚此行。

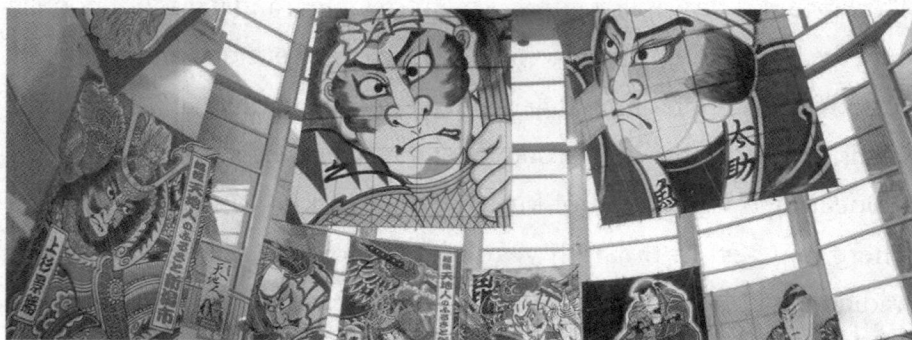

Shirane Giant Kite Historical Memorial Museum in Japan

The Japan Shirane Giant Kite History Memorial Hall is located in Shirane, Niigata. In the museum, you can feel the beauty of traditional Japanese kites. There are about 800 kites of the world and in Japan, including the same size kites that were actually used during the fight, toy kites of children, and kites from all over the world. The various patterns on the kite show the aesthetic consciousness and folk culture of the Japanese nation. Inside the museum, there are guidance on kite making to visitors. It will be worthwhile to make your own kite as a souvenir for travel.

马来西亚马六甲风筝馆

风筝博物馆位于马来西亚马六甲人民博物馆的三楼，这里不仅展示各种各样的风筝，还有许多的民俗展品，反映了马来西亚政治经济的各个方面。馆内陈列各式各样的大小风筝，造型丰富多彩，有的充满了浓郁的中华文化气息，有的也结合了当地的马来特色，所陈列的展品均是非常精美的民间艺术品。

Malacca Kite Museum in Malaysia

The Kite Museum is located on the third floor of the People's Museum in Malacca, Malaysia. It not only displays a variety of kites, but also many folk exhibits that reflect all aspects of Malaysia's politics and economy, etc. The museum displays a wide variety of kites of various sizes. The kites are rich in style, some are full of Chinese culture, and some also combine local features of Malaysia. The exhibits are very beautiful folk art.

印度尼西亚风筝博物馆

　　位于雅加达的印度尼西亚风筝博物馆，是一所以互动式交流为主题的风筝展馆，主要馆藏印尼雅加达地区特色风筝。参访的对象为当地学校课外教学或团体活动安排，就地教习制作简易风筝放飞。来参访的人员以相片同步制作参观纪念卡，并回赠风筝馆作为馆藏，成为非常有创意的亮点。

Indonesian Kite Museum

The Indonesian Kite Museum in Jakarta is an interactive exchange-themed kite museum that displays featured kite in the Jakarta region of Indonesia. The visitors come to the museum for local school extracurricular teaching or group activities. The visitors can learn making simple kites and flying. And the visitors can create commemorative cards with photos, and return them to the kite museum as a collection, which is a very creative highlight.

潍坊世界风筝博物馆

潍坊世界风筝博物馆坐落在山东省潍坊市奎文区行政街 66 号，建于 1987 年，1989 年启用，系全国第一座大型风筝专业性博物馆。博物馆建筑面积 8100 平方米。琳琅满目的风筝展品，展现了从春秋战国时期"鲁班风筝"至今的中外各式风筝。

潍坊世界风筝博物馆，其建筑造型选取了潍坊龙头蜈蚣风筝的特点，屋脊是一条完整的组合陶瓷巨龙，屋顶用孔雀蓝琉璃瓦铺成，似蛟龙遨游长空犹而又起，设计风格在国内独树一帜，是"世界风筝都"潍坊的标志性建筑。

展览以 2000 余只筒式、板式、硬翅、软翅、串式五大类风筝精品以及 300 余件翔实的风筝文物资料为主，较全面、客观地体现了潍坊风筝所独有的题材广泛、造型优美、绘画精细、色彩艳丽的风格；介绍了构思大方、造型夸张、色彩对比鲜明、注重飞翔性能、研究价值较高的近百只外国风筝；重现了历届潍坊国际风筝会的盛况，国家领导人的亲切关怀和题词；展示了在潍坊市委、市政府"文化搭台，经济唱戏"这一决策指导下各行各业发生的巨大变化。1988 年竞选"世界风筝都"，各国风筝组织一致推举潍坊为"世界风筝都"，1989 年"国际风筝联合会"成立，并将总部设在潍坊。潍坊成为传播和弘扬风筝文化的艺术交流中心。潍坊世界风筝博物馆每年免费接待数十万国内外观众，已成为潍坊市对外开放的一个重要窗口。

Weifang World Kite Museum

The Weifang World Kite Museum is located in No. 66, Xingzheng Street, Kuiwen District, Weifang, Shandong. It was built in 1987 and opened in 1989. It is the first large-scale professional kite museum in China. The museum covers an area of 8,100 square meters. A wide range of kite exhibits show various Chinese and foreign kites since the "Luban Kite" in the Spring and Autumn Period and the Warring States Period.

The architectural modeling of Weifang World Kite Museum selects the characteristics of Weifang dragon-head centipede-body kite. The roof ridge is a complete composite ceramic dragon and the roof is paved with peacock blue glazed tiles, which looks like a dragon flying in the sky. The design style is unique in China and becomes a landmark of Weifang, the "World Kite Capital".

The exhibition is based on more than 2000 pieces of five categories of kites, including tubular-type, plate-type, hard-winged, soft-winged, string-type kites, and more than 300 pieces of detailed cultural relics, which fully and objectively reflects the unique style of Weifang kites that has a wide range of subjects, beautiful shapes, delicate paintings and bright colors. It introduces nearly 100 foreign kites with generous concept, exaggerated modelling, contrasting colors, excellent flying performance and high research value; reproduces the grand occasion of all previous Weifang International Kite Festival; shows the great changes taken place in all walks of life under the guidance of the Weifang Municipal Party Committee and the Municipal Government, with the poicy of promoteing economy development by cultural activities. In 1988, Weifang was unanimously elected as the "World Kite Capital" by various kite organizations from the world. In 1989, the International Kite Federation was established. Weifang became the exchange center for spreading and promoting kite culture. Weifang World Kite Museum receives hundreds of thousands of domestic and foreign visitors free of charge every year, and has become an important window for Weifang to open to the outside world.

杨家埠风筝博物馆

杨家埠风筝博物馆坐落于杨家埠民间艺术大观园内，展示着千姿百态、异彩纷呈的风筝艺术精品。

博物馆的第一部分，主要介绍风筝的起源。春秋战国时期，鲁国的能工巧匠公输班为了刺探敌国军情，就曾经有过"选木鸢三日不下"的奇迹，在博物馆里，用的是高科技的动漫形式进行追溯展演，十分生动。

博物馆的第二部分则主要介绍了杨家埠风筝的历史地位。早在明代中叶，艺人把年画风筝艺术融为一体，有"放在天上是风筝，挂在墙上是年画"之说，在我国风筝史上独创一体，造就了潍坊的风筝文化。

博物馆第三部分，主要介绍了杨家埠风筝的艺术特点。其特点是以年画的艺术为根基，手绘点染，洒金点银，画龙点睛，做到了"飞到天上是风筝，贴在墙上是年画"的效果；按制作工艺分为硬式、软式、板式、串式、立体和特效6大类型。

博物馆第四部分，则介绍了中国"风筝王"杨同科。杨同科9岁学艺，11岁制作风筝。1986年与其三子杨其民共同研制了350米长的龙头蜈蚣，在第3届潍坊国际风筝会上获最佳奖，被誉为世界之最。

博物馆的第五部分为"杨家埠风筝与潍坊国际风筝会"。

博物馆的第六部分，展现的是融入了现代影动技术的杨家埠风筝。随着现代科技的发展，科技与传统工艺的完美结合，使风筝白天在蓝天中翱翔，晚上与星空斗艳。

Yangjiabu Kite Museum

The Yangjiabu Kite Museum is located in the Grand View Garden of Yangjiabu Folk Art, displaying the exquisite works of kite art in various shapes and forms.

The first part of the museum mainly introduces the origin of kites. In the Spring and Autumn Period and the Warring States Period, in order to spy on the enemy's military situation, the skillful craftsmen of the state of Lu named Gongshu Ban once performed the miracle of "made a kites of wood and flying it for three days". In the museum, the high-tech form of animation is used for retrospective performance, which is very vivid.

The second part of the museum shows the historical status of Yangjiabu kites. As early as the middle of the Ming Dynasty, the artist integrated the kite art with New Year paintings. There was a saying that "When flying in the sky, it is a kite; hanging on the wall, it is a New Year picture", which is unique in the history of Chinese kite and creates Weifang kite culture.

The third part of the museum demonstrates the artistic characteristics of Yangjiabu kites. Its characteristics are based on the art of New Year paintings, adopting techniques of hand-painted, to have the effect of "When flying in the sky, it is a kite; hanging on the wall, it is a New Year picture". According to the craftsmanship, kites are divided into six types which are hard, soft, plate, string, three-dimention, and special effects.

The fourth part of the museum introduces Yang Tongke, the Chinese "Kite King". Yang Tongke learned kite art and skills at 9 years old and made kites at 11. He spent 85 years of his life making more than 100,000 kites. In 1986, he made a 360-meter-long dragon-head centipede-body kite with his third son Yang Qimin, which won the Best Awards at the 3rd

Weifang International Kite Festival and was honored as the world's best.
The fifth part of the museum is "Yangjiabu Kite and Weifang International Kite Festival".

The sixth part of the museum shows the Yangjiabu kite incorporating modern animation techniques. With the development of modern science and technology, the perfect combination of technology and traditional crafts makes kites fly in the sky during the day and glitter with stars at night.

2004
Weifang China

潍坊国际风筝会主题馆

为了真实、客观地反映潍坊国际风筝会的辉煌历程以及办会所取得突出成效、经营做法，更好地宣传推介世界风筝都——潍坊，弘扬传承风筝文化，做大做强风筝会城市品牌，进一步加强对外合作交流，在潍坊市政府的支持下，潍坊国际风筝会办公室牵头，会同潍坊工艺美术研究所、山东大千工艺美术有限公司，在著名设计师梁文道指导下，于 2015 年 4 月，设计建立了世界上第一个以风筝盛会为题材的主题展馆——潍坊国际风筝会主题馆。

主题馆面积 137 ㎡，整体设计突出国际性、时尚性和风筝文化元素。展馆大门分左右两扇，使用电动控制，两扇门中间是一只栩栩如生的龙头蜈蚣风筝，门面两侧是多姿多彩的中外风筝图案。奇特的设计，使人仿佛进入了风筝的海洋。进入室内，迎面墙上是一副浮烟山国际风筝放飞场全景式放飞画面，在该图中间偏下位置，是一组夺人眼球的铜雕《儿童放风筝》，具有很强的视觉冲击。馆内中轴线两侧顶层处，悬挂着 2 只充满阳刚之美的龙头蜈蚣风筝，展示出潍坊传统风筝代表作的风采。

主题馆内容分前言，具有历史意义的决策，世界风筝都，国际风筝联合会，潍坊风筝的特点与种类，历届风筝会，风筝会会徽的来历，风筝会的"五种精神"，方兴未艾的节会经济，风筝会助推风筝产业大发展，精彩瞬间，对外文化交流，精品风筝展示，领导评价，结语。同时结合了风筝雕塑、风筝会视频播放、风筝书刊、风筝会票证、纪念品实物展示等，形式新颖，内容丰富。

Weifang International Kite Festival Theme Pavilion

In order to truly and objectively reflect the glorious history of Weifang International Kite Festival and its outstanding achievements and business practices, better promoting the World Kite Capital--Weifang, enriching and carrying forward kite culture, highlighting the brand of city of kite, as well as further strengthening foreign cooperation and exchanges, with the support of Weifang Municipal Government, Weifang International Kite Festival Office took the lead, together with Weifang Arts and Crafts Institute, Shandong Daqian Arts and Crafts Co. Ltd., under the guidance of the famous designer Liang Wendao, designed and established the Weifang International Kite Festival Theme Pavilion in April 2015. It is the world's first pavilion with the theme of kite festival.

The theme pavilion covers an area of 137 square meters and the overall design highlights the elements of international, fashion and kite culture. The entrance of the pavilion is two doors with electric control. Between the two doors there is a lifelike dragon-head and centipede-body kite. On both sides of the door there are colorful Chinese and foreign kite decorative patterns. The peculiar design makes people feel like enter the kite fantasy. There is a panoramic kite flying picture of Fuyan Mountain International Kite Flying Field on the front wall. Under the picture, there is a series of eye-catching bronze sculptures named "Children Fly Kites", which has a strong visual impact. On the top of both sides of the central axis of the pavilion, there are two dragon-head and centipede-body kites full of power, showing the elegant demeanor of Weifang traditional kites.

The content of the theme pavilion covers preface, historic decisions, World Kite Capital, International Kite Federation, characteristics and types of Weifang kite, all previous Weifang International Kite Festivals, the origin of emblem of Weifang International Kite Festivals, the "Five Spirits" of Weifang International Kite Festival, the ascendant festival economy, Weifang International Kite Festival promotes the development of kite industry, exciting moments, foreign cultural exchanges, boutique kite display, comments from leadership and conclusion. At the same time, it combines kite sculpture, video broadcast of Weifang International Kite Festival, kite publications, festival tickets, souvenir display, etc., which are of novel forms and rich content.

王家庄风筝文化馆

风筝文化馆位于潍坊市坊子工业发展区王家庄村，总投资400万元，占地2400平方米。于2015年年初施工，2015年4月16日建成投入使用。该展馆分为上、下两层，一层展厅主要展示风筝历史及本地风筝产业文化，二层展厅设有扎制体验区、电子商务区及贸易洽谈区等功能区域。

展馆的第一部分，主要介绍风筝的历史起源。风筝又称风琴、纸鹞、鹞子、纸鸢，在民间南方称"鹞子"，北方称"纸鸢"，故有"南鹞北鸢"之说。风筝是在竹篾等骨架上糊上纸或者绢，拉着系在上面的长线，趁着风势可以放上天空的一种深受人们喜爱的传统玩具。展馆的第二部分为产品展销区、传习室及电子商务区等功能区域。展馆的第三部分是风筝的流派：国内现主要分为5大派系，分别是北京风筝、天津风筝、潍坊风筝、南通风筝、阳江风筝。展馆的第四部分是风筝的种类，按照结构分为5种，分别是软翅风筝、硬翅风筝、串式风筝、筒式风筝和板式风筝。另外还有新兴的特技风筝和受人们喜爱的现代风筝。展馆的第五部分为历届潍坊国际风筝会的照片展示。展馆的第六部分，是工业发展区和王家庄子的基本情况。

Wangjiazhuang Kite Culture Museum

The Kite Culture Center is located in Wangjiazhuang, Fangzi Industrial Development Zone, Weifang with a total investment of 4 million yuan and covers an area of 2,400 square meters. The construction of the center started in early 2015 and was completed and put into use on April 16, 2015. The centre is divided into upper and lower floors. The first floor exhibition hall mainly displays the history of kites and the local kite industry culture. The second floor exhibition hall has functional areas such as kite-making experience zone, e-commerce zone and trade negotiations area.

The first part of the centre focuses on the historical origins of kites. Kite, also known as Fengqin, Zhiyao, Yaozi, and Zhiyuan, is called "Yaozi" in southern China and "Zhiyuan" in the north. So there is a saying that the name of kiteis "Southern Yao and Northern Yuan". Kite is a kind of traditional toy loved by people. Paper or silk are pasted on the bamboo sticks and pull long strings on them to put them in the sky while the wind is blowing. The second part of the centre is a functional area such as product exhibition area, study room and e-commerce area. The third part of the centre is the genre of kites: there are five major genres domestically, namely Beijing kites, Tianjin kites, Weifang kites, Nantong kites, and Yangjiang kites. The fourth part of the centre is the type of kites. According to the structure, it is divided into five types: soft-winged kites, hard-winged kites, string kites, tubular kites and plate kites. There are also emerging stunt kites and popular modern kites. The fifth part of the centre is a photo exhibition of all previous Weifang International Kite Festivals. The sixth part of the centre is the basic information of the Industrial Development Zone and Wangjiazhuangzi.

青州风筝博物馆

青州风筝博物馆对风筝的历史文化发展，风筝的流派、风格以及风筝的种类等作了介绍，展出了各具特色的中外精品风筝。

青州作为历朝历代的名城重镇，放风筝已成为青州民间一项节令性民俗活动。历经两千多年的发展，青州风筝已具备竞技性能良好、扎制工艺精湛、鲜明地方特色、不断创新发展的特点，也已成为潍坊风筝的重要组成部分和杰出代表。

Qingzhou Kite Museum

Historical and cultural development of kites, the genres, styles and types of kites are showed in the Qingzhou Kite Museum. It displays various Chinese and foreign exquisite kites with their own characteristics.

As a famous city in many dynasties, kite flying has become a seasonal folk activity in Qingzhou. After more than two thousand years of development, Qingzhou kite has become an important part and outstanding representative of Weifang kite because of its great competitive performance, exquisite craftsmanship, distinctive local characteristics and continuous innovation and development.

潍坊市民俗博物馆

潍坊市民俗博物馆于 2018 年 4 月份正式开馆，位于潍坊市奎文区机场路与宝通街路口南 200 米白浪绿洲湿地公园内。该馆建筑面积 4241 平方米，分为地上 3 层，地下 1 层，其中 1、2 层为固定展区，建筑面积 2000 余平方米，负 1 层为活动展区，建筑面积 1555 平方米。民俗博物馆共设有 8 个展区，分别为婚俗、潍县老照片、民间文学、多彩生活、节庆习俗、传统技艺、民间艺术和仿古铜铸造。展示内容涵盖潍坊人传统的生产、生活、饮食、起居、交通、服饰、禁忌、节庆礼俗等各个方面。

潍坊民俗文化资源丰富瑰丽，具有典型的地区特色和很高的艺术价值，是山东省民俗文化最富集的城市。全市入选国家级非物质文化遗产名录的项目有 16 项，省级 72 项，市级 276 项，县级 1226 项。其中，潍坊风筝、杨家埠木版年画、高密茂腔、高密扑灰年画、高密剪纸、聂家庄泥塑、诸城派古琴等 7 项入选第一批国家级非物质文化遗产名录。

潍坊市民俗博物馆对潍坊市蜚声中外的风筝、年画等非物质文化遗产项目设有专门展室，进行系统展示。

Weifang Folk-custom Museum

The Weifang Folk-custom Museum was opened in April 2018. It is located in Bailang Oasis Wetland Park, 200 meters south of Airport Road and Baotong Street intersection in Kuiwen District, Weifang. The museum covers an area of 4,241 square meters and has three floors above ground and one floor underground. The first and second floors are fixed exhibition areas with a construction area of over 2,000 square meters. The first-floor underground is an activity exhibition area with a construction area of 1555 square meters. There are eight exhibition areas in the Folk-custom Museum, which are wedding customs, old photos of Weixian, folk literature, colorful life, festival customs, traditional techniques, folk art and antique copper casting. The content of exhibition covers all aspects of Weifang people's traditional production, life-style, dietary habit, daily life, transportation, clothing and costume, taboos, festivals and customs.

With rich and magnificent folk culture resources, typical regional characteristics and high artistic value, Weifang is the city with the most abundant folk culture in Shandong Province. The city has 16 items selected for the national intangible cultural heritage list, 72 items on the provincial level, 276 items on the municipal level, and 1226 items on the county level. Among them, Weifang kite, Yangjiabu New Year paintings, Gaomi Maoqiang, Gaomi flashes New Year pictures, Gaomi paper-cutting, Niejiazhuang clay sculpture, Zhucheng Chinese zither were selected into the first batch of national intangible cultural heritage.

The Weifang Folk-custom Museum systematically displays the world famous intangible cultural heritage such as kites and New Year paintings etc. in Weifang in seperate display rooms.

李乃湘风筝会纪念品收藏馆

2018年4月22日，位于潍坊市奎文区健康街与四平路口西南角的世界风筝都李乃湘收藏馆正式开馆，这也是潍坊市首个私人风筝纪念品收藏馆。

已经76岁的李乃湘老人，对于风筝的痴爱，使他从第一届潍坊国际风筝会开始就搜集与风筝会有关的藏品，经过30余年

的苦心努力，他的风筝会纪念品数量之多、品种之多、品种之全、精品之最，堪称一流。截至目前，他收集的风筝纪念品达60余个大类，共计2万余件藏品，是名副其实的潍坊风筝纪念品收藏第一人。收藏馆里的藏品琳琅满目，包括历年的风筝会门票、风筝会首日封、风筝会纪念奖牌、风筝会纪念章、风筝会看盘等，甚至包括风筝火柴盒、扑克、邮票，应有尽有。

Li Naixiang Kite Festival Souvenir Collection

On April 22 2018, the World Kite Capital Li Naixiang Collection, located at the southwest corner of the Jiankang Street and Siping Road intersection, Kuiwen District, Weifang, was opened, which was the first private kite souvenir collection in Weifang.

At the age of 76, Li Naixiang has been collecting collections of kites for more than 30 years since the first Weifang International Kite Festival because of his kites fever. After more than 30 years of hard work, his kite collections are rated as first class collections due to the number and variety. Up to now, he has collected more than 60 categories of kite souvenirs, with a total of more than 20,000 pieces. He is the first person in the Weifang kite souvenir collection. The hall is full of collections, including kite festival tickets for past years, first day covers of Weifang International Kite Festival, memorial medals, souvenir medals, craft porcelain plate of Weifang International Kite Festival, and even kite matchboxes, poker, stamps, etc.

南通风筝博物馆

2005 年 5 月 18 日，南通风筝博物馆隆重开馆，地址选在风景秀丽的濠河边。以"风筝"为主题的南通风筝博物馆是一个"动""静"结合的综合博物馆，除了馆藏展示接待游客参观以外，还作为南通地域文化名片，承接涉外文化交流展览活动。让博物馆从一个高雅的文化殿堂更多地融入社会，贴近大众。

南通风筝博物馆栩栩如生地再现了风筝的起源、历史传说，记载了文化名人寄托情结的美丽诗句；有以风筝升空原理为启迪的 32 项国内外科学发明，有强身健体的中医传说等；有学生素质教育的教材；收藏了古今中外 100 余件风筝精品，并以南通特色——哨口板鹞为主。南通地方放风筝历史悠久，习俗成风。南通风筝俗称"板鹞"，为世界一绝，历来以其优美的造型，精巧的工艺和独特的音响效果而闻名于世，被国外友人称为"空中交响乐"。

在南通风筝博物馆，你还可以看到风筝与文化名人的轶事，历代著名诗人描写风筝的诗词、风筝邮品等，风筝文化在这里得到了全面的演绎，汇聚成一首动听的风中交响曲，久久回响。

Nantong Kite Museum

The Nantong Kite Museum was opened on May 18, 2005. It is located by the scenic Hao River. The kite-themed Nantong Kite Museum is a comprehensive museum with a combination of "movement" and "quietness". In addition to attracting visitors, it also serves as the name card of Nantong regional culture, undertaking foreign cultural exchange and exhibition activities. Therefore, the museum can be more integrated into the society and close to the public from an elegant cultural palace.

The Nantong Kite Museum vividly reproduces the origins and historical legends of kites and records the beautiful poems of cultural celebrities. There are 32 domestic and international scientific inventions inspired by the principle of kite flying. There are Traditional Chinese Medicine legends of physical fitness, etc. There are teaching materials of student in quality-oriented education. It has collected more than 100 pieces of kites all over the world, characterized by Nantong whistle Banyao kites. There is a long history for the customs of kites flying in Nantong. Nantong kite, commonly known as the "Banyao", is a unique kite in the world. It is famous for its beautiful shape, exquisite craft and unique acoustic effect. It is called "air symphony" by foreign friends.

In Nantong Kite Museum, you can also see the anecdotes of kites and cultural celebrities, the poems of famous poets depicting kites, kite philatelic products, etc. The kite culture has been fully showed here. It has become a beautiful symphony of the wind, echoing for a long time.

南通民间风筝第一馆

坐落于学田街道办事处三楼的"南通民间风筝第一馆"成立于 2009 年，是南通市首家民间风筝馆。风筝馆内陈列着 100 多只风筝，以南通哨口板鹞风筝为主，其中最大的长 2.6 米，最小的只有手掌大。南通民间风筝第一馆的建立为学田街办增添了一道靓丽多彩的人文风景，也为辖区居民群众了解南通风筝历史、培养风筝爱好、弘扬南通风筝文化搭建了坚实的平台。风筝馆建立以来，先后接待了观众数千人次。

风筝馆内的风筝主要由崇川区风筝协会会长朱军制作而成，朱军是学田街办辖区居民，在他的引导下，学田街道也成立了风筝协会，不少居民纷纷参与进来。朱军是个"风筝迷"，在风筝上投入了大量的精力，他曾成功研制了国际上第一只可折叠的哨口风筝，开发了"八仙过海"、"红楼梦"、"西游记"、"八卦"等多种系列的折叠板鹞，工艺精美、性能优良，为南通板鹞走出赛场、走进市场打下了基础。

Nantong First Folk Kite Pavilion

Established in 2009, Nantong First Folk Kite Pavilion, located on the third floor of Xuetian Sub-district Office, is the first folk kite pavilion in Nantong. More than 100 kites are displayed in the pavilion, mainly are the Nantong whistle Banyao kite, the largest of which is 2.6 meters long and the smallest of which is only about the size of a palm. The establishment of the pavilion not only adds a beautiful and colorful cultural scenery to Xuetian Sub-district Office, but also provides a solid platform for local residents to learn about the history of Nantong kites, cultivate kite hobbies and promote the kite culture of Nantong. Since its establishment, the pavilion has attracted thousands of visitors.

The kites in the pavilion were mainly made by Zhu Jun, president of the Chongchuan Kite Association. Zhu Jun is a resident of Xuetian Street District. Under his guidance, Xuetian Sub-district Office also established a kite association in which many residents have participated. Zhu Jun is a "kite fan" who has spent a lot of time in kites. He has successfully developed the world's first foldable whistle kite, and made a series of foldable Banyao with exquisite craft and excellent performance, such as the "the Eight Fairies crossing the Sea", "Dream of Red Mansions", "Journey to the West" and "the Eight Diagrams", etc., which laid a foundation for the marketing of Nantong Banyao kites.

贵阳中国风筝艺术馆

由中国风筝协会主办，贵阳市白云区人民政府投资 60 余万元承建的贵阳"中国风筝艺术馆"，坐落于高原锅城的白云公园内。该馆经过严密的方案设计、风筝收集和布展三个阶段近半年的筹建，于 2007 年 4 月 6 日完工交付使用。

"中国风筝艺术馆"按风筝的十二种类五种型号，从全国 5 大流派中精选收集具有典型代表意义的风筝 500 余只，同时还收集了许多珍贵的风筝历史资料。该馆有 6 个展室，共有面积 800 平方米。分别布展在倚云楼的一至六楼内，并依秩从中国风筝的发展简史、分类与流派、精品、文化艺术、传统风筝、工艺流程 6 个部分，把中国风筝的源流、发展、流派、风格、制作工艺和放飞技巧，以及外国风筝的特色都一一展现出来。

Guiyang China Kite Art Museum

Sponsored by China Kite Flying Association, the People's Government of Baiyun District, Guiyang invested more than 600,000 yuan to build Guiyang China Kite Art Museum, which is located in Baiyun Park, Guiyang. The museum was completed and delivered on April 6, 2007 after nearly half a year's preparation in three stages of rigorous program design, kite collection and exhibition layout.

According to the twelve kinds and five types of kites, the China Kite Art Museum collects more than 500 typical kites from five major genres in China. At the same time, it also collects many precious kite historical materials. The museum has six exhibition rooms with a total area of 800 square meters. They are respectively arranged on the first to sixth floors of Yiyun building. It is divided into six parts: a brief history of the development of Chinese kites, classifications of different genres, boutiques, culture and art, traditional kites and craft process. The origins, developments, genres, styles, manufacturing and flying techniques of the Chinese kite, as well as the characteristics of foreign kites are shown one by one.

阳江风筝馆

　　阳江风筝馆是一座独立建筑，座落在市区南国竞技场。建筑面积 2000 多平方米，建筑为三层结构。第一层、第二层分别介绍阳江风筝的历史传承、阳江风筝的特点，以灵芝为代表的各种传统风筝和代表性传承人，历届阳江风筝代表队获奖情况，国内外数百只精品风筝陈列展示等；第三层主要是阳江市风筝协会用于风筝人才培训、风筝技艺传习、风筝文化产业展览展示等。近年来，阳江市又投入 500 万元，对阳江风筝馆重新进行了设计和装修，提高了质量档次。阳江风筝馆与南国风筝竞技场成为阳江市著名的标志性建筑，每天吸引着大批市民和游客前来参观。

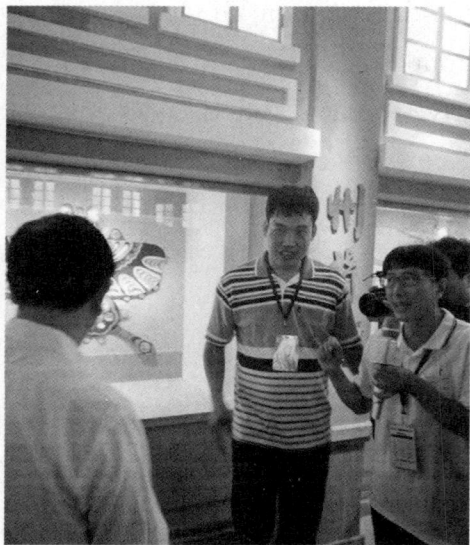

Yangjiang Kite Museum

The Yangjiang Kite Museum is an independent building located in the Nanguo Arena in the downtown. The building area is more than 2,000 square meters and the building has three layers. On the first and second floor, the historical inheritance of the Yangjiang kite and the characteristics of the Yangjiang kite, the traditional kites represented by Ganoderma and representative inheritors, the awards of the previous Yangjiang kite team, hundreds of boutique kites at home and abroad, etc. are introduced. The third floor is mainly used by the Yangjiang Kite Association for kite talent training, kite skill training, and kite culture industry exhibitions, etc. In recent years, Yangjiang has invested another 5 million yuan to redesign and decorate the Yangjiang Kite Museum and improved its quality. The Yangjiang Kite Museum and the Nanguo Kite Arena have become the famous landmarks in Yangjiang, attracting a large number of citizens and tourists every day.

太湖风筝博物馆

太湖风筝博物馆坐落于太湖西岸的宜兴周铁镇，作为太湖流域地区第一座以风筝文化为主题的博物馆，太湖风筝博物馆

总投资近300万元，总建筑面积约400平方米，旨在收藏、陈列中国风筝的精品及有关风筝的文史资料，促进风筝文化的推广与传承。馆内设风筝传统制作工艺、太湖风筝获奖荣誉、太湖风筝精品、中国风筝精品、太湖风筝历史文化五个展区，以实物、图片、文字、多媒体等形式对太湖风筝的发展历史、代表作品、制作技艺等方面进行回顾与展示。

太湖风筝是中国江南风筝流派的重要组成部分，因其得天独厚的地理优势，民间制作和放飞风筝活动有着悠久的传统和广泛的群众基础，特别是鹞笛、鹞灯风筝更是独具特色，别有风韵。

Taihu Kite Museum

Taihu Kite Museum is located in Zhoutie Town, Yixing, on the west bank of Taihu Lake. As the first museum in the Taihu Lake basin with the theme of kite culture, the Taihu Kite Museum has a total investment of nearly 3 million yuan and a total construction area of 400 square meters. It is designed to collect and display the kite boutiques in China and literature and history materials related to kites to promote and inherit of kite culture. The museum has traditional kite making techniques, awards for Taihu kite, Taihu kite boutiques, Chinese kite boutiques, and history and culture of Taihu kites. The development history, representative works and production skills of Taihu kites are displayed in the form of objects, pictures, texts and multimedia, etc.

Taihu kites are an important part of the kite genres in the South part of China. Due to its unique geographical advantage, folk production and flying kite activites have a long tradition and are very popular. Especially the whistle kites and the light kites are unique.

九份风筝博物馆（台湾）

　　九份风筝博物馆馆长赖文祥基于对风筝的热爱和儿时的童玩记忆，在九份成立了全台第一座以风筝为主题的博物馆，馆中收藏了各国地区千奇百怪的风筝和国际风筝比赛的部分获奖作品。馆内设有风筝教室，游客可以在这里亲手制作风筝，兼具承袭传统艺术与展览之用。

Jiufen Kite Museum (Taiwan)

Based on the love of kites and childhood memories, Lai Wenxiang, director of the Jiufen Kite Museum, set up the first kite-themed museum in Jiufen. Various kites from all over the world and kites won international kites competition awards were collected in the museum. There is a kite classroom in the museum where visitors can make their own kites and it has the function of inheriting traditional art and exhibitions.

冬山风筝馆（台湾）

冬山风筝馆设在台湾宜兰县冬山乡一学校内，于1997年11月正式建成。冬山风筝馆主要分为五间主题展示室，系统地把馆藏风筝依照类型、产地、习作过程，分门别类对外展示。馆内也收集各种与风筝相关的成品、文献资料与放飞图片等。冬山风筝馆内部设有视听教室，可播放多媒体影片及进行校区视讯系统教学。

Dongshan Kite Museum (Taiwan)

The Dongshan Kite Museum was established in November 1997 in Dongshan, Yilan, Taiwan. The Dongshan Kite Museum is divided into five theme pavilions, which systematically display the kites according to the type, origin and making process. Various kite-related finished products, literature materials and flying pictures are also collected in the museum. There is an audio-visual classroom inside the Dongshan Kite Museum, which can play multimedia videos and have teaching by the campus video system.

山东潍坊风筝文化馆（台湾）

　　山东潍坊风筝文化馆，于 2018 年 12 月 11 日，在台湾基隆市开馆。潍坊是风筝的发祥地和知名的世界风筝都。多年来，潍坊市以风筝为载体，开展了丰富多彩的两岸文化交流活动，搭建起了两岸民众相互了解、增进友谊的桥梁。为让台湾民众近距离了解和感知潍坊风筝之美。潍坊市台办、潍坊鲁台经贸洽谈会工作办公室和台湾基隆市山东同乡会数次洽商，决定在基隆市推动设立以风筝文化为主题的山东潍坊风筝文化馆，经多方努力，历经一年多筹备，终于建成。该馆展出面积达 1000 多平方米，展出了体现潍坊风筝文化精品的"龙头、蝴蝶、沙燕"等风筝 100多只。众多的到访者为文化馆的设立点赞。他们表示，在家门口就可以欣赏到来自大陆的文化艺术珍品，非常难得，期待两岸进一步加强文化交流，让更多的文化精品实现共享。本次文化馆的展品由潍坊风筝产业协会选送，并无偿赠送给基隆市以供长期展出。

Shandong Weifang Kite Culture Center (Taiwan)

Shandong Weifang Kite Culture Center was opened on December 11, 2018 in Keelung, Taiwan. Weifang is the birthplace of kites and the famous world kite capital. Over the years, Weifang has carried out a variety of cross-strait cultural exchange activities with kites as a carrier, and built a bridge for mutual understanding and friendship between the two sides of the strait. In order to provide an opportunity for the people of Taiwan to understand and perceive the beauty of the kite in Weifang, the Weifang Taiwan Affairs Office, the Work Office of Weifang Lu-Tai Economic and Trade Fair and the Shandong Fellowship Association of Keelung of Taiwan negotiated several times and decided to promote the establishment of the Shandong Weifang Kite Culture Center with the theme of kite culture in Keelung. After many efforts, it took more than one year to prepare and was finally finished. The exhibition area of the museum is more than 1,000 square meters, and more than 100 kites such as dragon-head, butterfly, swallow kites have been exhibited. Many visitors praised the establishment of the culture center. They said that it was very good opportunity to witness and appreciate the cultural and artistic treasures from the mainland And they expect to further strengthening cultural exchanges between the two sides of the strait, so that more cultural products can be shared. The items of the exhibition of this culture museum were selected by the Weifang Kite Industry Association and donated to Keelung for a long-term exhibition for free.

盘龙区栗树头社区风筝科普馆

　　盘龙区栗树头社区风筝科普馆位于昆明市盘龙区白塔路七彩俊园 8 幢栗树头社区工作站二楼，旨在收藏、陈列古今中外的风筝珍品及有关风筝的文物资料。整个博物馆设有风筝历史文化展、风筝精品展、世界精品风筝展、中国精品风筝展、微型风筝综合功能展、民族节庆风筝展、风筝制作全过程放映厅等。

　　在这里，人们可以了解到风筝的历史、应用及沿革发展，现代风筝的流派及分类等内容。展馆更侧重用翔实的风筝文物资料以及风筝实物、文字、操作及应用等，全面展示风筝的历史文化、现代文化、国际文化及延伸文化等，帮助人们特别是青少年了解风筝历史，特别是滇式风筝文化，普及风筝知识，传承和创新风筝文化。

Kite Science Museum in Lishutou, Panlong District

The Kite Science Museum in Lishutou, Panlong District is located on the second floor of the Lishutou Community Station, Building 8, Qicai Junyuan, Baita Road, Panlong District, Kunming. It aims to collect and display the kite treasures of ancient and modern China and foreign countries and the cultural relics related to kites. The museum has kite history and culture exhibition, kite boutique exhibition, world boutique kite exhibition, China boutique kite exhibition, comprehensive function of miniature kite exhibition, national festival and kite exhibition, and kite production process video hall.

Here, people can learn about the history, application and evolution of kites, the genre and classification of modern kites. The museum focuses on the show of the history culture, modern culture, international culture and extended culture of kites through detailed kite cultural relics and kite objects, texts, operations and applications etc, to help people, especially young people, understand the history of kites, especially kite culture in Yunnan, popularize kite knowledge, inherit and innovate kite culture.

张家港乐余镇风筝馆

乐余镇沙洲哨口板式类风筝特色鲜明，是江苏省非物质文化遗产。

2012 年乐余镇重新扩建了 400 平方米的风筝陈列馆与风筝扎制室；2019 年乐余镇风筝馆被命名为"苏州市第三批非物质文化遗产保护示范基地"，风筝制作技艺列为第一批江苏省级非物质文化遗产名录扩展项目。

Leyu Kite Museum in Zhangjiagang

The plate-type whistle kite of Shazhou in Leyu is distinctive and is the intangible cultural heritage of Jiangsu. In 2012, Leyu re-expanded a 400-square-meter kite exhibition hall and kite-making room; in 2019, Leyu Kite Museum was named as "the third batch of intangible cultural heritage protection demonstration base in Suzhou", kite production technology was listed in the first batch of Jiangsu Intangible Cultural Heritage List Expansion Project.

第什里风筝小镇规划馆

第什里风筝小镇规划馆于 2017 年 5 月 6 日投入使用，建筑面积是 1400 平方米。展馆由建筑规制厅、古城文化厅、规划陈列厅、永定河文化厅、风筝展厅及多功能厅六个展厅组成。一楼的古城文化厅主要通过艺术的手法体现安次历史及东安古城的人文景观。二楼的风筝展厅主要展示了第什里风筝的代表作品。

"第什里风筝小镇"位于廊坊市安次区调河头乡中部，是国家 AAA 级旅游景区。小镇占地面积 1000 公顷，以第什里村为中心，依托高新技术开发区，融合龙河湿地、永定河水系、廊南生态农业观光区，辐射京津走廊片区，是旅游文化休闲农业综合风景区，是河北省首批特色小镇、全国首批风筝小镇。

Planning Museum in Dishili Kite Town

The Planning Museum in Dishili Kite Town was put into use on May 6, 2017, with a construction area of 1,400 square meters. The museum consists of six exhibition halls, namely Building Regulation Hall, Ancient City Culture Hall, Planning and Exhibition Hall, Yongding River Culture Hall, Kite Exhibition Hall and Multi-function Hall. The Ancient City Cultural Hall on the first floor mainly reflects the history of Anci and the human landscape of the ancient city Dong'an through artistic practices. The Kite Exhibition Hall on the second floor mainly displays the typical works of Dishili kite.

Dishili Kite Town is located in the middle of Tiaohetou, Anci District, Langfang. It is a national AAA tourist attraction. The town covers an area of 1000 hectares. It is centered on the village of Dishili and covers the area of high-tech development zone. It integrates Longhe Wetland, Yongding River Water System, Langnan Ecological Agriculture Tourist Area, and near the Beijing-Tianjin Corridor area. It is a comprehensive landscape of tourism, culture, leisure and agriculture. The district is the first batch of characteristic towns in Hebei Province and the first batch of kite towns in China.

世界风筝都纪念广场

世界风筝都纪念广场，是以"风筝文化、民俗文化、人文文化"为主题规划设计的纪念广场，于 2006 年 4 月 15 日竣工开放，是潍坊城市建设史上的新亮点，是展示世界风筝都形象的标志性景观。

整个广场通过吉祥大道、鸢标广场等十大景观，追颂历史，咏颂现在，展颂未来，成为展示风筝文化与民俗文化、市民休闲娱乐、全民健身强体、商业购物消费以及举办大型集会活动的综合性城市广场。

广场布局

吉祥大道——步入风筝纪念广场，首先映入眼帘的是"世界风筝都纪念广场"9 个红色石刻大字；漫步吉祥物大道，依次摆放着 12 个风筝会代表吉祥物，神情可爱，栩栩如生。两侧迎宾墙正面层层跌水，迎宾墙南侧青铜浮雕，描绘的是《风筝史话》和《情满鸢都》。

主要景观

鸢标广场——位于广场正中，一座散发着现代气息的主题雕塑被风筝造型的喷泉所环绕。

咏筝栈桥——位于广场西侧，26根方柱支撑的全长75米钢木栈桥探身白浪河，观白浪美景，品古今诗韵。

芙蓉树阵——广场东北角以芙蓉树为主方形树阵，地面以硬质铺地和草地相交织，夜晚华灯初上，丛林漫步，树影婆娑，别有情趣。

民俗长廊——广场东人口至风筝博物馆轴线，布满剪纸地灯，《朝天锅》《和乐》《杨家埠年画》等民俗铸铜雕塑小品，充分体现潍坊的民间手工艺特色。

儿童乐园——位于广场东南方，各种鹅卵石图案别具匠心，新型材料树脂风筝地画，《打陀螺》《虎头鞋》《布老虎》《狮子》等儿童情趣铸铜雕塑、三个铸铜风筝拐子错落有致，是孩子们尽情玩耍的乐园。

森林公园——广场西南角胸径1.05米的天然大皂角树巍然耸立，成片的桃树林、樱花林、紫叶李、青桐、五角枫、广玉兰、合欢林郁郁葱葱、密不透风，白日红、连翘、迎春等点缀其中，给都市人提供了一个舒适温馨的休憩、晨练空间和天然氧吧。

风博广场——与广场通过斜轴相联系，形成风筝博物馆圆形小广场，世界风筝博物馆对面矗立有《鲁班梦》铸铜雕塑。

滨河景区——位于广场西侧白浪河东岸，河边鹅卵石小道弯弯曲曲，河边怪石嶙峋，馒头柳随风飘扬，木栈道、河边金色沙滩为游人休闲、购物提供休息观景平台。

露天剧场——位于滨河步行商业街中段，咏筝栈桥正下方。芬兰木铺就的木质阶梯圆形广场，是举行群众公益活动、群众自发表演的绝佳场所。

World Kite Capital Memorial Square

The World Kite Capital Memorial Square is designed on the theme of "Kite Culture, Folk Culture, Humanistic Culture". It was completed and opened on April 15, 2006. It is a new highlight in the history of city construction of Weifang and a name card displaying the image of the World Kite Capital.

People can trace history, extoll the present, and look into the future through the top ten views such as Jixiang Avenue and Kite Logo Square, etc. It has become a comprehensive urban square for kite and folk culture exhibition, resident's leisure entertainment, national fitness, shopping, as well as the venue for large gatherings and activities.

Layout of the square

Mascot Avenue - Stepping into the Kite Memorial Square, the first thing you will see is the nine Chinese characters carved in red, "World Kite Capital Memorial Plaza". Strolling down the Avenue, 12 Weifang International Kite Festival representative mascots are arranged in order, which look very cute and lifelike. The frontages of welcome walls on both sides have a scene of water, and the bronze embossment on the south side of the welcome walls depict "the History of Kites" and "Love of the World Kite Capital, Weifang".

Major landscape

Square with logo of kite- Located in the center of the square, a modern themed sculpture is surrounded by a kite-shaped fountain.

The landing stage of kite- Located on the west side of the square. The 75-meter long steel-wood landing stage supported by 26 square columns connects the Bailang River, which provides a place for visitors to view the beautiful scene along the riverside.

Hibiscus tree array - The northeast corner of the square is dominated by hibiscus trees. The ground is intertwined with hard paving and grass. At night, there is great fun to step on the square under the trees.

Folk corridor - from the east entrance to the axis of the kite museum, there are paper-cutting ground lights, art exhibition of Chaotianguo(a kind of traditional Weifang food boiled in the pot), Hele(a kind of traditional Weifang noodles), Yangjiabu Lunar New Year Paintings, etc, which fully demonstrated the folk craftsmanship features of Weifang.

Children's Paradise - Located in the southeast of the square. There are various cobblestone patterns, ground kite painting made of resin, a kind of new material and other bronze sculptures show children's fun, which are named Gyro, Tiger Head Shoes, Wood Tiger, Lion, etc. Three cast copper kites reels are located on the ground. It is really a paradise for children to have fun.

Forest park - The natural saponin tree with a diameter of 1.05 meters in the southwest corner of the square stands tall, and there are peach trees, cherry trees, purple-leaf plum trees, green paulownias, maples, southern magnolias, albizzias, etc. Red and yellow flowers of crape myrtle, forsythia, primrose are dotted among them, providing urban people with a comfortable rest space and natural oxygen bar for morning exercise.

Kite Museum Square - Connected with the square through the oblique axis to form the circular small square of the Kite Museum. There is a bronze sculpture of Dream of Luban on the opposite side of the World Kite Museum.

Binhe Scenic Area - Located on the east bank of the Bailang River on the west side of the square. There are zigzag cobblestone path, rocks, golden sandbeach along the riverside, which provide a platform to the tourists for leisure and shopping.

Outdoor theatre - Located in the middle of Binhe Pedestrian Commercial Street, just below the landing stage of kite. The round square with wooden stair is a a great place for public activity and a spontaneous performance venue for the masses.

潍坊浮烟山中国风筝放飞基地

潍坊浮烟山国际风筝放飞场，是潍坊市于 1992 年修建的标准化风筝放飞场，占地 300 亩。地处潍坊西南部，距市区仅 9.6 公里，与依傍天然山峰沟壑和林木植被而建成的浮烟山森林公园融为一体，自然风光和人文景观交相辉映，成为融科技、体育、文化、度假等为一体的综合风景区。

20 多年来，浮烟山风筝放飞场连年承接潍坊国际风筝会和全国风筝赛，为发展我国体育事业做出积

极贡献。2004 年 11 月，国家体育总局社会体育指导中心命名潍坊浮烟山国际风筝放飞场为"中国风筝放飞基地"。

Weifang Fuyan Mountain Kite Flying Base

Weifang Fuyan Mountain Kite Flying Field is a standardized kite flying field built by in 1992 in Weifang, covering an area of about 200 thousand square meters. It is located in the southwest of Weifang, and is only 9.6 kilometers away from the urban area. It is integrated with the Fuyan Mountain Forest Park built by natural mountain and forest. The natural scenery and human landscapes complement each other and it becomes a comprehensive scenic area of technology, sports, culture, holiday, etc.

Over more than 20 years, the Weifang International Kite Festival and the National Kite Competition have been held here for many times in the filed, which have made positive contributions to the development of sports in China. In November 2004, the Leisure Sports Center of the General Administration of Sport of China named it as "China Kite Flying Base".

潍坊滨海国际风筝放飞场

潍坊滨海国际风筝放飞场，占地 1000 亩，投资 3400 余万元，并邀请意大利知名设计师依据国际尖端设计理念，对风筝放飞场主席台、座席等相关配套设施进行优化设计，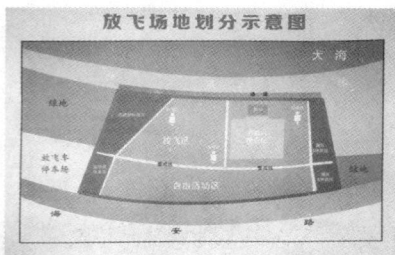于 2017 年 4 月 15 日，在第 34 届潍坊国际风筝会期间启用。

潍坊滨海国际风筝放飞场是世界上最大的陆地放飞场，也是南、北两面均临海的放飞场，同时，道路畅通，交通便捷。

潍坊滨海国际风筝放飞场的启用，为潍坊国际风筝会举办开辟了广阔的空间。从此，潍坊国际风筝会开幕式和万人放飞表演、世界风筝锦标赛都在此举行，吸引着更多的市民和中外客人莅临现场，放飞风筝，放飞梦想。

Weifang Binhai International Kite Flying Field

Weifang Binhai International Kite Flying Field, covering an area of more than 6,00 thousand square meters, the investment is more than 34 million yuan. Well-known Italian designers was invited to optimize the design of kite-flying venues, seats and other related facilities according to international cutting-edge design concepts. On April 15, 2017, it was opened during the 34th Weifang International Kite Festival.

Weifang Binhai International Kite Flying Field is the world's largest land-based flying field. The two sides of south and north face the sea. At the same time, the roads are smooth and the traffic is convenient.

The opening of the Weifang Binhai International Kite Flying Field opened up a vast space for the Weifang International Kite Festival. Since then, the opening ceremony of the Weifang International Kite Festival and the 10,000 people kite flying performance and the World Kite Championship have been held here, attracting more and more citizens, domestic and foreign guests to fly kites and fly their dreams here.

阳江南国风筝竞技场

　　为弘扬风筝文化，推动风筝运动深入持久的开展，1991年阳江市建成了南国风筝竞技场，占地面积12万平方米，可容纳30万人放飞，是目前全国最大的风筝放飞场之一。从1992年开始，每年农历九月初九重阳节，阳江都在南国风筝竞技场举办各种层次的风筝比赛，吸引了越来越多的国内外风筝选手和爱好者前来登台献艺。

Yangjiang Nanguo Kite Arena

In order to carry forward the kite culture and promote the deep and long-lasting development of the kite sport, in 1991, Yangjiang built the Nanguo Kite Arena, covering an area of 120,000 square meters and can accommodate 300,000 people for flying. It is one of the largest kite flying fields in China. Since 1992, every year at the Double Ninth Festival of the Lunar Year, various levels of kite competitions were held in the Nanguo Kite Arena in Yangjiang, attracting more and more domestic and foreign kite players and enthusiasts.

深圳大梅沙海滨公园

深圳大梅沙海滨公园于 1999 年 6 月 18 日建成，建设总投入 1.2 亿元，总面积 36 万平方米，其中沙滩全长约 1.8 公里，沙滩总面积 18 万平方米，公园绿地面积为 10 万平方米，内湖面积为 8 万平方米。是广东省 5A 级旅游景区，位于深圳特区的东部、风光旖旎的大鹏湾畔。这里三面环山，中间开阔平缓，一面临海，1800 米的沙滩就镶嵌在这环碧艺海路之间。深圳大梅沙公园是珠三角地区规模最大、条件最好的放飞场地之一，每年的深圳大梅沙风筝赛在这里举办。

Dameisha Waterfront Park in Shenzhen

Dameisha Waterfront Park in Shenzhen was completed on June 18, 1999. The total investment is 120 million yuan, with a total area of 360,000 square meters. The total length of the beach is about 1.8 kilometers, the space of the total beach area is 180,000 square meters, and the green area in the park is 100,000 square meters. The space of the inner lake area is 80,000 square meters. It is a 5A-level tourist attraction in Guangdong. It is located in the east of Shenzhen Special Economic Zone and on the banks of Dapeng Bay. It is surrounded by mountains on three sides, with a wide and gentle land in the middle, and facing the sea on one side. The 1800-meter beach is located between the Huanbi Road and the Yihai Road.

铜仁市万山放飞基地

万山放飞基地位于万山区行政中心对面，总占地面积22.7万平方米。该项目以"旅游观光目的地、休闲娱乐目的地"为目标进行打造，在此已举办过两届高水平的国际风筝赛事。

万山放飞基地项目包含风筝放飞基地、四季花海、旅游文化长廊（即16栋2层四合院精品民宿区）。四季花海项目包含健身跑道、花海、休闲长廊、景观风车、景观石、放飞场地。花海主要种植郁金香、薰衣草等花草，花草种植面积约4万平方米。旅游文化长廊包含16栋二层四合院建筑群及2栋

高层酒店建筑，已形成集旅游、娱乐、生活、运动健身为一体的一站式休闲天堂。

Wanshan Flying Base in Tongren

The Wanshan Flying Base is located to the opposite of the Wanshan District, with a total area of 227,000 square meters. The project is aimed at building "tourism destinations, leisure destinations" and has hosted two high-level international kite events.

The Wanshan Flying Base project includes a kite flying base, a four-season flower sea, and a tourism culture corridor (that is, 2nd Floor of No. 16 building of courtyard home stay facility area). The four-season flower sea project includes fitness running track, flower sea, leisure corridor, landscape windmill, landscape stone and flying field. There are flowers such as tulips and lavender in flower sea area, and the planting area of flowers and plants is about 40,000 square meters. The tourism culture corridor consists of 2nd Floor of No. 16 building of courtyard and two high-rise hotel buildings. It has formed a one-stop leisure paradise integrating tourism, entertainment, life, sports and fitness.

八里河旅游区风筝基地

安徽省首个风筝基地位于颍上县八里河旅游区。八里河旅游区始终坚持体育＋旅游融合发展，连续成功举办了"2016年全国运动风筝巡回赛和2017年国际运动风筝赛"。八里河风筝赛已成为交流提升风筝技艺，传承和普及风筝运动的重要平台。八里河风筝基地将打造成集风筝文化展示、风筝技艺观赏、风筝运动教学、风筝放飞体验、风筝文化旅游为一体的风筝文化旅游目的地，风筝产业也将成为八里河旅游经济新的增长点。

Bali River Tourist Area Kite Base

The first kite base in Anhui is located in the Bali River Tourist Area of Yingshang. The Bali River Tourist Area has always adhered to the development of the integration of sports and tourism, and has successfully held the 2016 National Sports Kite Tour and 2017 International Sport Kite Competition. The Bali River Kite Competition has become an important platform for exchange and promotion of kite skills, inheritance and popularization of kite sports. The Bali River Kite Base will be built into a kite cultural tourism destination integrating kite culture display, kite skill show, kite sport teaching, kite flying experience and kite culture tourism. The kite industry will also become a new growth point for the Bali River tourism economy.

王家庄现代风筝产业基地

王家庄中国现代风筝产业基地位于潍坊市坊子区工业发展区王家庄村。王家庄子村有着悠久的风筝传承历史，具有规模的生产企业达 53 家，风筝加工户近 600 家，从业人员近 2000 人，年生产能力 8000 万只，年产值 2 亿元，产品主要销往温州、义乌、广东等地以及欧美等国家，年产销量居全国首位。

王家庄子社区包括王家庄子一村、王家庄子二村、王家庄子三村、王家庄子四村四个村，位于坊子工业发展区的东北部，北依 309 国道，东靠潍河，共有农业人口 4400 人，耕地面积 3200 亩，劳动力 2200 人，人均纯收入 14500 元。王家庄子风筝产业优势明显，当地文化底蕴深厚，扎制风筝历史悠久。2015 年 王家庄村被国际风筝联合会授予"现代风筝产业基地"。

Wangjiazhuang Modern Kite Industry Base

Wangjiazhuang China Modern Kite Industry Base is located in Wangjiazhuang, Industrial Development Zone, Fangzi District, Weifang. Wangjiazhuang has a long history of kite inheritance. There are 53 large-scale production enterprises, nearly 600 kite processing households, nearly 2,000 employees, the annual production capacity is 80 million, and annual output value is 200 million yuan. The products are mainly sold to Wenzhou, Yiwu, Guangdong domestically and countries in Europe and America, and the annual output and sales rank first in China.

The community of Wangjiazhuang consists of Wangjiazhuang No. 1 Village, Wangjiazhuang No. 2 Village, Wangjiazhuang No.3 Village and Wangjiazhuang No.4 Village. It is located in the northeast of Fangzi Industrial Development Zone, south of 309 National Highway and west of Weihe River, with a total population of 4,400, people, about 2 million square meters of agricaltural land, and a per capita net income of 14,500 yuan. The kite industry has obvious advantages, and the local cultural heritage is profound, and the village has a long history of kite-making. In 2015, Wangjiazhuang was awarded the "Modern Kite Industry Base" by the International Kite Federation.

太湖风筝基地

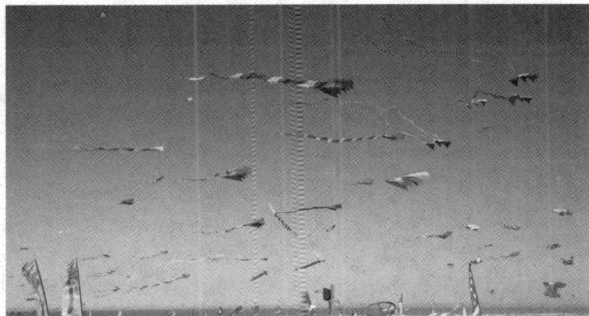

近年来，宜兴周铁镇加大投入，斥巨资建成了江苏省太湖风筝基地——竺山湖湿地公园。同时积极挖掘不同风筝技艺，并举办了 19 届太湖风筝节、5 届江苏省风筝公开赛，先后承办过全国风筝精英赛、国际风筝邀请赛。风筝已经成为周铁镇一个特殊的文化符号和靓丽名片。因周铁镇风筝运动成绩突出，被国家体育总局社会体育指导中心授予"中国风筝之乡"荣誉称号。

Taihu Kite Base

In recent years, the town of Zhoutie has invested much in the construction of the Taihu Lake Kite Base in Jiangsu Province, the Zhushan Lake Wetland Park. At the same time, it actively explored different kite techniques and held the 19th Taihu Kite Festival and the 5th Jiangsu Kite Open Competition. It has undertaken the National Kite Classic and the International Kite Invitational Tournament. The kite has become a special cultural symbol and beautiful business card of Zhoutie. Due to the outstanding achievements of the kite sports, Zhoutie was awarded the honorary title of "Hometown of Chinese Kite" by the Leisure Sports Center of the General Administration of Sport of China.

第四章 中外风筝之最

TOP KITES IN CHINA AND OVERSEAS

210-278

世界上第一只风筝

据史料记载，2400多年前世界第一只木鸢风筝由能工巧匠鲁班在潍坊境内的鲁山成功放飞，"飞三日而不败"。鲁班被后人尊称为建筑界和风筝界的鼻祖。从此，风筝文化逐步传承普及。

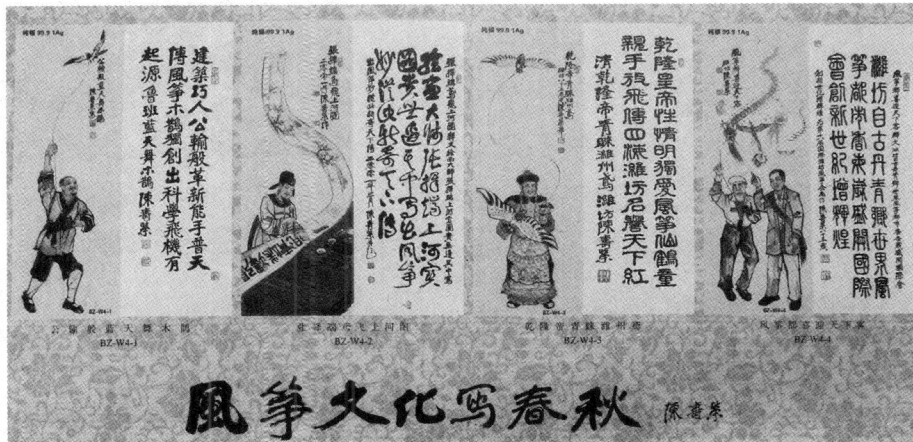

風箏文化寫春秋 陳壽榮

The world's first kite

According to historical records, more than 2,400 years ago, the world's first kite was successfully made by Luban, a skilled craftsman, and the kite was flewn in Lu Mountain in the territory of Weifang.The kite had been flying for three days. Luban was honored as the originator of the architectural and kite. The kite culture has gradually been inherited.

世界风筝都

1988 年 4 月 1 日至 10 日，第五届潍坊国际风筝会暨第三届全国风筝比赛在潍坊市隆重举行。期间，竞选"世界风筝都"是本届风筝会的一项重要议程。为此，4 月 1 日上午 10 时，召开了第五届潍坊国际风筝会主席团会议。会议由中国风协副主席、国家体委群体司副司长郭敏主持。会上，潍坊市风协主席、副市长宋希焕介绍了关于本届风筝会的筹备情况，美国风筝界知名人士、西雅图风协主席大卫·巧克列先生宣读了《提议潍坊市为"世界风筝都"的倡议书》。与会的中国、美国、英国、加拿大、法国、意大利、联邦德国、丹麦、澳大利亚、新西兰、日本、泰国等国家和中国香港的风筝协会负责人一致通过了大卫·巧克列的倡议。英国风协全权代表费莱德·瓦特豪斯在致辞中说："潍坊作为世界风筝活动中心和世界风协所在地是当之无愧的"。

潍坊市被推举为"世界风筝都"是世界风筝运动史上的一个重大事件，具有十分重要的意义，在海内外产生了巨大的反响，国内外先后有 200 多个风协组织和友好单位纷纷来电来函表示祝贺。

1988 年 4 月 10 日上午，与会的各个国家和地区的风协代表在《倡议书上》签字。

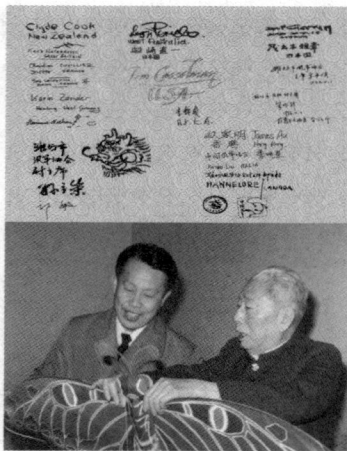

Capital of Kite in the World

From 1st to 10th, April 1988, the fifth Weifang International Kite Festival and the third National Kite Championship was held in Weifang, China. During the festival and championship, it was a very important agenda to elect the capital of kite in the world. At 10:00 am on April 1, the fifth Weifang International Kite Festival held a presidium meeting. The meeting was chaired by the Vice-Chairman of the China Kite Flying Association, deputy director of the Group Sport Department of the National Sports Commission, Mr. Guo Min. At the meeting, the Chairman of the Weifang Kite Association and Vice Mayor of Weifang, Mr. Song Xihuan introduced the preparations of the Weifang Internatioanl Kite Festival. Famous person fo American kite filed, president of Seattle Kite Association, Mr. Dave Checkley announced the initial written proposal on Selecting Weifang as the Capital of Kite in the World. Principals from the kite fliers associations of China, the United States, UK, Canada, France, Italy, the Federal Republic of Germany, Denmark, Australia, New Zealand, Japan, Thailand and other countries and Hong Kong , China unanimously approved the proposal. Plenipotentiary of BKFA said in his speech that Weifang was well deserved of the title of World Kite Event Center and the capital of International Kite Federation.

It is an important event in the history of kite sport in the world that Weifang was elected as capital of kite in the world. The news had been spread to the world, and more than 200 domestic and international organizations have called or sent letters to show their congratulations.

In the morning of April 10, 1988, representatives of the kite associations of various countries and regions participating in the meeting signed on the Proposal.

国际风筝联合会

国际风筝联合会现有理事国、地区 16 个，会员国、地区 67 个，于 1989 年 4 月 1 日经中国国务院批准，在中国潍坊正式成立。这是第一个由华人发起，第一个由华人牵头负责，第一个设在中国地级城市的国际性体育组织。成立大会上，来自美国、日本、英国、意大利等 16 个国家和地区的风筝组织的 84 名代表通过民主协商，选举产生了国际风联主席、副主席、秘书长和理事成员。经中国国务院批准，代表大会确定国际风联总部设在世界风筝都潍坊。国际风筝联合会的诞生，标志着世界风筝事业有了领导机构和活动中心，对推动全球风筝事业的蓬勃发展，增进各国风筝爱好者的友谊，促进世界和平和友好往来发挥了积极的作用。

2013 年 12 月 7 日，国际风筝联合会第三届代表大会进行了换届改选。现任主席冯建中，常务副主席孙起生，副主席刘北剑、刘建国、柏默·汉斯、史蒂夫·多诺万、汉斯·詹森、彼得·林恩、芭芭拉·梅耶、张松林，秘书长兼司库张崇高，副秘书长颜建海。

International Kite Federation

At present, International Kite Federation (IKF) has 16 existing council member states and regions, 67 district member states and regions. On April 1, 1989, approved by the China State Council of the PRC, the IKF was formally established in Weifang, China. This is the first international sports organization initiated and taken charge by the Chinese, and the first international organization headquartered in prefecture city of China. On the inaugural meeting, 84 representatives of kite organizations from

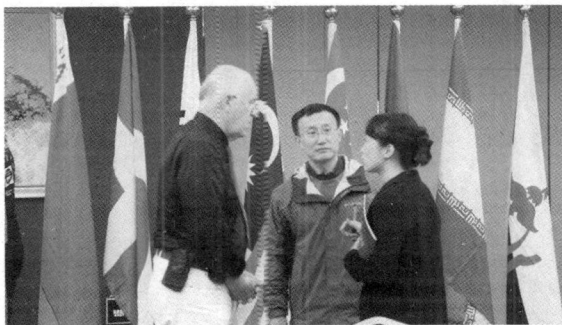

16 countries and regions, including the United States, Japan, UK, Italy, etc jointly elected, through democratic consultations, President, Vice President, Secretary General and the members of the council. It is approved by the State Council of the PRC that the headquarter of the IKF is located in Weifang, the capital of kite in the world. The birth of IKF means the establishment of the world's leading organization and event center of the kite cause, which plays a positive role in enhancing the kite development in the world, promoting the friendship among people who love kite all over the world, and enhancing world peace and friendship.

On Dec 7th, 2013, the IKF had election at expiration of prior terms of the executive members on the 3rd executive meeting. After the new election, the current president is Feng Jianzhong, the standing vice president is Sun Qisheng, the vice presidents are Liu Beijian, Liu Jianguo, Hans Peter Boehme, Steve Donovan, Hans Jansen op de Haar, Peter Lynn, Barbara Meyer, Zhang Songlin, the secretary general and treasurer is Zhang Chonggao, the deputy secretary general is Yan Jianhai.

中国风筝协会

中国风筝协会，简称"中国风协"，于 1987 年 1 月成立，是由热爱风筝运动的各地群众自愿结成的全国性、行业性社会团体，是非营利性社会组织。

中国风协的宗旨是，团结全国风筝运动的从业者和爱好者、风筝运动组织和热心支持风筝运动的机构、社会组织、各界人士等，调动一切积极因素，推动和普及风筝运动，提高风筝运动管理水平，加强与世界各国风筝组织的交往，促进中国风筝体育产业的发展。

中国风协负责人包括主席、副主席、秘书长。现任主席刘北剑，副主席冷世祥，曾晓红，吴保国，王爱军，王永训，宁友林，秘书长侯秋玲。

China Kite Flying Association

The China Kite Flying Association was established in January 1987. It is a national and industrial social group formed by the people who love kite sport. It is a non-profit social organization.

The aim of this association is to unite the practitioners and enthusiasts of the national kite sport, the kite sports organizations and the institutions, social organizations and people from all walks of life who enthusiastically support the kite sport, to integrate all positive factors, promote and popularize the kite sport, and improve the management of kite sport, strengthen exchanges with kite organizations around the world, and promote the development of kite sports industry in China.

The principals of the association include the chairman, vice chairman, secretary general. The current chairman is Liu Beijian, and the vice chairmen are Leng Shixiang, Zeng Xiaohong, Wu Baoguo, Wang Aijun, Wang Yongxun, Ning Youlin, and the secretary general is Hou Qiuling.

中国风筝协会创新实现"6个首次"

2014年以来，口国风筝协会加大推广风筝项目力度，开展了一系列比赛活动，实现了风筝运动6个"首次"：2015年首次举

办全国风筝精英赛分站赛，第一站内蒙古呼和浩特、第二站福建平潭、第三站福建厦门、第四站广东河源；首次举办了全国运动风筝巡回赛，第一站内蒙古乌兰察布，第二站内蒙古达茂旗，第三站上海；首次举办了全国风筝冲浪锦标赛福建平潭。2014年，首次在黑龙江大庆杜尔伯特县举办了中国雪地风筝赛，2017年，在贵州铜仁、兴仁分别首次举办了全国盘鹰风筝锦标赛和全国露营风筝大赛。2018年，首次组织开展了2018年全国风筝精英赛暨总决赛。

通过一系列风筝比赛，使更多的风筝爱好者参与比赛，扩大了风筝项目的影响力。

Six initiative steps in the innovation and development of China Kite Flying Association

Since 2014, the China Kite Flying Association has stepped up efforts to promote kite projects and has launched a series of competitions. Six initiative steps of kite sports were launched. Branch competitions of National Kite Classic Competition were held in 2015. The first stop was Hohhot, Inner Mongolia, the second stop was Pingtan, Fujian, the third stop was Xiamen, Fujian, and the fourth stop was Heyuan, Guangdong; The first National Sports Kite Tour was held. The first stop was Wulanchabu, Inner Mongolia, the second stop was Damaoqi, Inner Mongolia, and the third stop was Shanghai; the first National Kite Surfing Championship wa s held in Pingtan, Fujian. In 2014, the China Snow Kite Competition was hled in Dulbert, Daqing, Heilongjiang. In 2017, the National Eagle Kite Championship and the National Camping Kite Competition were held for the first time in Tongren and Xingren, Guizhou, 2018, respectively. The 2018 National Kite Classic and Finals were launched for the first time.

Through a series of kite competitions, more and more kite enthusiasts participated in the competition, the love for kite sports was significantly enhanced, and the influence of the kite project was expanded.

历史上第一部风筝竞赛规则

风筝竞赛规则(试行)

国家体育总局
一九八六年十二月

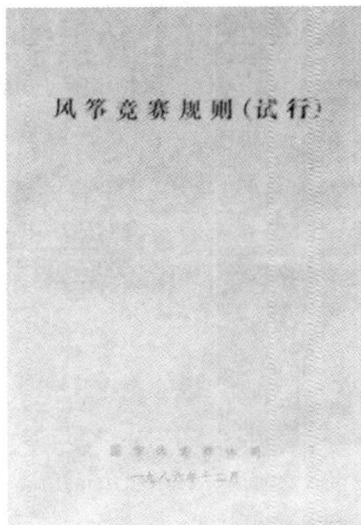

中国运动风筝的起步较晚，1984年4月第一届潍坊国际风筝会上只有放飞表演项目，到了1986年第三届潍坊国际风筝会上，美国运动员汤姆和凯斯放飞的带有很长彩色飘带的可操控的复线风筝，第一次在放飞场上空展示其"运动"风采。当风筝呼啸着上下翻飞时，其惊险动作和彩色飘带飞出的漂亮图形，吸引了数万名观众争相观看。

国外运动员精彩的放飞表演，既吸引了我国运动员的眼球，也激发了中国风筝专家和风筝爱好者的竞争意识。

有竞争才有发展。在潍坊国际风筝会和全国风筝邀请赛的推动、鼓励下，广大风筝爱好者和专家急切呼吁将复线操纵风筝纳入全国风筝比赛项目。

要比赛就要有规则。经过风筝界专家、运动员、爱好者的共同努力，《风筝竞赛规则》于1986年在潍坊完稿，并在当年被国家体委批准试行。1987年1月5日中国风筝协会成立后，对《风筝竞赛规则》又进行了补充修改，国家体委于1987年12月批准颁布了我国第一部《风筝竞赛规则》。经过5年的比赛实践，1990年下半年，国家体委正式批准发行《风筝竞赛规则》。

The first kite competition rule in history

The sports kite started late in China. In the first Weifang International Kite Festival in April 1984, there was only a flying performance project. In 1986, at the third Weifang International Kite Festival, American athletes Tom and his partner flew dual-line steerable kite with very long colorful streamer for the first time, showing its sports style over the flying field. When the kite whizzed up and down, its thrilling action and beautiful view made by the colorful streamers attracted tens of thousands of audiences.

The wonderful flying performance made by foreign fliers not only attracted the attention of Chinese fliers, but also stimulated the competition consciousness of Chinese kite experts and kite enthusiasts.

Competition always pushes forward development. Under the promotion and encouragement of the Weifang International Kite Festival and the National Kite Invitational Tournament, the majority of kite enthusiasts and experts eagerly called for putting the dual-line steerable kite into the national kite competition program.

Rules always come along with competition. After the joint efforts of kite experts, athletes and enthusiasts, the Kite Competition Rules was completed in Weifang in 1986 and was approved by the State Sports Commission in the same year. After the establishment of the China Kite Flying Association on January 5, 1987, the Kite Competition Rules was supplemented and revised. The National Sports Commission approved the promulgation of China's first Kite Competition Rules in December 1987. After five years of competition practice, in the second half of 1990, the National Sports Commission officially approved the issuance of the Kite Competition Rules.

历史上第一所风筝技校

1988 年，潍坊国际风筝会成功举办了五届以后，在市政府领导的肯定和支持下，潍坊国际风筝会办公室与潍坊劳动技校合作，成立了潍坊风筝技工学校。

办风筝学校的初衷主要是想通过学校来培养一批风筝专业人才，改变传统的师傅带徒弟的办法，把风筝生产从作坊式办成现代半工业的生产方式，提高生产效率和潍坊风筝的整体水平。

风筝技工学校从 1989 年开始招生，总共招了 89 级（20 人）、90 级（16 人）两级。办学规模不大，存在时间也不长，但无论在招生还是课程设置上都是很正规的。学制是 3 年。这两届学生掌握了比较扎实的有关风筝制作的知识和技能。

The first kite technical school in history

In 1988, after the Weifang International Kite Festival was successfully held for five sessions, with the support of the leaders of the municipal government, the Weifang International Kite Festival Office and the Weifang Labor Technical School established the Weifang Kite Technician Training School.

The original intention of running a kite school is mainly to train a group of kite professionals, change the traditional manners of training apprentices by masters, and make kite production from the workshop into a modern semi-industrial production mode, improve production efficiency and the overall level of Weifang kite.

The Weifang Kite Technician Training School began enrolling students in 1989, and recruited two years of 1989 (20 people) and 1990 (16 people). The scale of running a school is not large, and it does not last long. However, it is very formal in both enrollment and curriculum.The school system was 3 years. The students of the two grades mastered relatively good knowledge and skills related to kite making.

风筝装饰路灯最长的街道

潍坊市区北海路，是一条风筝文化元素突出的大道，是中国最长的街道，全长 120 里，比"神州第一街"长安街还要长。

每到夜晚，华灯初上，路两侧的蝴蝶风筝造型的路灯，就像一只只展翅欲飞的红蝴蝶，十分壮观；放眼望去，又像一条条长长的巨龙，腾空飞翔。

The longest street with kite shaped lamp

Beihai Road in Weifang, decorated with kite cultural elements, is the longest street in China, with a total length of 60 kilometers, which is longer than Chang'an Street, the No. 1 street in China.

Every night, when the road lamp are turned on, the street lights on both sides of the road are like a red butterfly that flies along the road. It is very spectacular. The road looks like a long dragon flying in the sky.

潍坊滨海万人放飞创造新的吉尼斯世界纪录

2011 年 4 月 16 日上午，在潍坊滨海海边，当地万余市民面对大海，携手结队同时放飞出 10000 余只五颜六色的风筝，向新的世界吉尼斯放飞风筝纪录冲击。

为体现此次创纪录活动的权威性，整个活动严格按照世界吉尼斯的规则，对放飞、场地、计算等规则进行了周密的部署，参与活动的每名放飞者只放飞一只风筝，线的长度 10 英尺以上，所有风筝在空中持续 30 秒以上。

活动举办方表示，由于参与人数众多，放飞时按照吉尼斯世界纪录许可的方阵式计算方法，将放飞人员分成了 22 个放飞区，每个放飞区 500 人。整个活动在独立监督员监督下进行，最后由吉尼斯现场认证官进行了确认并现场公布。英国吉尼斯世界纪录认证官吴晓红宣布，中国潍坊举办的万人同放风筝活动，以 10465 只同时放飞的风筝，刷新了 2010 年加沙 6198 人在此项目上保持的吉尼斯世界纪录。

Kite-flying by 10,000 people created a new Guinness World Record in Binhai, Weifang

On the morning of the 16th of April 2011, along the seaside of Weifang, China, more than 10,000 kites were flown by local citizens. They were attempting to make a new world Guinness record of kite flying.

In order to reflect the authority of this record-setting activity, the entire activity was strictly arranged in accordance with the rules of the Guinness. And the rules of flying, venue, calculation and other rules were carefully deployed, including each player who participated in the activity only flew one kite, the length of the line was more than 10 feet, all kites should last in the air for more than 30 seconds.

According to the organizer of the event, due to the large number of participants, the personnel were divided into 22 zones, with 500 people in each zone. The above was done according to the square matrix calculation method approved by the Guinness World Records. The entire event was conducted under the supervision of an independent supervisor and was finally confirmed by the Guinness Field Certified Officer and the result was published on site. Wu Xiaohong, Certified Officer of the Guinness World Records of the United Kingdom, announced that the 10,000-person kite-flying event in Weifang, China set a Guinness World Record with 10,465 kites flying at the same time, and refreshed the result of kite flying by 6,198 people in Gaza in 2010.

世界上最长串的风筝

  2016 年 10 月 29 日，世界最长串风筝记录在广东汕头澄海海岸线六合围堤上诞生，总长度 7250 米，大小串联一共 146 只风筝。

  该记录是"风筝王"陈旺松创造，超过了法国人创造的吉尼斯世界纪录 7 倍。

The longest string kites in the world

On October 29, 2016, the world's longest stringing kite record was made on the Liuhe dike in the Chenghai coastline of Shantou, Guangdong. The total length is 7,250 meters, and a total of 146 kites are connected in series. The record was created by the Kite King Chen Wangsong. The kite was more than seven times of the Guinness World Record created by the French people.

世界上最长的巨龙风筝

2016 年 12 月 18 日，在上海崇明，一条全长 6200 米的巨龙风筝放飞成功。

此风筝由镇江风筝协会会长吴杏桃一个人独立制作完成，共用 6 个月时间，耗资 2 万多元。这么一条大风筝放飞也不是一件容易的事，风筝协会的队员用了一个半小时也才放飞了 4000 多米，全部放完用了 4 个多小时。收风筝的时候费时近 7 个小时才完成。

随着整条巨龙上天，上海大世界基尼斯纪录工作人员现场认定并宣布，这一风筝以 6200 米的长度创造了大世界基尼斯之最。

The longest dragon kite in the world

On December 18, 2016, in Chongming, Shanghai, a 6,200-meter dragon kite was successfully flown.

The kite was independently produced by Wu Xingtao, the president of Zhenjiang Kite Association. It took 6 months and cost more than 20,000 yuan. It was not an easy task for flying of such a large kite. The members of the kite association took an hour and a half, and flew more than 4,000 meters of the kite. And they used more than 4 hours to fly the whole kite. And it took nearly 7 hours to collect the kite.

With the whole dragon flew in the sky, the Shanghai Great World Guinness record staff confirmed and announced that the kite created the world's longest kite record of Guinness with a length of 6,200 meters.

世界上最大的风筝

世界上最大的风筝，长 150 米、宽 75 米，面积 11250 平方米。此风筝第一次出现是在 2011 年 4 月 19 日法国北部海滨城市 Berck-Sur-Mer 举办的第 25 届国际风筝节上，当时吸引了非常多的人前来观看这只风筝。

这只风筝是由来自新西兰的巨型风筝专家彼得－林恩（Peter Lynn）制作。

The world's largest kite

The world's largest kite, which is 150 meters long, 75 meters wide, covers an area of 11,250 square meters. The kite first appeared on the 25th International Kite Festival in Berck-Sur-Mer, a coastal city in the north of France on April 19, 2011. A lot of people were attracted to watch the kite. The kite was produced by Peter Lynn, a giant kite expert from New Zealand.

世界上最重的风筝

2014 年 8 月 5 日，一只面积为 1500 平方米的"章鱼"软体风筝，在内蒙古呼和浩特市希拉穆仁草原举行的草原风筝节上放飞升空，成为世界上最重的风筝吉尼斯的创造者。它重 200 公斤，由来自天津的黑哥风筝队历时 3 个月制作而成。

The heaviest kite in the world

On August 5, 2014, an octopus inflation kite with an area of 1,500 square meters was flown over the grassland kite festival held in the Xilamuren grassland of Hohhot, Inner Mongolia and became the heaviest kite in the world recognized by the Guinness Record. It weighed 200 kilograms and was made by the Heige Kite Team from Tianjin.

世界上最小巧轻薄的风筝

　　1985 年 4 月，在山东省潍坊市举行的国际风筝盛会上，潍坊织布三厂工人唐延寿做的风筝，成为世界上最小的风筝。

　　唐延寿做的 3 只配套的小风筝，被取名为"子母燕"，造型别致，色彩明快，乍看像是从邮票上剪下来似的，细看才发现，这是扎、糊、绘都极为精细的半立体式风筝。骨架是薄若蝉翼的竹片，筝面是上等丝绢，制作得在放大镜下进行。其中，最小的一只长 2.5 厘米，宽 2.4 厘米。

The smallest and lightest kite in the world

At the International Kite Festival held in Weifang, Shandong in April 1985, the kite made by Tang Yanshou, a worker from 3rd Weaving Factory in Weifang, became the smallest kite in the world.

The kite sets composed of three small kites made by Tang Yanshou were named child-mother swallow. The shape was unique and the color was bright. It looked like that the kite was cut from a stamp. It was only after careful observation that it was a well tied and pasted, three-dimension kite with extremely fine paintings. The skeleton is a thin bamboo blade, and the surface of the kite is fine silk. It is made under a magnifying glass. Among them, the smallest one is 2.5 cm long and 2.4 cm wide.

马庆华一人一次放飞风筝数量最多创吉尼斯世界纪录

2006 年，潍坊市青州风筝艺人马庆华一人放飞 43 只风筝，创造了放飞风筝数量最多的世界纪录。项目参赛标准和要求是，

一人放飞风筝，风筝距手 3 米之外，单线牵拉一个风筝，飞起的风筝必须在天空飘舞 30 秒以上，同时具备这些要求的风筝才能计算数量。经吉尼斯认证官现场认证，马庆华成功放飞起 43 只风筝，成为当今世界一次放飞风筝最多的人，创造了新的吉尼斯世界纪录，并被邀请到中国中央电视台《吉尼斯之夜》节目参加颁奖。

Ma Qinghua set a Guinness World Record for the most kites flown by a person at a time

In 2006, kite artist Ma Qinghua of Qingzhou, Weifang flew 43 kites and created the world record for the most kites flown by a person at a time. The standards and requirements for the project were: one person flies a kite, the kite is 3 meters away from the hand, a single line pulls a kite, the kite must keep flying in the sky for more than 30 seconds, and then the quantity of kite can be calculated after meeting all the above requirements. After the on-site certification by the officer of Guinness Record, Ma Qinghua successfully flew 43 kites, becoming the person flying the most number of kite in the world, and created a new Guinness World Record. He was invited to Night of Guinness program for on-site awarding.

杨云胜创最大风筝吉尼斯世界纪录

2003 年，潍坊市青州风筝艺人杨云胜扎制的"眼镜王蛇"风筝，获得了吉尼斯世界纪录最大风筝称号。这只"眼镜王蛇"软体风筝，长 293.8 米，面积为 882.41 平方米，重为 123 公斤。在潍坊国际风筝会上，该风筝放飞性能良好，获得风筝创新一等奖。不久，该风筝被推荐申报"最大风筝"的吉尼斯纪录。经过专家实地考察、验收，吉尼斯总部正式批准该风筝为世界最大风筝。

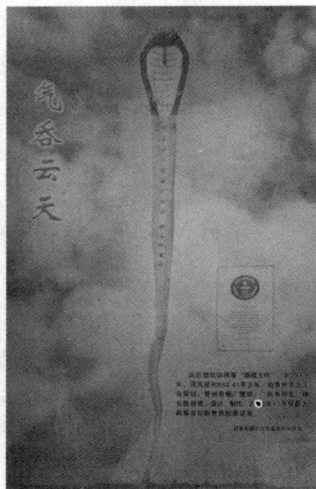

Yang Yunsheng creates the largest kite Guinness World Record

In 2003, the King Cobra kite made bykite artist Yang Yunsheng from Qingzhou, Weifang won the Guinness World Record for the largest kite. This King Cobra inflation kite is 293.8 meters long, covers an area of 882.41 square meters and weighs 123 kilograms. The kite was flown at the Weifang International Kite Festival and won the first prize for kite innovation. Soon, the kite was recommended to declare the Guinness Record of Largest Kite. After field visits and acceptance by experts, the Guinness headquarters officially approved the kite as the world's largest kite.

最大组合的风筝主题群雕

潍坊的《风筝魂》铜雕是中国最大的组合群雕，作者傅绍相、车秀申，已申报世界吉尼斯纪录。

中国最大的青铜民俗情景组合群雕《风筝魂》

大型青铜群雕《风筝魂》在首届中国（潍坊）文化艺术展示交易会上亮相。群雕共由 2008 件形象逼真、形态各异的人物雕塑和场景单体雕塑构成，以风筝放飞为主线，共分 6 个板块，生动地再现了潍坊风筝的历史变迁和潍坊的风土民情，同时还巧妙地把神六飞天、"嫦娥"奔月、放飞福娃迎奥运融入其中，有人称其为"立体版清明上河图"。此群雕是目前国内最大的组合群雕，用铜达 13 吨。

The largest group sculpture of kite theme

Bronze sculpture in Weifang named Kite Soul is the largest group sculpture in China. The authors are Fu Shaoxiang and Che Xiushen. The sculpture has already declared the Guinness Records.

The large bronze group sculpture Kite Soul was unveiled at the first China (Weifang) Cultural and Art Exhibition Fair. The group sculpture consists of 2008 vivid and different characters sculptures and single scene sculptures. The flying of kite is the theme of the group sculpture. It is divided into 6 sections, vividly reproducing the historical changes and the local customs of Weifang, at the same time, the sculpture contains the elements of No. 6 Shenzhou spacecraft flying to the space, the gods of Chang' e flying to the moon, flying Fuwa kite to welcome the Olympics, some people call it three-dimensional version of the Riverside Scene at Qingming Festival. The group sculpture is currently the largest group group sculpture in China, with a copper capacity of 13 tons.

1987 年世界十绝风筝

1987 年在第 4 届潍坊国际风筝会上，首次设立世界风筝"十绝"评比项目，当年获得世界"十绝"风筝的有：

①连接风筝 – 日本广岛风协 – 津田欣二

②蜻蜓 – 中国辽宁 – 郭庆玺

③麻姑献寿 – 中国天津 – 郭霄云

④双巨流型 – 美国罗德岛风协 – 汤姆·卡斯尔曼

⑤神风号中日友好 – 日本千叶县风协 – 川崎火吕志

⑥龙 – 联邦德国 – 伯纳德·布克

⑦马可·波罗 – 意大利 – 萨维亚·沃兰特

⑧三角风筝 – 美国华盛顿州风协 – 马歇尔

⑨长串连接体风筝 – 全日本风协 – 茂出木雅章

⑩龙飞凤舞 – 中国潍坊 – 康立本

The World Top Ten Kite in 1987

In 1987, at the 4th Weifang International Kite Festival, the world's Top Ten Kite was elected for the first time. The winners were:

1 Connected Kites-Japan-Hiroshima Kite Fliers Association

2 Dragonfly-Liaoning China

3 Fariy Magu Presenting Longevity Gift- Tianjin, China

4 Pairs of giant flow type - Rhode Island Kite Fliers Association, USA

5 Shenfeng China-Japan Friendship-Japan Chiba Kite Fliers Association

6 Dragon - Federal Germany

7 Marco Polo - Italy

8 Triangle Kite - Washington State Kite Fliers Association

9 Long string kites -Japan Kite Fliers Association

10 Dragon Fly & Phoenix Dance Kite- Weifang China

1988 年世界十绝风筝

①哪吒闹海 – 中国山东 – 于长坡

②龟 – 美国克劳莱德 – 斯哥特·斯金纳

③蓝星 – 联邦德国 – 皮特·马林斯克

④章鱼 – 意大利 – 比德

⑤节日队列 – 澳大利亚 – 里昂·派瑞里克斯

⑥电视 – 丹麦 – 乔里斯顿·沙特

⑦富士山 – 日本熊本县 A 队 – 船崎直一

⑧大龙 – 加拿大 – 汉娜罗拉

⑨串蝶 – 法国 – 约埃勒泰兹

⑩蛇 – 泰国 – 普伦亚叟智

The World Top Ten Kite in 1988

1 Nezha Fighting in the Sea - Shandong China

2 Turtles -USA

3 Blue Star - Federal Republic of Germany

4 Octopus - Italy

5 Festival Queue - Australia

6 TV - Denmark

7 Fujiyama - Japan's Kumamoto A team

8 Great Dragons - Canada

9 Butterflies string- France

10 Snakes - Thailand

1989 年世界十绝风筝

①蝴蝶 – 意大利 – 皮埃特罗·利维

②万花筒 – 美国罗德岛 – 威地·康纳斯

③火风筝 – 瑞典 – 拉斯·恩兰得

④彩龙 – 香港风筝总会 – 林祖泽

⑤六角风车 – 联邦德国 – 波耶·尼克尔森

⑥太国风筝 – 韩国釜山县风协 – 徐相守

⑦友好之桥 – 全日本风协（A）– 克里芒

⑧蓝色、红色、白色 – 法国（A）队 – 克里芒

⑨金龙腾飞 – 中国潍坊 – 康宝忠

⑩飞机 – 丹麦 – 乔斯顿·沙特

The World Top Ten Kite in 1989

1 Butterfly - Italy

2 Kaleidoscope - Rhode Island, USA

3 Fire Kite - Sweden

4 Colorful Dragon - Hong Kong Kite Association

5 Hexagonal Windmill - Federal Republic of Germany

6 Taiguo Kite - Republic of Korea Kite Fliers Association

7 Friendly Bridge - All Japan Kite Fliers Association (A)

8 Blue, Red, White - France (A) team

9 Golden Dragon Soaring - Weifang China - Kang Baozhong

10 Aircraft - Denmark

1990 年世界十绝风筝

①晨星 – 英国 – 费雷德·沃特豪斯

②捷克龙 – 捷克斯洛伐克 – 史凯特

③多彩六角星 – 联邦德国 – 本德·纽佛

④三角形 – 法国 – 塞奇·尼格尔

⑤展翅 – 意大利 – 皮埃特·洛利维

⑥角风筝 – 日本 – 茂出木雅章

⑦刘角风筝 – 土耳其 – 穆罕麦德·萨勃尔

⑧魟鱼 – 美国 – 汤姆凯瑟门

⑨灵芝 – 中国广东 – 冯光

⑩龙头蜈蚣 – 中国潍坊 – 蒯建民

The World Top Ten Kite in 1990

1 Morning Star - UK

2 Czech dragons - Czechoslovakia

3 Colorful Hexagon Stars - Federal Germany

4 Triangles - France

5 Wings - Italy

6 Angle Kite-Japan

7 Hexagonal Kite - Turkey

8 Ray- United States

9 Lucid Ganoderma -Guangdong China

10 Dragon-head Centipede-body Kite-China Weifang

风筝艺术潍坊第一

1984 年春，日本著名书法篆刻家梅舒适先生在潍坊参观书画展期间，正值潍坊国际风筝会即将开幕的前几天，他到潍坊工艺美术研究所，参观了风筝展览。他看到绚丽多姿的各式风筝，情不自禁地感叹道："嗬！不得了，真是不得了！此情此景我才发现了潍坊人民的勤劳和智慧。潍坊风筝给人以美的享受、奋扬的力量和求索的勇气。我是为潍坊书法艺术而来，但潍坊风筝却紧紧扣住了我的心弦。潍坊不仅是书道之乡，也是风筝界的明珠，是光辉的一页。"他还说："书画展刚开幕，风筝又凌空飞翔。真是方兴未艾，潍坊具有旺盛的生命力！我归国后，要让我的朋友、学生都知道中国有一个潍坊！"说毕，激情挥毫书写了"风筝艺术潍坊第一"8 个刚劲有力的篆体大字，赠给了潍坊市工艺美术研究所。

Weifang Ranked No. 1 in the Art of Kite

In the spring of 1984, during the visit to the calligraphy and painting exhibition in Weifang, the famous Japanese calligraphy engraver Meishushi arrived at the Weifang Arts and Crafts Institute and visited the kite exhibition a few days before the opening of the Weifang International Kite Festival. He saw a variety of kites, and he couldn't help saying,"Ah! It's really amazing! I found the hard work and wisdom of Weifang people here. Weifang kites give people a beautiful enjoyment and excitement, and the strength and the courage to seek. I came here for the calligraphy art of Weifang, but the Weifang kite shocked me so much. Weifang is not only the hometown of art of calligraphybooks, but also famous for the kite." He also said, "The painting and calligraphy exhibition has just opened, and the kite is flying in the air. It is really in the ascendant. Weifang has a strong vitality! After I returned to Japan, I want my friends and students to know that there is a Weifang in China!" He wrote the powerful characters of "Weifang Ranked No. 1 in the Art of Kite" and presented it to Weifang Arts and Crafts Institute.

潍坊国际风筝会纪念品收藏第一人
——李乃湘

李乃湘是潍坊的一名退休职工，对风筝的痴爱，促使他从第一届潍坊国际风筝会就开始收集与风筝有关的藏品，经过 30 多年的积累，老人收获颇丰。邮票、火柴盒、钥匙环、纪念币、剪纸、门票、采访证……在这些与风筝有关的纪念品上，都有栩栩如生的风筝翩翩展翅。

2002 年 11 月，老人在奎文区凤凰小区的家中首次展出风筝纪念品，在鸢都市民中引起很大反响。人们争相一睹。2004 年，潍坊国际风筝会办公室邀请老人来潍坊风筝博物馆展出，他的收藏精品一下子成为游人关注的焦点。

目前，李乃湘老人收藏的风筝纪念品已达到 40 多种、数万件。

No. 1 Person of Souvenir Collection of the Weifang International Kite Festival-Li Naixiang

Li Naixiang is a retired worker in Weifang. His love for kites has enabled him to collect kites related collections since the first Weifang International Kite Festival. After more than 30 years of accumulation, he has gained a lot. Stamps, matchboxes, key rings, commemorative coins, paper-cuts, tickets, interview cards... On these kite-related souvenirs, there are lifelike kites.

In November 2002, he exhibited the kite souvenir for the first time in the home of the Phoenix Community in Kuiwen District. The citizens of Weifang were greatly shocked. In 2004, the Weifang International Kite Festival Office invited him to exhibit his collections at the Weifang Kite Museum. His collections became a focus of attention by tourists.

At present, the kite souvenirs collected by Li Naixiang have reached more than 40 kinds and tens of thousands of pieces.

规模最大的万人风筝放飞表演活动

万人风筝放飞表演活动是潍坊国际风筝会的一项品牌活动，伴随风筝会已连续举办了35年。此活动与在放飞场举行的风筝会开幕式相连接，开幕仪式结束后即宣布举行万人风筝放飞表演活动。届时，中外来宾，当地市民，外地游客，国内外放飞队展开自由放飞，各种形态各异的风筝飞向蓝天，竞相飞翔，把世界风筝都的天空妆扮得绚丽多彩。在每届的万人放飞表演中，少则几万人，多则十几万人参加，场面宏大壮观。目睹这一壮观场景，国际风筝联合会原主席季明涛先生曾赞叹称，这真是风筝的海洋，这样超大规模的放飞场景，只有在世界风筝都潍坊才能亲身体验到。

The largest kite flying performance by 10,000 people

The 10,000 people kite flying performance is a featured event of the Weifang International Kite Festival, which has been held for 35 years. The event is held after the opening ceremony of the Weifang International Kite Festival held at the flying field. After the opening ceremony, a 10,000 people kite flying performance began. At that time, Chinese and foreign guests, local citizens, foreign tourists, domestic and foreign flying teams flew their kites. Different kinds of kites flew into the blue sky, making the blue sky into a colorful world. In the flying events, the number of participants would be tens of thousands people or more than that. It was very spectacle. In witness of this spectacular scene, Mr. Ji Mingtao, the former president of the International Kite Federation, praised that it is really an ocean of kites which can only be witnessed in Weifang, the capital of kite in the world.

潍坊风筝首次亮相国家重大政治活动

为庆贺中国共产党第十六次全国代表大会召开，2002年11月9日，潍坊市在市区白浪河公园绿地广场，组织广大市民开展了风筝放飞表演庆盛会活动。数百名风筝爱好者放飞了形式多样、各具特色的风筝，特别是由潍坊市供销社退休干部陆开国扎制的"灯笼一串红"风筝，16个红色灯笼飘在空中显得格外引人注目。据陆开国介绍，这16个灯笼象征党的十六大胜利召开，也代表祖国建设和各项事业在党的领导下红红火火、蒸蒸日上，同时也表达了潍坊市民对党的无比热爱之情。在活动现场，潍坊国际风筝会办公室副主任张崇高以市民身份随机接受了中央电视台采访，畅谈了收听党的十六大政治报告的心得体会。张崇高深有感触地说，党的十六大政治报告提出了"三个代表"和全面建设小康社会的奋斗目标，听了很受鼓舞，备感振奋。一个党始终想着人民，一切为人民谋福利，这样的党是我们老百姓无比信赖的党，我们坚决拥护。

此次风筝放飞活动和对市民张崇高的采访，各级媒体纷纷进行报道，特别是中央电视台先后在《新闻联播》《午间30分》《匚国新闻》等栏目中连续滚动播出了10多次，在国内产生了广泛影响，也创造了潍坊3方面的新纪录：一是潍坊地方民间活动首次与国家重大政治活动紧密联系；二是潍坊市最新的城市景观，如白浪河公园绿地广场、新建亚星桥首次出现在央视新闻联播；三是潍坊市单项活动在央视各频道滚动播出次数之多，创历史之最。

Weifang kites firstly showed in major national political events

To celebrate the convening of the 16th National Congress of the Communist Party of China, on November 9, 2002, the Weifang Municipal Government organized the Kite Flying Show in the Greenland Square of Bailang River Park. Hundreds of kite fans flew many kites of different styles and unique features. The Red Lantern kite, which was composed of 16 red lanterns, made by Lu Kaiguo, a retired cadre of the Weifang Supply and Marketing Cooperatives were particularly eye-catching in the air. According to the introduction by Lu Kaiguo, these 16 lanterns symbolized the victory of the 16th National Congress of the Communist Party of China. It represented the motherland's construction and various undertakings which are prosperous under the leadership of the party. And it expressed the Weifang people's incomparable love for the party. At the event, Zhang Chonggao, deputy director of the Weifang International Kite Festival Office, was randomly interviewed by CCTV as a citizen and talked about the experience of listening to the Political Report of 16th National Congress of the Communist Party of China. Zhang Chonggao said with deep feeling that the political report of the 16th National Congress of the Communist Party of China put forward the "three represents" and the goal of building a well-off society in an all-round way. He was very encouraged and excited. A party always thinks about the people and benefits the people is what people can trust. He showed that we would firmly support it.

The kite-flying activities and interviews with the citizen Zhang Chonggao have been reported in succession by the media at all levels. In particular, CCTV has successively published in the "Network News Broadcast",

"30 minutes in the afternoon", "China News" and other columns for more than 10 times. The news has produced widespread influence in China. It created new records in three aspects of Weifang: First, the local folk activities in Weifang were closely related to major national political activities; the second was the latest urban landscape in Weifang, such as Bailang River Park Greenland Square, newly built Yaxing Bridge, firstly appeared in CCTV news broadcast; the third was the news report of Weifang's single event became the most popular ones regarding Weifang in CCTV channels .

首届世界风筝小姐比赛

2004 年第 21 届潍坊国际风筝会推出了一台重头戏——闻名中外的世界风筝小姐选拔大赛。

该大赛旨在通过世界风筝小姐选拔大赛及系列活动，弘扬风筝文化，架起友谊桥梁，打造世界风筝都潍坊品牌，促进旅游经济大发展。"世界风筝小姐"评选时间跨度较大，从 2004 年 2 月开始发布公告，组织评选，到风筝会期间搞完初赛，到 2004 年 9 月鲁台经贸洽谈会期间举行决赛。整个比赛分初赛、复赛、决赛 3 个阶段，初赛分散在全球各地举行，复赛与决赛均在山东潍坊。其间，进行了北京登长城风筝放飞、潍坊入城仪式、风筝会开幕式、鲁台经贸洽谈会开幕式及庆典晚会、游园、购物、献爱心等活动。大赛经过知识问答、才艺表演、舞台展示等综合成绩测评后，来自斯洛文尼亚的朱利娅获得冠军和 60 万元的奖金。

中国选手董青、高晓倩分获亚军、季军。中国香港选手张乐获特邀选手代表奖。这次大赛还决出最佳上镜、最受传媒关注、最佳身材、最佳才艺、最佳气质、最佳容貌、最佳观众印象共 7 个单项奖。另外，还决出 20 名优秀选手奖，有 46 名选手获得"世界风筝小姐"荣誉奖。

这次大赛的举办，在世界上是首次。通过举办这次活动，进一步弘扬了风筝文化，增进了国际友谊，扩大了潍坊的知名度和影响力，进一步提高了潍坊作为世界风筝文化传播中心的地位。

The First World Miss Kite Competition

In 2004, during the 21st Weifang International Kite Festival, a major event was launched, the World Miss Kite Competition.

The aim of the competition was to promote the kite culture, build a bridge of friendship, build a world-class kite Weifang brand, and promote the development of the tourism economy through the selection and series of activities of the World Miss Kite Competition. The World Miss Kite Competition took a long time since its publishment of announcement from February 2004. The selection was organized, and then the preliminary competition was completed during the kite festival, and the final was held during the Lu-Tai Economic and Trade Fair in September 2004. The whole competition was divided into three stages: preliminary, semi-final and final. The preliminary competition was held all over the world. The semi-final and final were in Weifang, Shandong. In the meantime, the activities of kite flying was held on the Great Wall in Beijing, and the ceremony of entering Weifang, the opening ceremony of the Weifang International Kite Festival, the opening ceremony of the Lu-Taiwan Economic and Trade Fair, the celebration party, the garden visiting, shopping, and charity events were carried out. The contest covered knowledge quiz, talent show, stage show and other comprehensive performance evaluation. Julia from Slovenia won the championship and bonus of 600,000 yuan.

Chinese players Dong Qing and Gao Xiaoqian won the second place and the third place. Zhang Le, from Hong Kong,

China, was awarded the Special Representative Award. The competition also had the best photo, the most media focusing, the best figure, the best talent, the best temperament, the best appearance, the best audience impression, with a total of seven individual awards. In addition, 20 outstanding players were awarded, and 46 players won the honorary award of "Miss World Kite".

This competition is the first in the world. By holding this event, the kite culture was further promoted, international friendship was enhanced, Weifang's popularity and influence were expanded, and Weifang's position as the world's kite culture communication center was further enhanced.

飞越太空的最高风筝

2016年9月15日-11月17日，潍坊市选送了一只由风筝大师王永训先生特制的飞天木鸢风筝，伴随"天宫"二号空间实验室和神舟11号飞船胜利完成飞越太空之旅。

这只特制木鸢风筝是一只栩栩如生的飞鹰，重300克，呈折叠式，仅有A4纸大小，托在手中非常轻巧。在飞向太空过程中，距地面393公里，在太空遨游66天，成为全世界飞得最高的风筝。这只代表潍坊特色的"飞天木鸢"风筝，承载着928万潍坊人民的美好愿望，实现了人类风筝飞翔太空的梦想，创造了风筝飞天的最高纪录，进一步扩大了世界风筝都潍坊的知名度和影响力。

The Highest Flying Kite into Space

From September 15th, 2016 to November 17th, 2016, Weifang selected a kite specially made by Mr. Wang Yongxun, the kite master, and completed the flight over the space with the Tiangong No. 2 and Shenzhou No.11 spacecrafts.

The kite is a lifelike flying eagle. It weighs 300 grams and can be folded. It has only the size of a A4 paper and is very light in the hand. In the process of flying to space, it was 393 kilometers from the ground and flew 66 days in space, and it became the highest flying kite in the world. This represents the kite which carried the great wishes of 9.28 million Weifang people, realized the dream of flying in space, and created the highest record of kites flying, and further expanded the popularity and influence of Weifang, the capital of kite in the world.

首开国内节会标识先河的风筝会会徽

潍坊国际风筝会会徽于 1985 年正式推出。1984 年首届潍坊国际风筝会成功举办之后，为适应宣传推广的需要，潍坊市政府邀请山东工艺美院原院长张一民等专家，集体设计创作了潍坊国际风筝会会徽。会徽设计呈现三层含义：一是会徽由繁体字"風"变形而来。自然界之"风"本身与风筝关系密切。二是会徽像一只"蝴蝶"风筝。"蝴蝶"风筝是潍坊传统风筝的重要代表作，且在会徽问世前，潍坊市即以"蝴蝶"图形在国家工商总局将其注册为潍坊风筝商标。三是会徽的"五个圆"又有奥运五环的寓意。放风筝也是一种体育健身运动，"五个圆"体现了更高、更快、更强的奥运精神和开放性、国际性，也是友谊、和平的象征。会徽的主色调为蓝白两色，标志着潍坊蓝天白云、宜居宜业的良好生态环境。整个会徽图形设计构思巧妙，简洁明快，易识易记，视觉冲击力强，寓意吉祥丰富，体现了历史文化与现代时尚结合，地域特色和国际性结合，抽象与具象相结合，精致和谐与大气开放相结合。30 多年来，潍坊国际风筝会会徽成为宣传推介潍坊的一个重要标志，成为潍坊几代人的集体记忆，影响深远。

The emblem of Weifang International Kite Festival was the first in the logo design of domestic festivals

The emblem of the Weifang International Kite Festival was officially launched in 1985. After the success of the first Weifang International Kite Festival in 1984, in order to meet the needs of publicity and promotion, the Weifang Municipal Government invited Zhang Yimin, the former president of Shandong Arts and Crafts Institute, and other specialists to create and design the emblem of the Weifang International Kite Festival. The design of emblem has had three meanings: First, the emblem is transformed from the traditional Chinese character "wind". The "wind" of nature itself is closely related to kites. Second, the emblem looks like a butterfly kite. Butterfly kite is an important representative of Weifang traditional kites. Before the design of the emblem, Weifang has registered the "Butterfly" graphic as the Weifang kite trademark in the State Administration for Industry and Commerce. Third, the "five circles" of the emblem have the meaning of the Olympic rings. Flying a kite is also a kind of physical fitness. The "five circles" embodies a higher, faster and stronger Olympic spirit and openness and internationality. It is also a symbol of friendship and peace. The main color of the emblem is blue and white, which marks the good ecological environment of blue sky and white clouds and livable environment in Weifang. The design of emblem is concise and clear, easy to understand and easy to remember, and has strong visual impulse, meaning auspicious and rich, reflecting the combination of historical culture and modern fashion, regional characteristics and internationalism, abstract and figurative, exquisite harmony and open atmosphere. For more than 30 years, the emblem of Weifang International Kite Festival has become an important symbol for the promotion of Weifang, and has become a collective memory of several generations in Weifang, with far-reaching influence.

首批（潍坊）国际风筝工艺大师

2014年1月7日，首批（潍坊）国际风筝工艺大师颁证仪式在山东省交通职业学院举行。本次评出受奖的国际风筝工艺大师分为一级和二级，一级有韩福龄、王永训、张效东，二级有谭新波、杨云胜、杨红卫。

本次活动经国际风筝联合会同意，由国际风筝联合会秘书处、潍坊国际风筝会办公室组织实施。（潍坊）国际风筝工艺大师评选，目的是通过评选领军人物，提升潍坊风筝品牌价值，弘扬传承风筝文化，促进风筝产业发展，进一步扩大潍坊风筝的影响力。报名参评活动从2013年3月8日始至3月31日止，共收到代表作者最高水平的参评风筝作品60件，内容覆盖传统风筝、现代风筝，板式风筝、软体风筝，花、鸟、鱼、虫、人物、拐子、骨架等各类风筝工艺产品。各种作品均制作工艺精湛，加工考究。有的作品制作时间长达半年多，体现了作者的艺术造诣，基本代表了当前潍坊风筝艺人的最高水平，覆盖风筝产业链各环节。风筝产品也呈现多样化趋势，门类比较齐全。

韩福龄

男，汉族，1934年9月出生，国家级非物质文化遗产项目风筝制作技艺（潍坊风筝）代表性传承人，国际风筝工艺大师（一级）。

参加多届风筝会，多次获得最高奖，荣获历届潍坊市风筝明星称号。多次到国内外介绍潍坊风筝，研制成功了不需悬挂任何飘带类平衡物的硬翅足球风筝、紫荆花风筝和创新型飞机风筝。

张效东

男，汉族，1949年10月出生，山东省非物质文化遗产项目潍坊风筝代表性传承人，国际风筝工艺大师（一级）。

多次参加潍坊国际风筝会风筝比赛，屡获金奖，擅长180个种类的制作，研制出了集声、光、电于一体的动态风筝，荣获潍坊风筝专家、潍坊市民间艺术大师、潍坊市工艺美术大师、世界文艺当代艺圣等称号。

王永训

男，汉族，1972年11月出生，寒亭区非物质文化遗产项目潍坊风筝代表性传承人，国际风筝工艺大师（一级）。成立潍坊天成飞鸢风筝有限公司并任董事长。

王永训是中国风筝协会副主

席、潍坊风筝产业协会会长、潍坊市工艺美术大师、山东省十大民间艺术大师、潍坊风筝专家、潍坊市政协委员。从艺多年，获得的风筝奖项百余个，是潍坊市风筝产业的代表人物。

谭新波

男，汉族，1965 年出生，山东省工艺美术大师，国际风筝工艺大师（二级）。擅长设计和放飞巨型软体风筝，创立了潍坊凯旋风筝有限公司，是潍坊市风筝产业的代表人物。

美国风筝协会 AKA 的成员，潍坊风筝产业协会副会长，潍坊风筝专家，曾接受美国、马来西亚、韩国、英国、法国等十几个国家邀请，参加放飞表演，为中国夺得了诸多荣誉。

杨云胜

男，回族，1965 年出生于山东省青州市东关。国际风筝工艺大师（二级），连续三次获"潍坊市风筝明星"称号。自幼酷爱风筝艺术，遍寻名师刻苦钻研"扎、糊、绘、放"风筝"四艺"，多次代表潍坊参加国内外风筝比赛。

自参加潍坊国际风筝会以来，创作了巨龙、子母龙、九龙齐飞、民族同庆、千米蜈蚣、大戏楼、百蝶闹春、百猴闹春等大量经典作品并获创作一等奖。2002 年为庆祝北京申奥成功创作了 2008 米长的"中国龙"风筝，2008 年制作了 360 米长的"福娃龙"风筝。2003 年设计并制作的"眼镜王蛇"风筝，迎风面积 882.41 平方米，重量 123 公斤，获"吉尼斯"世界纪录（最大风筝）。

杨红卫

女，1966年7月出生，杨家埠"风筝之王"杨同科的孙女，"杨氏风筝"第16代传人，国际风筝工艺大师（二级）。

从艺30多年，扎制数万只风筝。1992年，在中国香港"世界同乐日"活动中，"龙头蜈蚣"和"百子呈龙"风筝，分别获最佳设计奖和最长风筝放飞奖；2007年10月，被山东省旅游文化博览会授予"手工艺制作大师"称号；2008年11月，"百子呈龙"风筝在首届山东国际大众艺术节——齐鲁民间手工艺精品博览会获银奖。

The first batch of (Weifang) international kite craft masters

On January 7, 2014, the first batch of (Weifang) International Kite Craft Master Awarding Ceremony was held at Shandong Transport Vocational College. The awards were divided into first-level and second-level. The first-level winners were Han Fuling, Wang Yongxun, Zhang Xiaodong, and the second-level winners were Tan Xinbo, Yang Yunsheng and Yang Hongwei.

The event was approved by the International Kite Federation and organized by the Secretariat of International Kite Federation and Weifang International Kite Festival Office. The purpose was to enhance the Weifang kite brand value, promote the inheritance of kite culture, promote the development of the kite industry, and further expand the influence of Weifang kites by electing the leading figures. From March 8th, 2013 to March 31st, the registration activities received 60 pieces of the highest level of participating kites, covering traditional kites, modern kites, board kites, inflation kites, and other kite craft products with shapes of flowers, birds, fish, insects, characters, etc. All kinds of works were exquisite in craftsmanship and well-processed. Some works had been produced for more than half a year, reflecting the author's artistic attainments. The works basically represented the highest level of the current Weifang kite artists, covering all aspects of the kite industry chain. The categories of kite products were diversified.

Han Fuling

Male, Han nationality, born in September 1934, the representative inheritors of national intangible cultural heritage items in kite-making skills (Weifang Kite); First level of international kite craft masters.

Han has taken part in Weifang International Kite Festival for many times, and has won the highest award for many times, and has won the title of Weifang Kite Star of the previous sessions. He has introduced Weifang kites domestically and abroad for many times, and has successful developed football-shaped hard wing kite, redbud-shaped kites and innovative aircraft kite unnecessary of hanging counterweight.

Zhang Xiaodong

Male, Han nationality, born in October 1949, the representative inheritors of Shandong intangible cultural heritage items in kite-making skills (Weifang Kite). First level of international kite craft masters.

Since the holding of Weifang International Kite Festival, he has participated for many times and has won gold medals for many times. He is good at production of one hundred and eighty types of kites. He developed dynamic kite with sound, light and electricity. And he has won title of Weifang kite expert, Weifang folk art masters, Weifang Master of Arts, contemporary art saint of world literary and art, etc.

Wang Yongxun

Male, Han nationality, born in November 1972. The representative inheritor of Hanting intangible cultural heritage items in kite-making skills of Weifang Kite. First level of international kite craft masters. He is the founder and president of Weifang Tiancheng Feiyuan Kite Co., Ltd.

Wang Yongxun is Vice Chairman of China Kite Flying Association, President of Weifang Kite Industry Association, master of arts and crafts in Weifang, one of top ten folk art masters in Shandong Province, Weifang kite experts, and CPPCC members of Weifang. He has been in this field for many years, and has won more than a hundred kite awards. He is one of the representatives in Weifang kite industry.

Tan Xinbo

Male, Han nationality, born in 1965, he is the arts and crafts masters in Shandong Province; second level of international kite craft masters. He is specialized in designing and flying giant inflation kite. He is the founder of the Weifang Kaixuan Kite Co., Ltd. He is the one of the representatives of the Weifang kite industry.

He is the member of the American Kite Association(AKA) and vice-chairman of Weifang Kite Industry Association and Weifang Kite expert. He has been invited to participate in kite flying in more than 10 countries, such as the United States, Malaysia, South Korea, UK and France, and has won numerous honors for China.

Yang Yunsheng

Male, Hui nationality, born in 1965 in Qingzhou, Shandong China. Second level of international kite craft masters. He has won Weifang Kite Star from three times. He loved kite art since childhood. He learned from many famous kite craftsmen and assiduously practiced kite making skills. He has participated in kite competitions domestically and overseas for many times on behalf of Weifang.

Since his participation in the Weifang International Kite Festival, he has created the kite of big dragon, mother and child dragon, nine dragons flying, celebration of nationalities, kilometer-long centipedes, large theater, a hundred butterflies in spring, a hundred monkeys in spring, etc, and has won first prize for innovation many times. In 2002, he produced 2,008 meters long Chinese Dragon kite to celebrate Beijing's successful bidding for Olympic Games. He produced 360 meters long Fuwa Dragon kite in 2008. He designed and produced the king cobra kite with a frontal area of 882.41 square meters and weight of 123kg in 2003, which has won the Guinness' World Records (the largest kite).

Yang Hongwei

Female, born in July 1966. She is the granddaughter of Yang Tongke, who is named the King of Kite in Yangjiabu. She is the 16th generation descendant of Yang's Kite and she is the second level of international kite craft masters.

She has been in this field for more than 30 years, and has made tens of thousands of kites. In 1992, in China Hong Kong World Fun Day activities, her dragon-head and centipede-body kite and dragon kite with a hundred kids were awarded the Best Design Award and the Longest Kite Award; in October 2007, she was awarded the title of handicrafts master by Shandong Tourism Culture Expo; In November 2008, her dragon kite with a hundred kids won Silver Award at the First Shandong International Mass Art Festival – Qi & Lu Folk Handicraft Boutique Expo.

阳江市风筝协会率先获得国家艺术基金扶持

近年来，阳江市风筝协会立足于传承弘扬风筝文化，制定规划，采取有效措施，加强对风筝非物质文化传承人的培养。2018年在上级有关部门、有关院校的大力支持配合下，成功申报国家艺术基金人才培训项目，获得了专项资金扶持，重点培养30名优秀的风筝文化传承人。此举开创了国家艺术基金扶持风筝文化人才培训的先河。

艺术人才培养资助项目（158项）

序号	项目名称	立项主体名称
101	阳江风筝技艺传承与创新人才培养	深圳大学

Yangjiang Kite Association took the lead in obtaining the support of National Art Fund

In recent years, Yangjiang Kite Association has established a plan based on inheriting and promoting the kite culture, taking effective measures to strengthen the cultivation of the intangible cultural heritage of kites. In 2018, with the support of relevant departments and relevant institutions at the higher levels, it successfully applied for the National Art Fund Talent Training Program and received special fund support to focus on training 30 outstanding kite culture inheritors. This action has created a precedent for the National Arts Foundation to support the training of kite culture talents.

"爱我潍坊" 全国大学生风筝知识大赛

为面向全国宣传风筝历史文化知识，推介潍坊城市品牌，大力弘扬优秀中华传统文化，加深大学生对中华文明的认识理解，积极培育社会主义核心价值观，山东省学生联合会秘书处、共青团潍坊市委、潍坊国际风筝会办公室、潍坊市地方史志办公室联合主办"爱我潍坊"全国大学生风筝知识大赛，已成功举办了4届。

全国各高校积极行动，热情参与，在校园里掀起了一场学习风筝文化历史，切磋风筝文化技艺，弘扬优秀中华传统文化的热潮，吸引了广大青年学生的广泛关注。各高校在宣传风筝文化的同时，积极组织开展了风筝知识大赛选拔活动，引领青年朋友争做优秀传统文化的引领者、传播者、践行者、极大地丰富了校园文化生活。

"Love Weifang" National College Student Kite Knowledge Contest

To promote the history and culture of kites to the whole country, promote the city of Weifang, vigorously promote the excellent Chinese traditional culture, deepen the understanding of Chinese civilization, and actively cultivate the core values of socialism, the Secretariat of Shandong Student Union, the Weifang Municipal Committee of Communist Youth League, Weifang International Kite Festival Office and the Local History Office of Weifang jointly hosted the "Love Weifang" National College Student Kite Knowledge Contest, which has been successfully held for 4 sessions.

All colleges and universities across the country took active actions and participated enthusiastically. They set up a great mass fervour of learning kite culture on campus and promoting the excellent Chinese traditional culture, which attracted the attention of young students. While promoting the kite culture, colleges and universities actively organized the kite knowledge contests, leading young friends to become the leaders, communicators and practitioners of excellent traditional culture, which greatly enriched the cultural life on campus.

鸢都之邀
——首届全国诗书画风筝文化主题双年展

为弘扬传统艺术和风筝文化，促进国际风筝文化的传播、交流与合作，由国际风筝联合会、中国书画家联谊会和中国诗词家联谊会主办，潍坊市书画家联谊会、国际风筝联合会秘书处承办的"鸢都之邀——首届国际诗书画风筝文化主题双年展"，于2016年4月1日至21日，在世界风筝都潍坊鲁台国际会展中心展出。

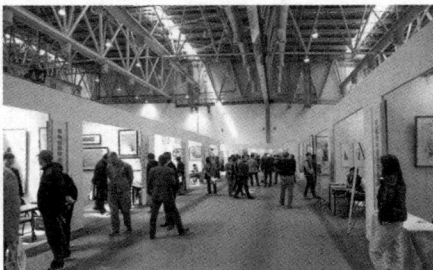

此次展览是潍坊第33届国际风筝会重点活动之一。活动自2月下旬开始，首先发起了咏风筝诗和国画作品的征集。海内外诗家群起响应，佳作迭见，到3月14日短短半月内，即收到咏风筝诗（词）328首。3月16日，经诗词专家学者严格认真的评审，最终有百首诗作入选，当日便启动了书写《咏风筝诗百首》的书法作品征集工作。广大书画家饱含激情，精心创作，在有限的时间里提供了一批高水平的诗书画作品。截至4月5日，共收到海内外书画作品1320幅。经过评审委员会公正客观的评审，最终选出书画作品各100幅入展，并收入《鸢都之邀——首届全国诗书画风筝文化主题双年展作品集》。

The invitation from the capital of kite in the world - the first National Poetry, Calligraphy, Painting, Kite & Culture Theme Biennale Exhibition

In order to promote traditional art and kite culture, and promote the spreading, exchange and cooperation of international kite culture, hosted by the International Kite Federation, China Calligraphers and Painters Association and China Poetry Association, undertaken by Weifang Calligraphers and Painters Association, Secretary of the International Kite Federation, the invitation from the capital of kite in the world - the first National Poetry, Calligraphy, Painting, Kite & Culture Theme Biennale Exhibition, was held on April 1, 2016, in the Shandong Weifang Lu-Tai International Exhibition Center in the World Kite Capital, Weifang.

This exhibition was one of the key activities of the 33rd Weifang International Kite Festival. Since the late February, the collection of kites poems and traditional Chinese paintings has been initiated. The poets at home and abroad responded quickly, and many masterpieces were supplied. Within a short period of half a month, on March 14, 328 poems were received. On March 16th, after a strict and serious evaluation by poetry experts and scholars, a hundred of poems were selected. On the same day, the collection of calligraphy works written in the book "100 Kite Poems" was initiated. Many calligraphers and painters provided a number of high-level poetry and calligraphy works, which were full of passion, in a limited time. As of April 5, a total of 1,320 paintings and calligraphy works at home and abroad were received. After a fair and objective review by the jury, 100 pieces of paintings and paintings were selected and entered into the exhibition, and they were included in the

"The invitation from the World Kite Capital - the first National Poetry, Calligraphy, Painting, Kite & Culture Theme Biennale Exhibition Works Collection".

"放飞梦想"首届世界风筝都潍坊楹联大赛

"放飞梦想"世界风筝都潍坊楹联大赛是第34届国际风筝会创新项目之一，以楹联这种中华文化特有的形式宣传潍坊、宣传潍坊国际风筝会，弘扬风筝文化。

此次楹联大赛，在海内外征得联稿4108副，经初评入围近3000副并从中评选出联作一等奖2名，二等奖5名、三等奖10名、优秀奖100名；联墨作品一等奖2名、二等奖4名、三等奖6名、优秀奖45名。本次大赛参选作者范围之广、作品数量之多、立意之新、质量之高是此次大赛不同以往的鲜明特点。

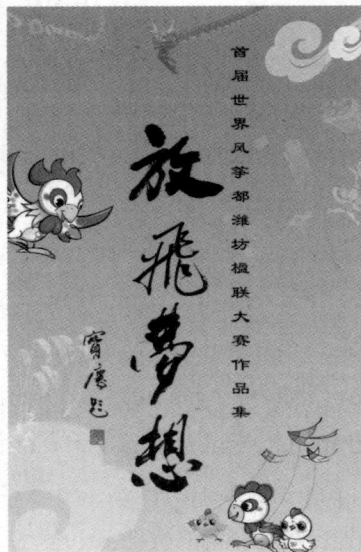

"Flying the Dream" The First Couplet Contest in World Kite Capital Weifang

The"Flying the Dream" First Couplet Contest in World Kite Capital Weifang was one of the innovation projects of the 34th Weifang International Kite Festival. The purpose of the event was to promote Weifang, Weifang International Kite Festival and the kite culture in a unique form of Chinese culture .

In this contest, 4108 couplets at home and abroad were collected. After the initial evaluation, nearly 3,000 couplets were selected for the next round of contest. Two couplets won the first prizes, 5 won second prizes, 10 won third prizes and 100 won outstanding prizes. 2 first prize, 4 second prizes, 6 third prizes and 45 outstanding prizes of the couplets and calligraphy works were issued. The wide range of participation, great number of works, excellent innovations and high quality are the distinctive features of this contest.

上海世博会墨西哥国家馆风筝夺人眼球

2010 年上海世博会墨西哥馆是唯一一个以风筝元素搭建的展馆。展馆外观是由色彩斑斓的风筝和碧绿的草地组成的"风筝森林"。草地广场上竖起 135 根柱子，组成了风筝森林，每根柱子的顶端有一只大风筝，最高 13 米，最低 2.4 米。这片"风筝森林"代表着墨西哥人对未来的期待，游客可以在这里读书、休憩、放风筝。

风筝在西班牙语中称为蝴蝶。风筝是连接墨西哥文化和中国文化的一个要素。参观者可以在墨西哥馆里购买风筝，或者亲手做一个风筝，然后在绿地广场上放飞。由风筝组成的森林代表着墨西哥人对未来的期待，广场上的人造绿草表达了墨西哥人对城市绿地的关注。

The design of kite elements of the Mexican National Pavilion at the Shanghai World Expo are eye-catching

The Mexico Pavilion at the 2010 Shanghai World Expo was the only pavilion built with kite elements. The exterior of the pavilion was a "kite forest" made up of colorful kites and green grass. There were 135 pillars on the grass square, which formed a kite forest. There was a big kite at the top of each pillar. The pillars were from 2.4 meters to 13 meters high. This Kite Forest represented the expectations of Mexicans for the future. The visitors can read, relax and fly kites here.

Kite is called a butterfly in Spanish. Kite is an element that connects Mexican culture with Chinese culture. Visitors can buy kites in the Mexican Pavilion, or make a kite by hand and then fly on the Greenland Square. The forest of kites represents the expectations of the Mexicans for the future, and the artificial green grass on the square expresses the attention of Mexicans to the urban green space.

全世界最大的妈祖风筝

2014 年 8 月 29 日，为期 3 天的首届海峡两岸夏季沙滩风筝节在莆田湄洲岛开幕，以妈祖文化为主题的特制大型风筝成功放飞。特制的高 14.35 米的大型妈祖主题风筝，是由潍坊风筝工艺大师王永训先生精心设计制作，此风筝放飞成功后引来众多的市民和游客前来观赏。

湄洲岛是"海上和平女神"——妈祖文化发祥地。近年来，湄洲岛积极以各种创新活动来推动旅游业的发展，此次风筝节的举办旨在依托潍坊风筝文化，进一步打响湄洲岛旅游品牌。

The world's largest Mazu kite

On August 29th, 2014, the first three-day Cross-strait Summer Beach Kite Festival was held in Meizhou Island, Putian, and a special large-scale kite with the theme of Mazu culture was successfully flown. The special Mazu theme kite with a height of 14.35 meters was carefully designed and produced by Weifang kite craft master Wang Yongxun. Many citizens and tourists came to witness the flying.

Meizhou Island is the birthplace of "Mother of Peace at Sea" - the birthplace of Mazu culture. In recent years, Meizhou Island actively promotes tourism with various innovative activities. The purpose of the holding of the kite festival is to further promote the tourism of Meizhou Island, and promote the economic development of Meizhou Island.

全球最大的风筝产业基地

世界风筝都潍坊是全球最大的风筝产业基地。据统计，现有风筝企业 400 余家，年产值近 30 亿元人民币，从业人员 12 万人，潍坊风筝在国内外市场所占份额分别为 80％、65％以上。

The world's largest kite industry base

Capital of kite in the world, Weifang, is the world's largest kite industry base. According to statistic, there are more than 400 kite companies with an annual output value of nearly 3 billion yuan and 120,000 employees. The share of Weifang kites in the domestic and foreign markets is above 80% and 65% respectively

潍坊园获世界园艺博览会创意金奖

2014 年 10 月 30 日，在 2014 青岛世界园艺博览会上，潍坊园荣获室外展园竞赛创意金奖。潍坊园位于青岛世园会中华园中部，作为"齐鲁园"的组成部分，北邻青岛、南接济南，总面积约 1518 平方米，整个地形西低东高。在潍坊园园区景观设计上，采用"遵从自然、以人为本"的设计原则，以"鸢飞花舞，美丽潍坊"为设计主题，引入潍坊风筝、莫言文化、高密剪纸等传统特色文化元素，让游客在赏景的同时了解潍坊、感受潍坊，展现了潍坊的新形象。

Weifang Garden won the Gold Award of Innovation of the Outdoor Garden in the World Horticultural Exposition

On October 30th, 2014, at the 2014 World Horticultural Exposition in Qingdao, Weifang Garden won the Gold Award of Creative in the Outdoor Exhibition Competition. Weifang Garden is located in the middle of China Garden of World Horticultural Exposition in Qingdao. As part of Qilu Garden, it is adjacent to Qingdao Garden in the north and Jinan Garden in the south. The total area is about 1518 square meters, and the whole terrain is low in the west and high in the east. In the landscape design of Weifang Garden, it adopted the design principle of "following the nature and human-oriented". With the theme of "Beautiful Weifang with kite flying and flowers blooming", traditional cultural elements such as Weifang kites, the culture of Moyan and paper-cutting of Gaomi are introduced to the design to make tourists understand Weifang and feel the cluture of Weifang while enjoying the scenery.

山东交通职业学院开设风筝设计
与制作高级研修班

2009 年 10 月，山东交通职业学院民间传统工艺风筝设计与制作高级研修班正式开班，研修班的学员集中了潍坊市风筝企业中优秀的管理人员和设计人员，有不少学员甚至拥有"风筝大师"称号。

潍坊风筝产业已经成为一个不断发展壮大的产业，急需大量人才和智力支持。参加此次学习的学员共 60 人，经过 2 年正规培训均取得了中专学历，成为传播风筝文化，发展风筝产业的领军人才。

Shandong Transport Vocational College took a lead in opening a high-level training course on kite design and production

In October 2009, senior training seminar of traditional crafts kite design and production was officially started in the Shandong Transport Vocational College. Most of the participants of the seminar were the excellent managers and designers of kite enterprises in Weifang. Many students even have the title of "Kites Master".

The kite industry has become a growing industry in Weifang, and it is in great need of a large number of talents and intellectual support. A total of 60 students participated in the study, after 2 years of formal training, they all obtained secondary education. They have become top talents in spreading kite culture and the developing the kite industry.

首届中国（潍坊）国际风筝文化创意设计作品
暨风筝扎制作品大赛

　　2016首届中国（潍坊）国际风筝文化创意作品暨风筝扎制作品大赛，是第33届潍坊国际风筝会创新设立的一项重点活动，以"风筝成就梦想"为主题，旨在传承弘扬风筝文化，创新提升风筝创意设计和扎制创新水平，大力开发风筝工艺美术产品，促进潍坊风筝文化产业的繁荣与转型发展。

　　历经2个多月的努力，大赛组委会共收到参赛作品300多件，经评委严格评选，对风筝文化创意设计作品暨风筝扎制作品，各评出特等奖1名，金奖3名，银奖5名，铜奖10名。其中，周红刚、丁松江等创作的工艺版画《风筝魂》长卷，获风筝文化创意设计类特等奖，张国华设计作的《木鸢》风筝，获风筝扎制类特等奖。颁奖仪式上，为各位获作者颁发了证书和相应的奖金。其中，特等奖奖金6000元，金奖奖金3000元、银奖奖金2000元、铜奖奖金1000元。

The first China (Weifang) International Kite Culture Creative Design Works and Kite-making Contest

The first China (Weifang) International Kite Culture Creative Design Works and Kite-making Contest in 2016 was a key activity of the 33rd Weifang International Kite Festival. It is based on the theme of "Kite Accomplishes Dream" and aimed to inherit and promote the kite culture, innovate and enhance the creative design and innovation level of kites, vigorously develop kite arts and crafts products, and promote the prosperity and transformation of the kite culture industry in Weifang.

After more than two months of hard work, the organizing committee of the contest received more than 300 pieces of works. The judges strictly selected and finally made one outstanding prize, 3 gold medals, 5 silver medals and 10 bronze medals. Among them, the "Kite Soul" long scroll made by Zhou Honggang, Ding Songjiang and other craftsmen, won the outstanding prize for kite culture creative design, wooden kite designed and made by Zhang Guohua, won the outstanding prize for kite making. At the award ceremony, the certificates and corresponding bonuses were awarded to the winners. Among them, the bonus for the outstanding prize, the gold prize, the silver prize and the bronze prize were 6,000 yuan, the 3,000 yuan, 2,000 yuan, and 1,000 yuan respectively.

最早开展风筝冲浪的地方

20 世纪 90 年代，风筝冲浪运动最早是在欧美国家率先开展的，至今只有 20 多年的历史。中国开展这项运动，已有 10 多年的历史。这是一项借助大型充气风筝，脚踏风筝浪板或冲浪板在水面滑行的运动。

风筝冲浪的原理相当简单，就是将充气风筝用两条或四条强韧的绳子连接到手持横杆上，操作横杆来控制风筝上升、下降及转向，并结合脚下踩着的各式滑板，在海面上滑行，甚至将人带离水面做出各种花样的翻腾动作。全球玩风筝冲浪的人正以几何数字增长。据统计，2007 年全球仅有 20 万玩家，而到 2012 年，这一数字已接近 100 万人。

The first place to start kite surfing

In the 1990s, kite surfing was first developed in Europe and the United States, and it only has a history of more than 20 years. The kite surfing in China has a history of more than 10 years. This is a sport that uses a large inflatable kite, a kite-surfing board or a surfboard to slide on the surface of the water.

The theory of kite surfing is quite simple. It is to slide on the sea by connecting the inflatable kite with two or four strong ropes to the hand-held crossbar, and operating the crossbar to control the rise, fall and turn of the kite, and control the various skateboards by foot. It can even take people off the water to make a variety of tricks. The number of people who play kite surfing around the world is growing dramatically. According to statistics, there were only 200,000 players in the world in 2007, and by 2012, this number is close to 1 million.

第 35 届潍坊国际风筝会创 "三个之最"

2018 年 4 月 21 日至 5 月 11 日，第 35 届潍坊国际风筝会成功举办。多达 60 个国家地区风筝团队参赛，创历届参赛国家地区代表队数量最多。多达 100 多万人参与各种活动，参与性创历届最强。吸引 30 多家企业投入冠名和广告宣传，市场运作力度创历届最大。

The 35th Weifang International Kite Festival created the "Three of the Most"

From April 21 to May 11, 2018, the 35th Weifang International Kite Festival was successfully held. Kite teams from 60 countries and regions participated in the competition, more than 1 million people participated in various activities, and the event attracted more than 30 companies to participate in the advertising, the above three aspects are the most in history of Weifang International Kite Festival.

第五章 中外风筝文化交流

KITE CUTURAL EXCHANGE AT HOME AND ABROAD

282-414

形形色色的国外风筝

风筝是世界文化宝库中的一颗璀璨夺目的明珠，是人类世代相传的一种独特的艺术门类，各国的风筝都有自己的发展历史和有趣的传闻。

相传，公元13世纪，随着《马可·波罗游记》一书在欧洲引起的中国热，风筝开始进入洋人的天地，并迅速传播开来且被广泛应用于科学试验。1794年，英国哥拉斯哥大学天文家亚历山大·威尔逊用6只风筝当作运载工具，把一些天文仪器升入高空，测量空中温度、湿度和风力，制造了世界第一架空中气象测量器。滑翔机及飞机的问世都是受益于风筝的原理。1800年，英国人乔治·凯利为了探索人类飞行的奥秘，曾经做过若干宽翼风筝，用来测试物体在空中时的重心和逆风而上压力中心的关系，终于成功地制造了世界第一架滑翔机。随着科学的发展，欧洲及各国风筝制作水平也有极大的提高，英国生产了一种风筝照相机，用尼龙线放飞，升入空中，从各个角度拍摄地球表面的目标，这很像现在的人造卫星。

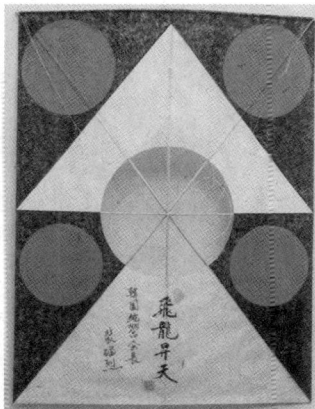

哥伦布发现新大陆以后，大批移民迁移美洲，同时也把风筝带入新的境地。电的发明者——美国著名的科学家富兰克林就是一位风筝爱好者。1752年，他把自己用金属做的风筝送上电雨交加的空中，电流顺着风筝的金属牵线传下来，从而揭示了雷电的秘密。人类航天飞行史，也应给风筝记一大功，飞机发明者莱特兄弟的第一架飞机实际上就是用薄槐木作肋条的一个"大风筝"，尽管那时在空中仅停留了99秒半，飞行距离41米，但在人类历史上，却有着划时代的意义。

前苏联放风筝的历史由来已久，早在 200 年前，俄国就出了一位乘风筝飞行的人。此人名叫莫扎伊斯基，是位勇敢的海军军官，善于冒险，也爱好飞行，他曾一人乘坐在自制的一个特大风筝上，用马车拉着他和风筝，逆风在公路上飞跑。

日本风筝与中国风筝同出一辙，最早是在公元 794 年，由中国传入的。起初是用布麻裱糊的风筝为主，后来纸制风筝普及更受人们喜爱。随着日本政治经济的繁荣兴衰，风筝的命运也历经坎坷，直到第二次世界大战后，作为民间工艺品的风筝才重新受到欢迎。1975 年，用乙烯薄膜铺张在塑料骨架上制作的扇形面洋风筝输入日本，这种风筝即使在微风中也能升空，与成人放的风

筝比较，更受儿童的喜爱。近几年有种被称作箱形风筝的立体风筝也开始在日本流行起来。

日本的风筝形状和花纹大体可分为以下几种：方形风筝和由此变形而成的风筝；带箱风筝；长崎旗系列风筝；中国风筝和由此变形而成的多角形风筝；特殊的风筝。

在日本因地域风俗各异，放风筝的含意也不同，有的视其为祈子的吉祥物，有的则用于占卜农作物丰歉及军事、测量等方面，静同地区放风筝表示喜庆；新潟地区则为祈祷丰收，而名古屋一带则把风筝作为男女联姻的手段，意在同牵一线，系百年之好。

在朝鲜，风筝的起源虽不可考，但在古代交通不发达，战事

频繁，武器落后的情况下，把风筝作为通讯联络的工具和武器的记载却不少见。

据历史文献记载，高丽末期公元1374年崔莹将军在平定济州岛耽罗国叛乱的时候，利用风筝使军士飞登悬崖峭壁，同时又用风筝带着火种入城中放火，从而攻占了耽罗国的城堡，平息了叛乱。

李朝英租时，放风筝逐渐成为民间的岁时风俗，据《东国岁时记》载，儿童于岁朝，把"去厄消灾""送厄迎福"等字样写在风筝尾部，然后把它放掉，希望放走厄运，迎来幸福之意。朝鲜有关大事典记载，农历正月初一到十五为放风筝的时间。现在韩国首尔每年于正月十五前一二天举办大型风筝会，参加者来自全国各地，观众更是人山人海，每到这时，天空绣满五彩风筝，地上充盈欢声笑语，人们头望蓝天，脚涉溪水，翻墙越脊追赶风筝，场面甚是壮观。

居住在亚洲东南部的马来西亚，视风筝为神明之物，人们把制作和放飞风筝看作是一件非常严肃认真的事情，对风筝的装点更讲究，从图案设计到剪贴、绘画都一丝不苟。

马来西亚人喜欢隼、鹰、猫、孔雀、青蛙、鹦鹉等形状的风筝，最喜欢的是月亮风筝，它的样子很特别，头部是一轮弯月，月口朝下，两端的角上各挂有一条彩穗，风筝尾巴也是小月牙形，月口朝上。行云变幻和花卉是人们最喜爱的图案，有的地区还把爪哇的蜡染花法和具有地方风格的绘画结合起来装扮风筝，在有些正式的官方场合，还见到姑娘们用图形优美的月亮风筝隆重欢迎贵宾。

澳大利亚人很讲究风筝的华美，在1987年第四届潍坊国际风筝会上，一种叫万花筒的风筝被人称为"最华丽的风筝"，它代表了澳大利亚的风格。

新西兰人也喜欢放风筝，尤其是毛利族人，他们经常在村庄上空飘放一只风筝表示太平无事。

他们的风筝也很特别，叫"独木舟"，是用大大小小的菱形方块交错结合组成的，上天后，在天空摇摇摆摆，很像船在波浪里颠簸一样。近年来，以尼龙塔夫绸为面料，配有三种颜色的翼伞式风筝在新西兰也很流行。

荷兰风筝迷把风筝装在一个二尺见方的纸箱里，放飞时，从纸箱里扯出一串约有十六开杂志大小的塑料纸做的不同颜色的菱角形小风筝，微风吹拂，风筝悠然飘出，五颜六色，如虹贯空，这种片串式风筝近年来很受群众喜爱。

排子式风筝在欧洲比较流行。英国制作的一种排子式风筝，是由红、蓝、黄组成的小帆船为主体，带动一只旋转的红、绿、黄、紫的圆桶，又在这条放飞线上，排列了国旗、彩旗、彩屏、彩带和7个圆角，一条尼龙绳带动了17种物体，在空中飘飞。

美国华盛顿的风筝乍看像一只降落伞，不同的是它不从天而降，却是平地升空。

各国根据自己不同的爱好、习俗及文化素养创造出风格迥异的民族艺术——风筝。潍坊国际风筝会的召开，又为大家提供了一个文化交流和艺术欣赏的好机会。

（作者刘镇，系潍坊国际风筝会办公室原副主任）

风格各异的中国风筝流派

中国风筝已经有2000多年的历史，作为一种民间艺术，在丰富多彩的地域文化熏陶下，逐渐形成了北京风筝、天津风筝、潍坊风筝、南通风筝、阳江风筝、西藏风筝、滇式风筝等风格各异的流派。

北京风筝

北京风筝源于清朝初期，作为别具兴味的玩物，最初在京城达官贵人中流行，后来才渐渐在普通百姓中风靡开来。清人潘荣陛所著《帝京岁时纪胜》中就描述了北京民众清明时节放飞风筝的情形："清明扫墓，倾城男女，纷出四郊，提酌挈盒，轮毂相望。各携纸鸢线轴，祭扫毕，即于坟前施放较胜。"

北京风筝品种繁多，在传为曹雪芹所著的《南鹞北鸢考工志》中就有四十多种制作方法。结构造型上主要有五种：硬翅、软翅、拍子、串儿、筒儿。翅膀的边缘框架固定的风筝称为硬翅风筝。外形像一个"大"字的扎燕风筝就属于硬翅风筝，因明清时期"扎"音同"沙"所以又称沙燕风筝，其属于北京风筝的代表，飞行的效果最好，对全国影响也最大。软翅风筝大多是立体仿生形的，如凤凰、蝴蝶等。所谓拍子风筝，是一种板状结构的风筝，也名板子风筝。串儿风筝三要是蜈蚣或龙形风筝。筒儿风筝是指宫灯、水桶形状的风筝。

扎燕风筝有各种造型，顾名思义，这种风筝让人看上去就会想到燕子。风筝的头部是燕子头形状的平面变形，眉梢则上挑，两眼有神，再加上那对剪刀尾巴，活脱脱一只带着人类情感的俏燕。曹雪芹在《南鹞北鸢考工志》里创造了一个完整的燕子风筝家族："肥燕"代表成熟稳重的壮年男子，"瘦燕"代表婀娜多姿的成年女子，"比翼燕"代表相濡以沫的夫妻，"半瘦燕"代表生气勃勃的少年，"小燕"代表天真可爱的儿童，"雏燕"代表蹒跚学步的胖娃娃。除了燕子模样变化外，人们在扎燕的前胸、膀窝等处加上牡丹、蜜桃等图案，寓意花开富贵、长寿幸福。这样一来，原本黑色的燕子变得生动活泼、多姿多彩。

北京风筝原有"四大门派"，即"哈氏""马氏""曹氏"和"金氏"，如今只有"哈氏"和"曹氏"传了下来。2011年，北京扎燕风筝制作技艺列入第三批国家级非物质文化遗产名录，曹氏风筝艺术家、自学而成的一代大师费保龄是代表性传承人。

天津风筝

天津风筝历史悠久，清代杨柳青年画《十美图放风筝》里就有蝴蝶、老鹰、斗鸡和唐僧师徒过通天河等不同造型的风筝。到清末民初时期，风筝作坊遍地、艺人云集，比较有名的有李和曾、李和林开设的"志远斋"等。

天津风筝种类繁多，但以软翅为主。所谓软翅，就是风筝翅膀的后半部分是软性的，没有主条的限制，可以更立体、多层次地呈现，类似蜜蜂、凤凰、螳螂、仙鹤等禽鸟或昆虫大多采取软翅造型。另外，在以神话故事为题材的风筝作品中，运用软翅结构，可以做成漂浮在神仙周围的云雾或是天兵天将背后飞扬的旌旗等等。和其他形式的风筝比较起来，软翅风筝有更好的起飞性能。

天津风筝在结构上的特点是可以拆装折叠。天津风筝的骨架部分采取类似建筑上的卯榫结构，不用线绑，其躯干与首、尾、翅等部分可以拆开，所以一只很大的风筝都能拆解下随身携带，等要放飞时通过翎毛管联结起来就可以了。另外一个特点是风筝的头部都是用事先做好的模子扣的，如此一来，风筝头可以不受扎架糊纸的限制，有利于整体制作。这种模子头部叫"盔头"，质量很轻，精致而美观。

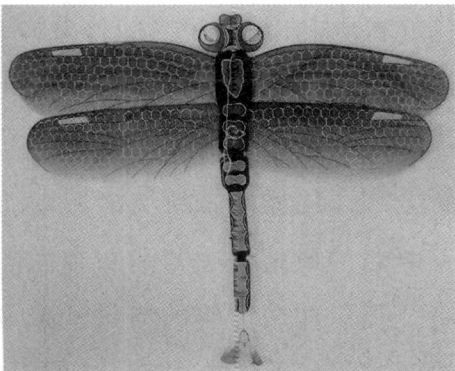

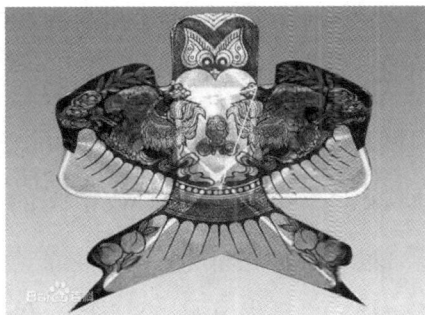

对天津风筝制作技术做出重要贡献的，是从清末开始崭露头角的风筝艺人魏元泰。在他漫长的风筝制作生涯里，研制了多种软翅风筝，进一步改进了软翅的折叠技艺，比如他认识到翎毛管有容易遭受虫蚀而损坏较快的缺点，找到了用锡（或铜）箍代替翎毛管衔接骨架的方法。他的风筝技艺在天津首屈一指。1915年，魏元泰的11件风筝作品在巴拿马万国博览会上获得银牌，"风筝魏"成了天津风筝的招牌。

2008年，"风筝魏"风筝制作技艺被列入第二批国家级非物质文化遗产名录。现如今，"风筝魏"已发展到了上千个品种，第四代传人魏国秋是代表性传承人。

潍坊风筝

　　据史料记载，世界上第一只风筝，是由春秋战国时期的能工巧匠鲁班，在潍坊境内的鲁山脚下放飞成功的，"飞三日而不败"。潍坊风筝自宋代开始流行于民间，明代更加普及。潍坊的很多文人墨客与风筝有不解之缘，比如北宋潍坊诸城籍的张择端在其著名的风俗画卷《清明上河图》中，画有儿童引线放风筝的情景。风筝的入画，给后人留下了研究风筝历史的宝贵资料。

　　曾任潍县县令的郑板桥在《怀潍县》一诗中形象地描绘了清明时节潍坊百姓放飞风筝的情景："纸花如雪满天飞，娇女秋千打四围。五色罗裙风摆动，好将蝴蝶斗春归。"清道光年间潍县诗人郭麟在《潍县竹枝词》有言："一百四日小寒食，冶游争上白浪河。纸鸢儿子秋千女，乱比新来春燕多。"诗句描述了当地民众在春风和煦、花香袭人的清明时节，竞相到白浪河两岸游春放风筝的热闹场面。

　　潍坊风筝经过众多艺人刻苦钻研探索，把国画、木版年画的技巧融入风筝制作中，形成了题材广泛、色彩艳丽、扎制牢靠、放飞平稳等特点。最能代表潍坊风筝技艺的是龙头蜈蚣风筝、硬翅人物类风筝等。龙头蜈蚣风筝一般体型巨大，加上龙头有些可达数百米，扎制的工艺则相当精妙复杂，仅龙头就需要用 100 多根竹条细致扎制，长短间隔、比例轻重都需要经过科学地计算和定制，耗时可达一个月至两个月之久。

　　2006 年 5 月，潍坊风筝制作技艺被列为第一批国家级非物质文化遗产名录，代表性传承人有韩福龄、张效东、王永训、杨红卫等。

南通风筝

中国北方称风筝为"纸鸢"，南方则称"鹞子"。南通风筝以板鹞最富特色，最为典型。大型的南通板鹞风筝多以六角形、八角形为基本框架，在鹞面上放置由葫芦、竹子或苇子等制成的哨口，哨口大小不一，数目从一百到三百只不等。板鹞外形古朴，工笔彩绘富丽典雅。巨大板鹞放飞时，发出高低不一的声音，像一支气势宏大的空中交响乐，响遏行云。南通板鹞虽框架结构较为简单，但其鹞面的绘画非常精细工整，装饰性极强，尤其哨口的制作，工艺复杂细腻，整个风筝融灯彩、绘画、雕刻、声音于一体，是一种复合性的艺术品。

以前，放板鹞是南通地区一项重要的集体活动，有着隆重的仪式。民众先将板鹞供在堂屋里，香烛纸马皆需齐备，一番恭敬祈愿之后方能放飞。放飞时要由一个很有经验的老手做"头把手"，带着十几个人拉绳，另外还要一伙人扶着风筝放飞，叫"丢"。风筝顺利高翔，预示着粮食丰收、生活如意，民众也是欢欣鼓舞。

经过一代代人的传承，集体放板鹞活动成了

南通的风筝文化传统，体现了团结协作、勇于拼搏、人天和谐的精神品质，也成了南通一道令人温暖的风景。2006 年 5 月，南通板鹞风筝制作技艺被列入第一批国家级非物质文化遗产名录，郭承毅为该文化遗产项目代表性传承人。

阳江风筝

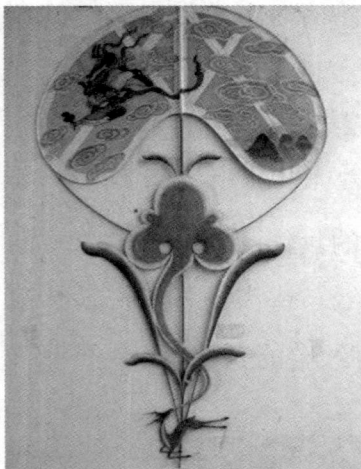

广东阳江风筝是南派风筝的代表之一。传说早在南朝至隋时期，阳江在一次战乱中被叛军所围，情况非常危急，岭南巾帼英雄冼太夫人命人放纸鹞于高空，把险情传递了出去，最后援兵来到，阳江城得以解围，民间百姓遂将放鹞子作为习俗延续至今。另外，阳江面朝大海，背倚青山，有非常好的放飞条件，阳江市也因此被称为"纸鹞城"。

阳江风筝种类繁多，精巧别致是其主要特征。最能体现这种风格特点的是灵芝风筝，其灵感源于民间传说《白蛇传》中白素贞去昆仑山盗取灵芝仙草救许仙的故事。灵芝风筝由三部分组成，中间通过一根长竿子联系起来，最下面是一只活泼可爱的小鹿，中间部分是小鹿口衔着的一朵巨大灵芝草，上端则像是一朵白云，里面画有白娘子手拿灵芝腾云驾雾离开昆仑山的场景，整体美感十足，具有浓厚的文化韵味。另外、花草与鸟类主题的风筝在阳江风筝中占比最大，常见形象有双桃、双凤、百鸟归巢、孔雀开屏等。

阳江风筝制作技艺于 2005 年入选广东省第一批非物质文化遗产名录。2007 年，梁汝兴、阮加培被评为阳江风筝省级非物质文化遗产代表性传承人，随后几年，冯光以及梁汝兴的儿子梁玉泉、徒弟梁治昂等三人也先后入选。

西藏风筝

西藏风筝流行于西藏拉萨、日喀则、泽当等地，并传播到邻国尼泊尔、不丹，清代盛行于藏族上层。十三世达赖喇嘛偏爱风筝，曾为专供风筝和加工筝线的"上哉"加封印章。

藏历八月卫藏地区风力较足，是放风筝的季节。民间认为，风筝放早了，秋季就会过早终结。拉萨风筝的放飞有许多规定。在时间上，拉萨在雪顿节后放飞，日喀则必须由东头宗的俗官先行放飞。风筝的形制与使用有年龄的规定，如六轴、八轴、十轴风筝，必须按年龄大小分开选择。

西藏风筝形态较为单一，多为菱形平面，但讲究彩绘图案，有"加沃"（大胡子）、"古玛或古那"（钉头或黑头）、"米洛"（瞪眼）、"其瓦"（龇牙）、"帮典"（围裙）、"嘎林"（腿骨号）六种。

因色彩艳丽，放飞时天空一片斑斓。平时这些风筝悬挂在墙，视为升腾运气的圣物。

拉萨风筝的放飞技巧体现在空中的争斗玩耍。放线与收线的微妙变化，可以使风筝在空中迅速地升降、旋转、左右打滚。最大的特点是"打架斗殴"，最后断线飘走者为败。

各种打斗技巧最后都集中在"绞线"上，线的质量至关重要，故在制作时有一道工序即上"那"。"那"的主要成分是玻璃碎粉，加入一种黏性较好的植物"旺拉"，调上捣碎的大米、白糖和水搅拌煎熬。等冷却到一定温度时，将"那"放在手心，将风筝的线从指间穿过，使粘上粗细不等的"那"如同锯齿。拉萨风筝的制作具有季节性。

每年秋季在拉萨、日喀则等城镇有人专门做风筝出售。日喀则的拉达卡其和拉萨的次仁等家族风筝制作技术精湛、特色鲜明，颇有影响。但现在一批有造诣的风筝艺人相继去世或年，年逾古稀，技艺面临失传。

滇式风筝

昆明特有的南派滇式风筝是根据昆明独特的天气和风的特点，在传统的风筝上改良后而成。勤劳聪慧的"滇人"经多番研究，巧妙运用了物体受风御风原理，发明了"元宝型"翅翼与三角形身体结合滇式风筝，是继四大风筝流派后的又一主流风筝流派，被列入国家非物质文化遗产名录。

"滇式风筝"的特点是风槽特别深，角度特别大。每只风筝上都有一个"坠力面"，即在风筝底部设计出具有流线型的气流通道，致使升力越大，坠力就越大，保持了风筝适合的高度，不会忽升忽降。

在外观上，多似蝴蝶的形状，风筝的头部较大，剪裁绘制成各种传统文化形象。

朱家祥是一位"南派滇筝"传承人，在"滇筝"上精益求精，勇于创新，在确保南派滇式风筝结构不变的基础上，也在不断对滇式风筝的制作进行改良。朱家祥认为，"非遗"的传承不仅仅是对技艺的传承，更是对中华传统文化、中国历史记忆、风土人情的承载。所以朱家祥制作的每一个风筝都是一个故事，"中华二十四孝""精忠报国"各种文化图腾等等，让风筝更具文化感和艺术感。为了将南派滇式风筝文化更好地传承下去，朱家祥老人在昆明市文化馆以及盘龙区文体局的支持下成立了"尚义社区滇式风筝传习所"，希望通过社区的努力将这项民俗艺术、传统文化发扬光大并有效传承。

（作者邓华，系潍坊著名文化学者）

中国风筝的四大产地

中国风筝起源于远古时代，据研究，最初是由巫师做巫术时，沟通天地所用。后来，逐步演变为民间青少年的游戏活动用品，成为传统的娱乐活动工具，同时也成为世代相传的民间工艺品，还有运用于军事战争的事例。

自古以来，我国民间扎制放飞风筝，形成了四大产地：山东潍坊、北京、天津和江苏南通。风筝的制作方法很多，有用棉纸糊的，有用绢做成的；有单线引子的，也有多线引子的；有的还能旋转或附挂灯笼、响器等。通常流行的有蝴蝶、蝙蝠、鹰形风筝等。也有以"天女散花"、"哪吒闹海"、"钟馗"、"孙悟空"等神话为题材的风筝。风筝有南北之分。南方风和，风筝多软翅，模拟飞鸟、蝴蝶、生动逼真；北方风烈，风筝多硬翅，如金鱼、沙燕等，在扎、糊、绘、放四艺上较讲究。20世纪70年代，发现一部《南鹞北鸢考工志》，评记各种风筝的扎、糊、绘、放等技法，上有口诀、绘图谱。据考为《红楼梦》作者曹雪芹所作。同时，曹雪芹也是位扎工绘画技艺双绝的艺人。

在我国四大产地中，历史上没有上下高低之分，只有风格的差异。但在改革开放以来的几十年，潍坊市尤其注重发掘民间工艺，每年举办国际风筝会，并被推举为世界风筝都；潍坊倡导风筝艺术活动，以风筝文化牵线搭台，引导经济唱戏，频繁地与全国各地乃至世界各国进行风筝文化交流活动；同时，潍坊的风筝扎制创新和生产销售也与日俱增，成为国内首屈一指的放大风筝产地。

早在清代乾隆年间，潍坊已有专门从事风筝制作的民间作坊。扬州八怪之一、做过潍县县令的郑板桥，在《怀潍县》诗中有"纸花如雪满天飞，娇女秋千打四围。五色罗裙风摆动，好将蝴蝶斗春归"的佳句。可见当时清明时节，放风筝游春已成当地习俗。清末，五福斋艺人制作的"仙鹤童子"和"霍震子背文王"风筝，已很精致。潍坊风筝，以"龙头蜈蚣"、"苍鹰"为最好。结构分平面、浮雕式、立体三种。八卦、七星和鱼等，属平面、立体平稳，飘带摇曳生姿。浮雕式做工精细，多为飞禽之类。立体最复杂，又分串式和筒式两种。风筝的彩绘风格，与当地木版年画相近，有的直接使月木版印制的单色纸（花纹轮廓），糊贴后再上色涂彩。

潍坊的传统风筝本来有软翅、硬翅、串式、板式和碰风筝五种类型。近 40 年来又发展了巨型立体风筝、微型观赏风筝、盒装礼品风筝、大型展览风筝，以及从国外引进的现代自由式风筝、运动风筝、冲浪风筝、花样品种日益翻新，已达千余种之多。

北京风筝从清代就有了名气，当时不仅民间放飞，就连宫廷中也形成了春天放风筝娱乐的习惯。据传，曹雪芹扎制的精品风

筝，在王府中能卖出很高的价钱，八旗子弟中不少是风筝迷。

北京的春天由于风沙大，气流猛烈，所以硬翅风筝和板工式风筝居多。从清末至今，有四个著名技艺流派：一是金忠福，作品带有浓郁粗犷的造型装饰色彩；二是哈国良，人称"风筝哈"，做工精湛，技艺过人；三是孔祥泽，主要仿效曹雪芹的艺术匠意；四是马晋，他本人是画家，作品带有文人画意。北京风筝的造型有五种基本形式：硬翅、软翅、拍子、长串和筒形。工艺大致分扎、糊、绘、放四项。在装饰上强调图案化，特点是以形引人，以画动人。

北京金家的几代人，都曾在地安门大街火神庙前摆摊卖风筝，尤以黑沙燕最为著名。这种风筝图案线条分明，只有黑白两色，但放飞实效好，很受一代代风筝迷的喜爱。

北京哈记风筝的一大特色是吃风力准确，即根据风力大小而制作不同的风筝。吃风大的风筝小风放不起来，反之则一放就散架子。全靠多年的经验来准确地衡量竹料的厚薄和制作的技巧。随着经济的发展和哈记风筝知名度的提高，据说现在哈记生产的精品风筝，以克为重量单位计价销售。

北京马晋风筝的特点是绘画生动雅丽，精致细腻，是典型的艺术品，可以陈设观赏，也可以放飞娱乐，深受一些较高层次人士的喜爱。

天津风筝是以杨柳青风筝和"风筝魏"扎制的风筝为代表，杨柳青年画与风筝，就像潍坊杨家埠年画与风筝并举一样，相辅相成，相互促进，相映成趣。杨柳青的风筝品种有二百多种。大部分产品出口，远销世界多个国家和地区。杨柳青风筝，骨架精巧，体轻，易携带；图案以动物、飞禽为主，形象逼真。为适应出口和旅游事业的发展，首先试制成功了具有我国民族风格的塑料风筝。

天津老艺人魏元泰一家扎制的风筝，代表作品有活眼绢制蝴蝶。风筝上扎制有 260 个活眼，升空后，活眼随风转，翅膀动忽明忽暗，变化万千。

魏家风筝大的近丈，小不盈尺，式样很多。如蝴蝶、鹰雁、仙鹤、美女以及一些神话人物风筝等，制作精巧。有的风筝还能拆卸折叠。一个五六尺的风筝，能装在一尺左右的盒子里。"风筝魏"在设计方面善于见景生情，创立新意，造型真实优美。在扎架工艺上，他的风格是"穿眼带榫、前后见平"，竹架的纵横交叉点竹条绝不重叠。

江苏南通扎制的风筝，也是以工艺精巧，造型优美而闻名，但比其它产地的风筝独特处在于有独特音响，最具特色的是板鹞风筝，俗称"六角鹞子"。这种风筝，小的三尺以下，大的一二丈。风筝用竹架糊土布，彩绘，鹞尾拴粗草绳长二、三丈，风筝上布满用大小葫芦、竹管、白果壳、栗子壳、鸽蛋壳、花生壳等材料做成哨子，大约 200 多组，分高、中、低三个声部，构成较完整的音程体系，须多人同心协力才能将它送上天空。其声尤如千马齐鸣，回荡苍穹，形成独特景观，是群体性、娱乐性非常突出的风筝类型。这种在风中鸣响的风筝，才是真正意义上的风筝，因为古筝本是一种古代乐器，能借风像筝一样鸣响，便是风筝名称的起源和字义。唐代诗人高骈在一首著名绝句中描绘道："夜静弦音响碧空，宫商信任往来风，依稀似曲才堪听，又被风吹别调中。"就是对鸣响风筝的绝妙写照。

另外，南通风筝还有一种夜间放飞的灯风筝，人们在扎制的立体风筝中点上灯，一盏盏或一串串地升上高空，灯光闪烁，音响奏鸣，颇有情趣。

总之，中国风筝的四大产地风格各异，各具特色，它们是群众智慧的结晶，一代代民间艺人聪明才智的结晶，是民族传统艺术中十分靓丽的一道风景线，牵动着千千万万人民群众的兴趣和心灵，也为历代文化和经济发展做出了自己的贡献。

（作者邓华，系潍坊著名文化学者）

潍坊风筝代表团出访美国西雅图

飞机穿越大洋，1984年8月的一天，潍坊风筝代表团，应邀来到美国西北部名城西雅图，这里是美国风筝运动和飞机制造业中心。八十多年前，莱特兄弟运用巨型风筝研制出来的世界第一架动力飞机，就在这里驾飞云天。到这儿来访问，我们充满敬意。

好客的主人盛情款待我们，招待会在西雅图最有名的希尔顿饭店举行。饭店有一大厅用风筝装饰，专供乘客欣赏，实不多见。据了解，风筝在美国人民生活中起多种作用：成年人视风筝为一种运动；孩子们把风筝作为玩具；用于室内装饰和广告宣传，风筝则是精美的艺术品。

为了让人们真切地观赏潍坊风筝和交流技艺，我们在西雅图举办了风筝展览、扎制表演，还进行了三次放飞。

在西雅图太平洋科学中心举办的潍坊风筝展览，为期7天，展出52件展品，其中有大、中、小三种龙头蜈蚣。大龙头蜈蚣由百余节组成，长50米，小龙头蜈蚣则可装进火柴盒里。还有孙悟空一手执棒，一手托盘迎风转动的金盘托玉；五彩缤纷的金凤凰等等。这些风筝既是历年创新之作，又是体现传统水平的代表作。观众赞扬他们做工精细，形象逼真、美丽。西雅图市市长罗亚说："你们的风筝展览很成功，你们的到来，是美国人民学习中国工艺品的好时机。"

与展览同时进行的风筝扎制表演，同样引起人们极大兴趣。加拿大温哥华风协主席哈里森带着风筝爱好者赶来了，他这是第二次与中国同行交流技艺。

放飞表演的情景，更是精彩动人，令人难忘。第三次放飞，是在华盛顿州风筝协会为交流团来访而专门举行的风筝节这天进行的。这天，中美两国的风筝比翼高飞，当地报纸报道说："整个公园上空都飞满了五彩缤纷的风筝。"放飞的高潮是在天空出现一只大型降落伞式和一只长达40米的潍坊蜈蚣风筝时，公园里响起一阵阵欢呼声和掌声。人们为这两只中美风筝高空媲美欢呼、鼓掌。

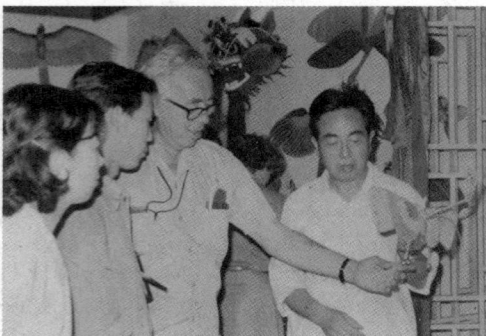

这只降落伞式风筝是西雅图风筝协会扎制的。看上去，它分明是一只降落伞，但它不是从天而降，却从平地飞起，并带动起12条鱼式风向风筝和串式菱形风筝，垂着五颜六色的飘带在空中旋转飞舞。此外，我们还看到双线旋转风筝，它能在空中轮番旋转表演；还有比两

间房子还大的特大风筝。这是一些有突破的创新风筝。它们展示了美国风筝的特点：空气流体力学原理运用得好。这里流行的盒式、瓦片式、降落伞式都能造成气流向上的推动力。因此，容易起飞，飞得高，大小风皆可放飞，人们放风筝也就不限于春天，而是四季皆宜了。这样，人们对风筝的需求量就很大，在美国，风筝生产是工厂化的，有统一的规格和型号。用的材质也很现代化，表糊料是呢绒绸和强塑料，质底轻薄，拉力强，能防水。全国各地约有三四百家商店经营风筝。商品化生产是美国风筝的又一个特点。

访问是取得相互了解的钥匙。过去美国西海岸的人们，不了解山东有个潍坊，不知道潍坊有这么好的风筝工艺。现在知道了，看到了，而且深深被潍坊风筝的真切形象所吸引。善于经营的风筝销售客商，自然不放过任何做生意的机会，他们纷纷登门与我们洽谈风筝贸易。华盛顿风筝协会副主席钱大卫要在全美国推销潍坊风筝，他与纽约的汤姆森电影公司合作，在我们访问后不久，将来中国拍摄风筝风光影片。

为期不长的访问结束了，然而，风筝架起的友谊之桥，通往五洲四海。我们与各国风筝人士的交流在继续，在扩大。

（作者孙立荣，系潍坊市风筝协会原副主席，潍坊市工艺美术研究所原所长）

潍坊风筝意大利夺魁记

　　1990 年 5 月 23 日，大型波音 747 客机降落在意大利罗马国际机场。300 多名乘客中有中国的风筝代表团，其中就有潍坊风筝专家韩福龄。此时正值世界杯足球赛前夕，从机场到通向市中心的交通要道上，到处悬挂着各式各样的国旗，唯独缺少一面五星红旗。中国驻意大利使馆文化参赞王振茂同志对代表团成员说："我们的足球队没能进军意大利，可中国的风筝来了，你们同样代表着十一亿中国人民，一定要把金牌夺到手。哪天决赛，我们去给你们当啦啦队！"听了这些话，代表团成员们仿佛觉得肩上担负着一面铁打钢铸的五星红旗！

　　6 月 1 日至 3 日，在古老的文化名城乌尔比诺市举行风筝放飞决赛。

　　6 月 1 日，没进入雨期的意大利反而一天不停地下雨。6 月 2 日，大风七到八级，赛场上别说风筝了，就是临时搭起的野餐帐篷也几乎被吹翻。6 月 3 日，天气晴朗，老天爷像是在故意捉弄人们，一丝风也没有，急得匈牙利的一位风筝迷不停地在胸前划十字，乞求上帝赐风。

中国驻意大使馆的"啦啦队"从 600 公里外的罗马驱车赶到赛场，参赞、二秘、武官司机、厨师全都来了，就像给我们注了一支兴奋剂，顿觉精神抖擞，跃跃欲试。

下午三点，决赛开始，风还是很微弱，各国的风筝虽在造型、扎制、创新方面各有所长，但在起飞时都显示不出优势来。四点二十分，该 21 号参赛了，这是代表团的龙头蜈蚣风筝和凤凰风筝的赛号。突然间，起风了，代表团队员和侯馆的同志们不禁欢呼起来。二秘崔志新同志高兴地说："上帝没给他们赐风，我们的诸葛亮却把东风借来啦！"

随后，代表团几十米长的龙头蜈蚣风筝腾空而起，摇胡须，摆长尾，双眼滚动着，如长吼，似施威，遨游在天空。金色的大型凤凰抖动着羽翅，摇曳着彩尾，在蓝天上鸣唱着一支动听的乐曲……

比赛结束了，大赛裁判长公布中国的"21 号"获总分第一。代表团成员们高兴极了，大家欢呼雀跃，有的将头上的帽子抛向空中。韩福龄更是激动万分，眼睛里闪动着泪花……

（引自潍坊国际风筝会信息导报）

"潍燕" 风筝韩国放飞记

以潍坊呢绒服装厂厂长袁文和为团长的中国风筝代表团，于1994 年 2 月 16-17 日在韩国首尔举行的韩国国际风筝会上取得佳绩，314 米的 "潍燕" 风筝获得银牌。

韩国国际风筝会在汉江岸边的风筝放飞场开幕了，当五彩缤纷的风筝伴着隆隆礼炮声升起的时候，拉开了 1994 韩国国际风筝会的序幕。

中国风筝代表团团长，潍坊呢绒服装厂厂长袁文和被聘为本届国际风筝会比赛的裁判长。

大会比赛定为两天。2 月 16 日开幕预演，17 日决赛。2 月 16 日上午，美国、中国、日本、德国、马来西亚等 12 个国家 20 个放飞队的造型奇特、色彩鲜艳、飞动灵活的风筝陆续飞向碧空，各展风采。这时中国风筝代表团的 314 米长的 "潍燕走向世界" 风筝也扶摇而上。虽然天公不作美，风力不足，但是 "潍燕" 风筝仍放飞成功。它那新颖的造型， 艳丽的色彩，特别引人注目。

中国风筝代表团一行 5 人，一踏上韩国，便得到了东道主热情周到的欢迎和接待。 代表团的向导是一位 20 岁出头的青年人。他熟悉汉语，对代表团的成员彬彬有礼，他说，他的任务是服务，能为中国代表团服务感到非常高兴和荣幸，不周到的地方请多多原谅。

"潍燕" 风筝全长 314 米，风筝由 156 名时装模特造型组成，

放飞比较困难。韩国国际风筝会的组织者，早已察觉，主动派出20名青年人，帮助风筝起飞。在组织放飞中，虽然语言不通，难以统一指挥，佳众心所向，一定要把中国的"潍燕"风筝送上蓝天，他们个个兴高采烈，助跑、放飞累得满头大汗，但还是坚持助跑。"潍燕"风筝上天了，引来观众一片欢呼和喝彩。照相机、摄像机"卡卡"不断。不少记者围上来采访，了解"潍燕"风筝的情况。可惜言语不通，难以回答记者的提问，他们只好按"潍燕"风筝的156名模特造型一一介绍，记者们个个欣赏，边照相边记录。

韩国国际风筝会形式灵活，竞争激烈。美国、日本、德国、马来西亚等国家的风筝代表团都具有一定实力。其中有的风筝参加过潍坊国际风筝会，还有进入世界风筝"十绝"行列的美国的龟、法国的串蝶和澳大利亚的节日队列风筝。各种造型独特、风格各异的风筝在蓝天中尽情翱翔，多姿多彩，变幻无穷，引起了观众们的浓厚兴趣。"潍燕"风筝的造型，征服了韩国观众和各国的风筝爱好者。美国风筝放飞队员纷纷称赞中国的"潍燕"风筝，有一位放飞队员还满面笑容地说，我们能与中国人一起放风筝，不是比高低，而是为友谊，为交流文化。我向往中国，盼望再到中国去放风筝。韩国当地的电视台、报纸、电台都以整版篇幅和专题节目介绍中国的"潍燕"风筝。韩国服装商对中国潍坊"潍燕"时装十分熟悉，见到放飞以"潍燕"命名的服装系列风筝，特别高兴。有的韩国朋友站在自己挑选的模特风筝前拍照留念，祝愿中国"潍燕"服装早日成为世界名牌。

2月17日下午国际风筝会举行风筝评比发奖。"潍燕"风筝在中国风筝代表团的护拥下走上了主席台。这时全场观众报以热烈的掌声，场内观众情不自禁地高呼："中国－韩国！""中韩友谊万岁！"

"潍燕"风筝在本次风筝会比赛中名列前茅。大会主席当场宣布"潍燕"风筝夺得国际比赛银牌。接着向中国风筝代表团发了奖牌，赠送了鲜花，颁发了奖金。全场再一次热烈鼓掌，又一次响起了"欢迎，中国风筝代表团"，又一次有节奏地响起："中国－潍坊"的欢呼声。

（引自潍坊国际风筝会信息导报）

潍坊市工艺美术研究所打造风筝展品牌

潍坊市工艺美术研究所，充分发挥技术力量雄厚的优势，在风筝的研发创新，弘扬传承风筝技艺，促进风筝产业发展等方面

做出不懈努力，取得了突出成绩。其中，每年坚持"走出去"，与有关方面密切合作，在国内外举办大型风筝艺术展，成为该所发展的一条成功之路和主打品牌，不仅取得了良好的经济效益，而且宣传推介了潍坊，传承了风筝技艺，与国内外同行建立了密切联系，使风筝文化不断发扬光大。

多年来，该所先后在北京、杭州、大连、福州、广州、山西、河北等几十处文化旅游场馆举办大型风筝艺术展；并到新加坡举办过风筝和风车展览，时间长达两个月。除外，还到美国、泰国、荷兰等举办风筝艺术展，深受当地人民喜爱。

潍坊市工艺美术研究所举办的风筝艺术展活动，展出的内容丰富多彩，主要包括四个方面的内容：

展出各类大型景点风筝。如海洋动物、飞禽走兽、古典人物、卡通人物、其中最高的风筝"雄鹰展翅"高15米，宽14米；最新的风筝"恐龙再现"210平方米；最长的"龙头蜈蚣"风筝高2.5米，长120米，并推出了世界吉尼斯风筝"鲤鱼跳龙门"。

组织高水平放飞表演。由潍坊风筝放飞明星组成的放飞表演队，在活动期间，每天进行现场放飞表演，放飞的风筝有30余种，其中潍坊最具代表性的"龙头蜈蚣"风筝放飞场面壮观，深受观

众欢迎。

开展风筝有奖猜谜竞赛。为吸引游客参与活动，制作了上千条风筝谜语，让观众自由选择，即席猜题，猜中者可领取风筝一只。

精彩的文字照片资料展。推出了党和国家领导人在潍坊放飞的珍贵镜头及为潍坊风筝的题词、题字，同时详尽地展出了潍坊风筝文化悠久的历史、潍坊国际风筝会开幕式盛况。

（作者丁传信，系潍坊市工艺美术协会常务会长兼秘书长，潍坊市工艺美术研究所党支部书记）

别开生面的法国风筝节

应法国迪耶普国际风筝节组委会的邀请，我随潍坊市风筝代表团，于 2006 年 9 月 19 日至 18 日参加了法国第 14 届迪耶普国际风筝节。包括中国在内的 37 个国家和地区的风筝专业与业余选手参加了本届风筝节。

迪耶普是位于法国西北部诺曼底地区的一座海滨旅游城市，有 10 万人口。迪耶普国际风筝节创始于 1978 年，每两年举办一届，以注重国际化和多样性闻名，是世界著名的风筝赛事之一。它不光是风筝爱好者的乐园，也是一个多民族文化、展示的平台。本届风筝节突出环保主题："我们的星球，漫步于动植物间。"顺应这一主题，在海边约 8 公顷的绿色放飞场上，借着大西洋的秋风，参赛选手放飞了颇具匠心的风筝作品，有相当一部分是各种各样的动物和植物形状，在充分展示异域风情的同时，唤起人们关注环境保护和生态平衡、共同维护地球家园的意识。本届风筝节传统类风筝以放飞表演为主，运动类风筝进行了正式比赛。潍坊代表团成功放飞表演的 100 多米长的龙头蜈蚣风筝、巨型软体蛇风筝、组合式菱形风筝等，引起人们关注，当地媒体多次采访，会刊上刊发了我们放飞的照片。代表团向组委会赠送了以弘扬风筝文化为内容的中国书法作品和具有潍坊特色的民俗产品，受到组委会和观众的高度评价，新华社巴黎分社、中央电视台都对此做了报道。

本届法国风筝节特点突出，组织形式新颖，令人印象深刻。

国际化特色突出。每届风筝节，他们都邀请数十个国家、地区的专业选手和风筝制作者参加，人数不是很多，但精品风筝门类齐全。

这对于各国风筝爱好者来说，也是一个展现各国不同风筝文化和相互学习交流的宝贵机会。

办节模式独特。风筝放飞与展示密切结合。组委会设立专门的风筝作品展示区，各国风筝作者近距离与游客交流，展示扎制、绘画技艺，并与销售、订货等经济活动密切结合，被邀请的国家和地区的参赛选手大都能获取一定的经济效益。组委会对知名的风筝作者和专业放飞队员，除免费接待外，还解决这些人士的往返机票。组委会人员精干、务实，为放飞表演者创造宽松环境。迪耶普组委会是一个只有几个人的精干班子，但工作效率高，不搞形式主义，开幕式只用几分钟。在整个 10 天放飞比赛过程中，时间安排相对宽松，每天上午 10 点开始放飞比赛，遇到急的事情由联络员随时通知代表队。风筝创新的类型众多，如有单线、双线、多线操控的运动风筝，有与声光电结合的夜光风筝，有造型夸张的软体风筝，有海上冲浪风筝等。现场还有 5 个观摩风筝助阵表演，其中 2 只动漫风筝声色并茂，十分有趣。在近 8 公顷的草坪上，划分出不同的功能区，让世界各国专业和业余风筝爱好者尽情放飞五彩斑斓的风筝，风筝专家适时提供现场解说，乐队和民间文艺表演也适时助兴。这些安排，拉近了市民、游客与风筝之间的距离。

宣传力度大。迪耶普国际风筝节组委会通过印发海报，市区狂欢巡游活动，风筝图片展，组织青少年赴现场参观学习，推出纪念邮票、连环画、电影、音乐会等多种途径，营造了红红火火的节日氛围。

接待工作以人为本。组委会除在放飞现场设置餐饮区外，还在距离放飞现场 3 公里以内，指定了 20 余个接待饭店，由组委会统一发放餐券，各代表队可自由选择餐饮饭店，不需要组委会派人陪同。

拉动旅游的作用大。本届风筝节，地方政府投入 400 万欧元，在为期 10 天的风筝节期间，有近 40 万游客来到迪耶普观看了风筝放飞活动。在此期间，游客络绎不绝，所产生的经济效益是显而易见的。

（作者张崇高，系国际风筝联合会秘书长，潍坊国际风筝会办公室原主任）

潍坊风筝"飞进"北京奥运会

潍坊风筝作为山东省仅有的一个主打展示项目，在 2008 年北京奥运会期间举办的"中国故事"文化展示活动中，向来自世界各地的观众展现了其独特魅力。

据了解，"中国故事"是 2008 年奥运会期间唯一在奥林匹克公园中心区举办的文化活动。该活动以"关注中国国家级非物质文化遗产和传统民族、民俗、民间文化"为主旨，历时一个多月，贯穿北京奥运会、残奥会始终。主办方为各省、市、自治区参展方临时搭建了 30 多个面积 80 — 100 ㎡的"祥云小屋"。参展方在各自的"祥云小屋"里，通过图片、实物、多媒体视听艺术、现场表演和与观众互动等多种形式进行展示。

此次活动中，山东仅有一个主打展示项目的名额。经反复论证，山东省政府确定，将潍坊风筝作为此次山东参展活动的主打展示项目。山东"祥云小屋"展示内容以潍坊风筝为主打，题材方面既有传统潍坊风筝，又有八仙过海、梁山好汉等极具山东地方特色的风筝。

另外，在"祥云小屋"内还有泥塑、木版年画、扑灰年画等非遗项目的展示，力争通过多种表现形式来展示山东和潍坊独特的地域文化魅力。

在为期一个多月的展示中，前来山东"祥云小屋"参观的人络绎不绝，美丽的潍坊风筝给中外观众留下了美好记忆。

（作者王永训，系中国风筝协会副主席，潍坊市风筝产业协会会长）

潍坊风筝放飞雪域高原

2010年9月17日至20日，应西藏自治区旅游局邀请，潍坊市由初宝杰副市长带队，潍坊国际风筝会办公室有关人员赴西藏参加了由西藏自治区旅游局主办的拉萨风筝旅游文化展。活动期间，精心组织了潍坊风筝放飞表演和展览展示活动。

风筝放飞表演和展览展示活动取得良好效果。9月19日上午，拉萨风筝旅游文化展隆重开幕，西藏自治区副主席甲热·洛桑丹增出席了开幕式并宣布开幕，初宝杰副市长代表潍坊市政府致辞。风筝放飞表演和展览展示活动在市区赛马场举行。在为期两天的风筝放飞表演和展览展示活动中，拉萨市独具特色的菱形风筝的设计制作、风筝线的精巧加工，以及以打斗为主的表演形式，都给潍坊代表团留下了深刻印象，受到很大启发。潍坊市带去的上千只大中小搭配、传统与现代结合的各种风筝，在放飞表演和展览展示中也令拉萨市民耳目一新，特别是潍坊风筝的传统代表作龙头蜈蚣，长串风筝及象征56个民族大团结的特色风筝等，展示了丰富的风筝文化和一流的扎制放飞水平，引来众多市民观赏。在现场，代表团还向拉萨市民赠送了易于放飞的500余只小型风筝，同时，向西藏博物馆赠送了1200余米的长串风筝。在活动期间，潍坊市代表团还与西藏自治区旅游局就加强风筝业务交流进行了深入探讨，就双方的进一步合作达成了共识。

（作者张崇高，系国际风筝联合会秘书长，潍坊国际风筝会办公室原主任）

潍坊风筝放飞上海世博会

2010 年 9 月 28 日—10 月 15 日，潍坊国际风筝会办公室与哥伦比亚国家馆在上海世博园区共同组织了由 30 个国家参展的 "世界风筝展"，其中潍坊市参展风筝最多，有 200 多只风筝参展，有力地宣传推介了潍坊风筝文化，促进了潍坊风筝产品销售。在此期间，潍坊国际风筝会办公室与上海世博会哥伦比亚馆进行了风筝文化交流洽谈及签约仪式。经双方友好协商，委托潍坊天成飞鸢有限公司为哥伦比亚馆定做并交付了象征中哥两方友好的鹦鹉风筝 150 套。这些设计制作精美的风筝，赢得了各方的高度评价。

（作者王永训，系中国风筝协会副主席，潍坊市风筝产业协会会长）

潍坊风筝代表团出访美国、加拿大

2011 年 5 月 27 日至 6 月 4 日，潍坊市组成由张崇高任团长的风筝代表团，参加了美国、加拿大的风筝节和风筝文化交流活动。

5 月 27 日至 6 月 1 日，潍坊市风筝代表团首先前往美国加州圣拉蒙市，参加了国际艺术风筝节。潍坊市风筝代表团是该市邀请的唯一国外代表队。

在圣拉蒙市参加开幕式后潍坊市风筝代表团在该市少年艺术馆进行了风筝扎制表演、年画印制、剪纸表演。在社区文化中心，举办潍坊精品风筝展览和表演活动，共有 300 只龙头蜈蚣、蝴蝶、老鹰、人物、动物等各种各样的传统风筝参展，吸引了一万多名参观者。随后，潍坊市风筝代表团还在该市中央公园绿地广场举办了 4 次潍坊传统风筝放飞表演，受到当地观众的一致赞赏。

6 月 2 日到 4 日，潍坊市风筝代表团又前往加拿大多伦多山东商会、当地风协组织，开展风筝文化交流。风筝代表团带去的精品风筝受到当地各界人士的喜爱和称赞。山东商会与潍坊市风筝代表团还就深入开展风筝展览、风筝贸易等事宜进行了友好商榷，并就提升风筝产业，促进风筝贸易达成了深入合作的共识。

此次出访，不但在美国、加拿大展示了潍坊的风筝、年画和剪纸艺术，还传播了潍坊风筝文化，增强了两国文化交流，为共同弘扬风筝文化，推动运动风筝的普及与推广做出了积极贡献。

（作者王永训，系中国风筝协会副主席，潍坊市风筝产业协会会长）

"潍坊展馆"获第二届世界风筝博览会三项大奖

2011年9月17日，第2届世界休闲博览会在杭州开幕，为期60天，潍坊国际风筝会办公室承办的"潍坊展馆"大放异彩，吸引了众多参与者的注意。

"潍坊展馆"凸显了"风筝之都，魅力潍坊"的主题，体现了大气、洋气与地方传统特色设计风格的紧密结合，比较全面地宣传和推介了潍坊市以风筝为代表的传统文化，展示了潍坊宜居宜业宜休闲的城市形象。该展馆面积100 m²，以文字、图片、实物、视频和现场制作等形式，全面、立体地宣传推介潍坊，是潍坊市参展史上设计最精美、内容最丰富、展示最全面、展览时间最长的一次。中央和省级媒体先后对"潍坊展馆"做过重点报道，通过长达两个月的展览展示，进一步扩大了潍坊在国内外的知名度和影响力。

展览结束后，因"潍坊展馆"在160个国内外参展城市展馆中表现突出，被评为"2011世界休闲博览会最佳设计奖""2011世界休闲博览会最佳观众满意奖""2011世界休闲博览会最佳展品展示奖"三项大奖，是获奖最多、奖项最高的城市。

（作者张崇高，系国际风筝联合会秘书长，潍坊国际风筝会办公室原主任）

潍坊风筝制作技艺助力伦敦奥运

2012年夏季的伦敦奥运会举世瞩目，作为奥运会文化节一个重要组成部分，歌剧《诺亚方舟》向全球亮相，而其中的舞台道具皆出自潍坊市寒亭区杨家埠天成飞鸢风筝有限公司的王永训之手，这些道具都是运用潍坊传统的风筝扎制工艺制作而成。这一不寻常的任务之所以能够顺利完成，王永训功不可没。

王永训曾多次出国参加各种与风筝相关的巡展活动，结识了英国大使馆的朋友。机缘巧合之下，伦敦奥组委负责舞台道具的Simon找到了他。作为"考试"项目，Simon要求王永训先做一只老虎，王永训按照要求完成，交了一份满意的答卷。

这样的订单最大的困难在于将平面图上的动物立体化，让它们活起来。《诺亚方舟》传说中，方舟要载上畜类和飞鸟，这些东西在舞台上表现要求色彩艳丽、体态轻盈、不易松散。"满打满算只有40天的时间，现在只有几张平面图，时间不够用。"

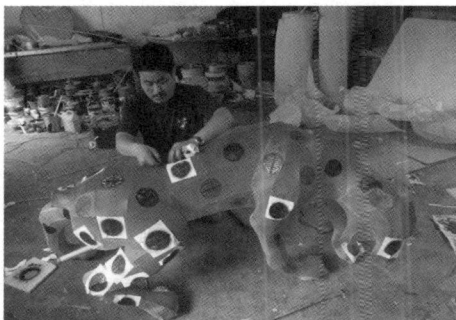

王永训说，他深知这样的订单要求高、难度大，如果做不出来是要砸牌子的。

王永训考虑再三之后告诉Simon，这个订单工期太紧，正常工作时间肯定无法高质量完成。这时，Simon才告诉王永训要在伦敦奥运会上用，"我觉得只有你才能完成。"

王永训又认真地想了想，并做了时间规划，只要在一个多月的时间内每天加班，还是有希望完成的。"中国的东西能上奥运会这样的舞台，比什么都重要。"王永训和爱人达成了这样的共识。

所能依据的只有平面图纸，而 Simon 要求做出的成品必须和图纸造型颜色完全一致。颜色好说，造型方面依靠双方协商也不是问题，但是要用潍坊传统的风筝扎制工艺来做各种动物，造型取材上就得花点功夫了。

在整个创作的过程中，王永训总是能产生意想不到的灵感。想要一个什么东西，他就会走出工作间，在自家院子里转一圈，多半会有成果。辣椒、保温材料等等都是他的独门秘技。不过最令大家叫绝的还是一条老鼠尾巴。

有一个创作是猫追老鼠，老鼠的尾长超过 1 米。按照图纸，老鼠的尾巴用竹子烤成一个卷即可，但是力求完美的王永训觉得竹子缺乏立体感和灵动效果。那几天他一直在琢磨用什么东西做老鼠尾巴。突然有一天刮风，家里一根用来拉门的弹簧跳入他的视野。王永训二话不说，拆下了门上的弹簧，拉成前粗后细的老鼠尾巴再用尼丝纺布一包，活灵活现的效果引得大家称奇。

"咱干这个东西，有义务为潍坊风筝争一席之地，能上奥运会这样的舞台，比什么都重要。"王永训说。

（潍坊天成飞鸢风筝有限公司供稿）

万里之遥风筝情

2012年11月19日至21日，应特立尼达和多巴哥共和国旅游部邀请，潍坊市组成风筝文化代表团，由我（时任潍坊国际风筝会办公室主任）任团长，代表团成员包括风筝专家刘秋萍、石岳、韩军、王永训、翻译杨永花。我们一行6人，按计划飞赴特立尼达和多巴哥共和国，开展了为期3天的风筝文化交流活动。访问时间短促，活动内容丰富，代表团高效运作，达到了超出预期的效果。经过积极努力，成功地进行了潍坊风筝展览展示和放飞表演，展示了潍坊精湛的风筝制作技艺和放飞技巧，与特多有关方面进行了友好交流，加深了彼此间的了解和友谊，弘扬了中国传统风筝文化，受到当地人们的热情欢迎。可以说，整个出访活动取得了圆满成功，开创了与特立尼达和多巴哥共和国（以下简称特多）风筝文化交流的新局面，留下了令人难以忘怀的美好记忆。

代表团与特多旅游部进行了友好座谈交流。当地时间11月19日上午，代表团与特多旅游部进行了工作座谈。特多旅游部部长卡迪

茨，部长助理克里兹汀·侯赛因，中国驻特多使馆商务参赞兰和平女士、商务一秘刘鹰女士等出席座谈会。座谈会上，我着重介绍了潍坊市的市情，风筝文化历史，举办国际风筝会和风筝文化

产业发展情况，国际风筝联合会总部及工作开展情况。特多旅游部部长卡迪茨在发言中，热烈欢迎潍坊代表团到访，并称赞此次代表团的到访，开启了两国在风筝文化领域交流的先河，表示今后将共同努力，进一步推动双方在这一领域的交流与合作。同时，他热情地为潍坊国际风筝会题词"希望潍坊国际风筝会一帆风顺，期盼特多有幸参与"。

成功地开展了潍坊风筝展览展示和放飞表演活动。访问期间，代表团先后在特多三所中小学校（企业家公立小学、圣费尔南多市公立中学、多巴哥公立小学，土生华人协会所在地千里达华人会馆，分别进行了数百只精品传统潍坊风筝展览展示，播放了潍坊国际风筝会万人风筝放飞表演视频和历届风筝会简介幻灯片，风筝专家们向中小学生传授潍坊传统风筝制作技艺，开展现场放飞表演活动，并免费向上述三所学校、土生华人协会、一所儿童福利院赠送了数千只特色小风筝。11 月 21 日，在特多儿童福利院附近的萨瓦那广场上，代表团成功地放飞了潍坊风筝的代表作龙头蜈蚣，长串喇叭花等各式风筝，吸引了当地众多市民驻足观赏并参与放飞，放飞现场充满欢歌笑语，友好气氛十分热烈融洽。

代表团在特多的风筝展演活动，该国对此非常重视，代表团的出色工作也在当地产生了良好影响。该国旅游部部长卡迪茨对各项活动亲自安排和陪同，同时饶有兴致地多次放飞潍坊风筝。在上述活动中，卡迪茨部长所在选区内的企业家公立小学及该国总理故乡的圣费尔南多市公立中学，是这次风筝展演的两处重点场所，广大师生对精美的潍坊风筝表现出了极大兴趣，纷纷参与扎制和试飞风筝，对风筝专家精彩的风筝展演不时报以热烈的掌声。

举行了潍坊风筝展演媒体推介活动。在中国驻特多大使馆和特多旅游部协调下，于 11 月 21 日举行了潍坊风筝文化展演媒体见面会，展示了精美的潍坊风筝，回答了记者们感兴趣的话题，

中国驻特多大使杨优明和特多旅游部长卡迪茨和我本人分别接受了记者专访。特多主流媒体包括特多外交部媒体事务所，特多著名网站 Tnnview，位列特多国三大报纸前列的《快报》、《每日新闻》，以及特多匼独立媒体人 Damian Lvkpak 等，分别对潍坊风筝展演作了报道，并配发了多幅展演照片。

拜会了中国驻特多大使杨优明先生。中国驻特多使馆十分重视潍坊风筝文化代表团的到访。按照约定，代表团准时到达中国驻特多使馆。杨尤明大使在百忙之中会见了代表团一行，并出席了 21 日的媒体见面会和风筝展演活动。在与代表团交谈中，杨大使希望以此次访闬为起点，进一步加强潍坊与特多在风筝领域的交流合作，使之成为两国交流的新亮点。杨大使还欣然为潍坊国际风筝会题写了"祝潍坊国际风筝会越办越好！"的祝福语。

本次出访，是潍坊市乃至山东省文化类代表团首次访问特多，通过访问，我感到收获很大，体会很深。主要有这样几点：

宣传推介了潍坊和独具特色的风筝文化。以风筝为载体，通过潍坊风筝的展览展示和现场制作以及放飞表演，弘扬了风筝文化，宣传了潍坊，扩大了潍坊市的知名度，同时，加深了相互间的了解和友谊，密切了与特多有关方面的联系。

看到了特多发展风筝文化产业的巨大潜力和美好前景。该国人民生活富裕，市民注重休闲运动，从上层到民众，喜欢风筝的人很多，同时，该国属于加勒比海地区，风力适宜，适合放飞，城区到处是开阔的绿地，为风筝运动开展和风筝文化产业深入合作提供了良好基础和条件。

土生华人协会是未来合作的重要平台。在特多的华人是特多的第4大族群，已有200余年历史。特多土生华人协会拥有的千里达华人会馆，室内空间很大，可以长期举办各种展览、展销活动。通过深入洽谈，对方也有与我们开展合作的愿望。今后，潍坊市可以来特多举办风筝、民俗工艺品展览，以此为平台，拓展在特多的风筝文化产业合作，加大潍坊风筝和工艺品的营销力度。

中国驻特多大使馆是靠山。此次出访得到了中国驻特多使馆全力协助，从大使到工作人员，都满腔热情，认真负责，全力支持，而且他们也都对风筝文化情有独钟。今后对特多的深入合作和交流，必须继续紧紧依靠驻特多使馆的正确领导和大力支持。

（作者张崇高，系国际风筝联合会秘书长，潍坊国际风筝会办公室原主任）

潍坊风筝万里行活动

2013 年，为进一步提升和扩大潍坊风筝以及潍坊这座城市的品牌影响力，潍坊国际风筝会办公室会同有关部门组织了潍坊风筝万里行大型宣传活动。

活动共分三期进行。第一期于 2013 年 3 月下旬，分别走进了南京、上海、杭州、芜湖、济南；第二期，于 2013 年 5 月下旬至 6 月上旬，分别走进了武汉、贵阳、北川；第三期，于 2013 年 12 月中旬，分别走进了合肥、南昌、安阳、菏泽。

在每一次活动中，潍坊国际风筝会办公室都精心组织，邀请全市最具实力的风筝放飞专家，带着各式各样的潍坊风筝，与当地市民共同分享风筝放飞的乐趣。每到一地，风筝艺人们不管天气如何，都会想方设法把风筝放飞做到极致，让当地市民能够真正领略到来到世界风筝都艺人们的不凡水准。

潍坊日报等主流媒体也参加了这次风筝万里行活动，走进了每一个城市。记者们深切感受到当地民众对风筝这项运动的喜爱，也深切感受到潍坊风筝的巨大影响力。记者们用自己的笔触和镜头，记录了每一站精彩各异的瞬间，在笔下，在镜头里，有多彩的潍坊风筝，有敬业的风筝艺人，有对潍坊风筝赞不绝口的各地市民，以及各地风筝爱好者对潍坊风筝的向往与期盼。

（一）潍坊风筝万里行正式出征

2013 年 3 月 20 日上午，由潍坊市政府主办，潍坊国际风筝会办公室、潍坊市旅游局等单位承办的潍坊风筝万里行活动，从市人民广场正式出发。这次参加万里行活动的均为我市知名的风筝艺人，包括连续参加过 30 届风筝会的风筝艺人谭洪、谭鹤亭以及潍坊知名的风筝明星等。据了解，这些风筝艺人均带来了自己的代表作品，包括软体、串式、板式以及运动风筝等，包含了潍坊风筝的各个门类，也代表着潍坊风筝的最高扎制技艺。

据了解，举办这次风筝

万里行活动，旨在大力推进潍坊风筝"走出去"，通过进行风筝放飞，风筝及民俗工艺品、潍坊景观名胜图片展演，媒体互动等一系列活动，宣传推介潍坊，促进潍坊与当地文化旅游交流与合作，打响潍坊城市品牌，扩大潍坊的影响力和吸引力。

风筝万里行活动分三期进行，计划巡游国内 10 多个重点城市，首批出发的风筝艺人们将走进南京、上海、杭州、芜湖、济南等城市。参加万里行的风筝艺人纷纷表示，将会以一流的状态向所到城市展示潍坊风筝的风采，让更多的外地人了解潍坊风筝，喜欢上潍坊风筝。

（二）燕子矶下鸢竞飞
——潍坊风筝万里行第一期首站在南京举行放飞活动

燕子矶被称作长江三大名矶之首，有着"万里长江第一矶"的称号，"燕矶夕照"为清初金陵南京四十八景之一。2013 年 3 月 21 日，风光如画的燕子矶平添了一道别致的景观，来自世界风筝都潍坊的风筝艺人们在这里放飞起各式各样的潍坊风筝，让南京市民领略了潍坊风筝的独特风采。

南京是潍坊风筝万里行活动的第一站，为了迎接远道而来的客人，南京风筝运动协会也组织了当地的风筝艺人来与潍坊的艺人们进行现场交流。10 时许，当我们赶到放飞地点时，当地的风筝艺人们早早地放起了风筝。为使这次潍坊风筝万里行活动充分展示潍坊风筝的风采，参加放飞的艺人们也是做足了准备工作，为应付不同的放飞天气，风筝艺人都带来了大大小小多个风筝，大的有长达 100 米的软体蛇，80 米的龙头蜈蚣，小的有不足一米的彩虹、三角风筝等。经过商量，风筝艺人们决定首先放飞潍坊风筝的代表作品——龙头蜈蚣。天公作美，据气象预报说当天的风力达到了 4 级，足以能让 80 多米的龙头蜈蚣飞上天。在风筝老艺人谭洪的指挥下，褚光亮、张建华等几名放飞队员们干净麻利快，毫不费力便把龙头蜈蚣送上蓝天。但见这龙头蜈蚣摇摇摆摆的刚飞上蓝天，便引来围观群众的一片啧啧赞叹之声。

"太漂亮了！"一位女士情不自禁地喊道。

首炮打响，风筝艺人们都纷纷拿出了自己的看家作品，谭洪带来了100米的软体蛇，潍坊工艺美术研究所带来了40米多的章鱼，这两个都算是大块头，飞到天上都会让其他风筝敬而远之的。很快，五彩斑斓的潍坊风筝便成了空中的主角，喜羊羊与灰太狼三角风筝天上飘飘悠悠，还有嗖嗖作声的运动三角都成为现场观众的最爱，尤其是那软体蛇，摆着长长的尾巴，简直就是蓝天上的霸主，煞是壮观。

在潍坊风筝艺人大显身手的同时，南京当地的风筝艺人也不肯错过这次学习交流的机会，他们有的自己放起了风筝，有的参与到了潍坊放飞队伍之中。南京风筝运动协会的秘书长刘长胜先生，曾10多次担任潍坊国际风筝会的风筝裁判，对潍坊风筝一往情深，说起这次潍坊举办风筝万里行，刘长胜表示，这样的活动会带动更多地方风筝运动的发展。潍坊是风筝的故乡，也是风筝爱好者心中的圣地，在潍坊的带动下，全国的风筝运动有了很大发展，也希望通过这次活动，能够让更多的南京市民加入到风筝运动中来。

在现场，除了这些放飞的风筝艺人，还有一群长枪短炮的摄影爱好者，听说潍坊风筝要到这里进行放飞表演的时候，他们也纷纷拿起手中的相机，记录下潍坊风筝最美的一刻。一位女摄影家，在现场拍了一上午，直到我们的放飞活动结束，她才离去。她说，本来是想到江边随便拍拍，没想到遇到这么壮观的风筝放飞活动，真是太幸运了。

（三）潍坊风筝万里行在上海举行放飞活动

2013年3月23日上午，潍坊风筝万里行活动来到上海，在浦东新区世纪广场举行了放飞活动，并现场为市民派送印有世界风筝都标志的风筝，当天也是上海市民文化节的首日，潍坊市的风筝艺人与当地风筝爱好者共同放飞风筝，把世纪广场上空装扮得五彩缤纷。

与首站南京放飞的都是"大块头"不同，上海的放飞更显示出潍坊风筝的多样性。既有龙头蜈蚣这样的传统风筝，也有"嫦娥奔月"题材的大型软体风筝；既有"五福献寿"这样的主题风筝，也有形象逼真的QQ风筝等。特别是同时放飞的软体彩虹风筝，几名艺人共同放飞多个彩虹，利用手中的双线，使彩虹风筝在天空中变幻出多个阵式，一会儿互相盘绕，一会儿一字排开，变化无穷的空中造型让现场观众看得大呼过瘾，也展现了潍坊风筝的放飞技巧。

在放飞现场，还向市民派送了潍坊风筝。许多市民拿到风筝

后立马就加入到了放飞的行列。据浦东新区潍坊街道群工部有关负责人介绍，由于当天是上海市民文化节的第一天，各地都组织了丰富多彩的活动，潍坊风筝万里行活动恰巧来到上海，也是为当地市民文化活动助兴添彩，希望通过这个活动能够促进两地更多的风筝交流与合作。现场的放飞活动也带动了世纪广场上几个风筝小贩的生意，这几个专卖潍坊风筝的小伙都来自于山东枣庄，说起潍坊风筝，他们也是一脸的自豪，因为潍坊风筝名气大，一年只卖春秋两季，就有不菲的收入。

近三个小时的放飞活动，一根根细细的银线，把潍坊风筝的独特魅力展现在上海人民面前，也让更多的上海市民认识了潍坊风筝，也认识了潍坊这座充满活力和生机的世界风筝之都。

（作者窦浩智，系潍坊日报记者）

（四）西湖上空景亦美

2013年3月25日，风光如画的杭州西湖，白堤两岸，桃红柳绿，游人如织，一派春意盎然的景象。当天下午，潍坊风筝万里行活动来到这里，10多位潍坊风筝艺人通过展示和放飞向游人推介潍坊最亮的一张名片——风筝。

并不宽阔的西湖白堤因为潍坊风筝艺人的到来而显得格外拥挤，格外热闹。而刚刚亮相的风筝艺人们，简直称得上人人都是焦点。在现场，他们个个都是明星，有的接受媒体采访，有的接受游客咨询，有的与当地风筝爱好者进行交流学习，忙得是不亦乐乎。为了让游客直观地了解潍坊风筝，几位风筝艺人先把两个庞然大物，80多米的龙头蜈蚣和100米长的软体青蛇在白堤两岸的草坪上向游人进行展示。

"龙头蜈蚣是潍坊风筝的代表，这只风筝尽管80多米长，但很容易起飞"，风筝艺人褚光亮一边忙活着展示风筝，一边向游人介绍着。

"白蛇传的故事人人皆知，能在西子湖畔放飞 100 米长的青蛇风筝，绝对是道风景。"风筝艺人谭洪向游客介绍道。

为了欢迎远道而来的潍坊风筝艺人，杭州风筝协会也组织了 30 多名风筝迷前来助兴，也借机向世界风筝都的同行取经。潍坊市风筝艺人钱建国刚刚拿出他的盘鹰风筝，就被当地的"鹰友"们围了起来，问这问那，钱师傅不厌其烦地给他们解释着盘鹰扎制的技巧，讲的不过瘾，就现场演示放飞，一边放飞一边讲。之所以有这么多人求教盘鹰，原来当地有专门的盘鹰风筝俱乐部，据杭州风筝协会副会长陆佑授介绍，盘鹰风筝是杭州人最喜欢的一种风筝，也是放的最多的一种风筝，为了能跟潍坊的风筝艺人学习取经，当地的风筝艺人有的上午 9 点钟就到了现场，等候着潍坊风筝艺人的到来。

龙头蜈蚣的放飞堪称是最壮观的一幕。由于白堤路窄人多，必须先蹚出一片空地，展开风筝，几位风筝艺人便需要先"打场子"，三五名老艺人前呼后唤，硬是在人群中开出了一条道，摆好风筝。谭洪、褚光亮手执龙头，其他几位风筝艺人各执几段龙身，一阵风来，但见龙头一跃，整个龙身腾空而起，随之而来的便是一片惊叹，整个白堤上游人的目光便聚焦在了这摇摇摆摆的龙头蜈蚣上。

随后，在碧波荡漾的西湖上空，各式各样的潍坊风筝便成为最夺目的一道风景：软体老板鱼、五福献寿、龙头三角、软体彩虹、对燕，等等，还有新题材的传统风筝，喜羊羊与灰太狼，这时也来凑热闹，成为西湖上空最可爱的一员。当然最受游客欢迎的，还是风筝万里行活动带来的简易三角风筝，这些风筝印有世界风筝都的标志，既是礼品风筝，也是宣传风筝，每到一地，都会成为当地市民的最爱。由于轻便易起飞，现场派送的这些三角风筝，很快便加入到了放飞的方阵。

潍坊风筝绚丽夺目，杭州当地风筝爱好者自然不甘示弱，他们放飞的盘鹰以及各式各样的微型风筝也是随风起舞，争奇斗艳。82 岁的杨迪生是个盘鹰爱好者，对潍坊风筝向往已久，这次听说潍坊风筝要到杭州放飞，便早早地来到了活动现场。他说，潍坊国际风筝会对全国风筝爱好者来说，吸引力非常大，很遗憾这么多年我没去过潍坊的风筝会，但今年终于可以实现这个夙愿，4月 20 日我将随杭州风筝协会前往潍坊，观摩潍坊国际风筝会。

碧波画舫、蓝天风筝，此时的西湖，潍坊与杭州两地风筝爱好者共同描绘出一道最美丽的风景。

（作者窦浩智，系潍坊日报记者 ）

（五）潍坊风筝亮相安徽芜湖

2013 年 3 月 29 日，来自安徽 17 地市的百余位风筝高手云集芜湖，各展拿手绝活，展开一番激烈角逐。当天进行的是第三届安徽风筝大赛。不过在赛场之外，一场由潍坊风筝大师举行的放飞表演则让安徽的这些风筝高手们看得如醉如痴，直夸过瘾。受赛事主办方的邀请，潍坊风筝万里行活动在经过南京、上海、杭

州等城市的巡游放飞之后，特意转道芜湖，到第三届安徽风筝大赛暨芜湖风筝文化节的开幕式上进行放飞表演，让现场观众看得可谓畅快淋漓。

对于潍坊风筝的到来，当地期待已久，当地媒体把潍坊风筝在开幕式上的表演称作是"体会世界顶级风筝竞技的艺术魅力。"29日早晨，离正式的放飞表演还有两个小时，潍坊风筝艺人们便早早地来到了现场。开幕式现场的背景墙是专为潍坊风筝留下的，艺人们有的组装，有的固定，两块背景墙很快便成为潍坊风筝的展板，蝴蝶、蜻蜓、金鱼、雄鹰，造型各异的潍坊风筝把背景墙装扮的五彩斑斓。不等放飞，单就这钉在板上的风筝，早早地便抢足了观众眼球。

挂在板上，毕竟只能过过眼瘾。重头戏当然还是放飞。

最先起飞的当然还是首推一号明星——龙头蜈蚣。几位风筝艺人撒开龙节，80多米的龙身光是摆在地上就足以让现场观众瞠目，尽管是个大家伙，但起飞并不费劲，一人控制着龙头，一人把龙尾一抛，那龙身便挺着脊梁直入云霄，引来现场观众一片叫好。由于风大，这龙头蜈蚣几次摇摇摆摆，但见几个风筝艺人稍稍调整了一下线，它便安安稳稳地飞翔在蓝天。

"这属于传统的中式风筝，有100多节、是潍坊风筝的代表。"一边放飞，风筝艺人还要一边向观众介绍着潍坊龙头蜈蚣风筝。

这次放飞表演还有一个庞然大物，软式立体的泰迪熊风筝，这家伙风小飞不起来，地方小了更不用考虑，前几站的放飞，这家伙一直偷懒，在南京、上海、杭州，不是地方小，就是风力不足，一直没个露脸的机会。不过这次总算有它露面的机会了。这个庞然大物高30多米，宽达8米，充满气足足有200多个立方米。

几位放飞队员首先调整好姿势，让风灌进风筝体内，然后稍稍一送，泰迪熊就像踱步似的慢悠悠地升了空。憨态可掬的泰迪熊一飞上天空，便成了焦点，大家都愿意去拽一拽，拖一拖，跟逗着玩似的，就连参加开幕式表演的锣鼓队的几位大妈，也禁不住忙里偷闲，一起玩起了泰迪熊，现场不时地笑声连连。

还有那双线控制的百米青蛇，通体绿色，张着大大的嘴巴，摇着长长的尾巴，在天上飘飘悠悠，活灵活现地宛如一条活体蛇游走在蓝天。

除了这几个庞然大物，双线运动风筝、各式的软体风筝自然也缺不了。各式各样的潍坊风筝把赛场上空装扮的异常夺目，放的畅快，看得过瘾，芜湖市民对于潍坊风筝也不吝溢美之词，夸赞潍坊风筝做工精美，放飞气势恢宏，不愧是世界一流的放飞表演。几位来参加比赛的风筝选手表示，潍坊风筝世界一流，我们能在家门口看到顶尖的风筝放飞，是一次很好的学习！

（作者窦浩智，系潍坊日报记者）

（六）潍坊风筝进泉城进高校

2013 年 4 月 4 日清明节，由山东省民俗学会、潍坊国际风筝会办公室共同主

办"潍坊风筝进泉城进高校"活动，在位于济南大学西校区的山东民俗文化陈列馆开幕，潍坊的五彩斑斓的风筝为山东民俗文化陈列馆的里里外外涂上了一层春天的色彩。这是潍坊风筝万里行活动第一阶段最后一个活动。

风筝源于春秋战国时代，至今已有 2000 多年发展历史。一直以来，作为我国民俗特色文化，风筝渗透着诸多民族传统和民间习俗，并广为流传。到清代，风筝的制作工艺更加完美，并且形成了北京、天津、潍坊、南通四大风筝产地。每年的三、四月份，都是人们走出家门放飞风筝的最好时节。

据《墨子·鲁问》篇记载"公输般竹木为鹊，成而飞之，三日不下"；又说"公输般作木鸢，以窥宋城"。公输般就是后人所说的七巧匠鲁班。他制作的"鹊"或"鸢"，其原材料是极薄的木片或竹片。汉朝以后，由于纸的发明和应用，在制作风筝时，逐渐以纸代木，称为"纸鸢"。五代时，又在纸鸢上系竹哨，风吹竹哨，声如筝鸣故以后称"风筝"。唐宋时期，现属潍坊各地扎放风筝已很普遍。北宋著名画家张择端（今潍坊诸城人）的《清明上河图》就有儿童在放风筝。明清时期，潍坊的风筝在民间比较普及。每年清明节前后，风和日丽，家家户户扶老携幼，踏青

登场，竞相把自己的得意之作送上蓝天。《潍县志》记载：清明，小儿女作纸鸢，秋千之戏，纸鸢其制不一，于鹤、燕、蝶、蝉各类之外，兼作种种人物，无不惟妙惟肖，奇巧百出。清代扬州八怪之一的郑板桥在《怀潍县》诗中说："纸花如雪满天飞，娇女秋千打四围。五色罗裙风摆动，好将蝴蝶斗春归。"生动地描写了清明时节潍坊风筝放飞的情景。这种春意盎然的民间活动，既是相互观摩、评比的机会，又是呼吸早春空气、享受大自然的恩赐、锻炼身体的好时光。

潍坊风筝扎工精美，画工别致，造型新颖，构图合理。它还吸收了木版年画的某些特点，博采京津画技之长，线条优美，色彩鲜明，善以夸张的手法，突出主题。风格独特，栩栩如生。其种类有软翅类，硬翅类，龙头串式类，板子类和立体筒子类等，其中以龙头蜈蚣最为突出。据说是受了龙骨水车的启发而制造的。现在已发展许多品种，小的可放在掌上，大的有几百米长，造型、色彩也各不相同，从很简单的白纸糊身，红纸糊头，不画一笔，不染一色的蜈蚣风筝，到色彩缤纷，绘金描银的九头神龙风筝。从构思奇妙的二龙戏珠到三条巨龙在空中呈"y"字形飞行的"哪吒闹海"，千变万化，奇巧百出。潍坊的长串风筝除蜈蚣之外，还有各种不同的题材。如"梁山一百单八将"是把梁山的一百零八位好汉做得个个形态不同，栩栩如生，放上天去排成一队，各持兵刃，随风飘动，这时你也许会隐约地感到有战鼓催阵，好像他们正要出发，去打下大宋朝廷……

1984年4月，在潍坊的北海滩上放起了一条巨型龙头蜈蚣，头高4米，长4米，腰节直径1.2米，这个风筝共长360米，当时在全国是最大的了。"龙头蜈蚣"扶摇蓝天，气势千里，蔚为壮观。赢得国内外的普遍赞誉。自1984年第一届潍坊国际风筝会以来，每年的四月，都要举办一届国际风筝盛会，至今已举办30届。1988年，第五届国际风筝会将潍坊定为"世界风筝都"。每年都要吸引来自世界的几十个国家和地区代表队参加。潍坊风筝它不仅被广泛用于放飞、比赛、娱乐，而且已经成为美化人们生活的时尚装饰品。风筝是潍坊的象征，每年的风筝会是潍坊以风筝拉动经济发展的一个活动。

2006年，潍坊风筝制作技艺被列入第一批国家级非物质文化遗产名录。

潍坊风筝万里行活动，目前已走进南京、上海、杭州、芜湖等城市。由山东省民俗学会、潍坊国际风筝会办公室共同主办"潍坊风筝进泉城进高校"即是潍坊风筝万里行活动的重要组成部分。

放风筝是清明时节人们所喜爱的活动。清明时节，碧空万里，惠风和畅，草木萌发，是放风筝的好时候，人们不仅白天放，夜间也放。夜里在风筝下或风筝拉线上挂上一串串彩色的小灯笼，像闪烁的明星，被称为"神灯"。放风筝，一般人只知道是一种文化娱乐活动，但在古代，还包括一项古老的习俗——"放晦气"。过去，人们把风筝放上蓝天后，便剪断牵线，任凭清风把它们送往天涯海角，据说这样能除病消灾，给自己带来好运。从而，风筝也成为古代人们节日避邪的一种护身符。

（七）潍坊风筝万里行第二期启动
首站潍坊龙头蜈蚣腾飞"江城"武汉

由潍坊市人民政府主办，潍坊国际风筝会办公室、潍坊市旅游局等单位承办的潍坊风筝万里行活动第二阶段日前启动。2013年5月28日上午，由潍坊风筝艺人组成的放飞队，在江城武汉进行放飞活动，这是本次活动的第一站。

好风凭借力，扶我上青云。当天，来自世界风筝都潍坊的传统风筝龙头蜈蚣，在江城腾空而起，自由地飞翔在江城上空，引起阵阵地叫好声。两地风筝艺人、爱好者共同放飞，其他的各类风筝也逐渐升空，一时间空中千鸢飞舞，为江城增添了一道亮丽的景观。

龙头蜈蚣惊艳江城

武汉是中部地区最大都市及唯一的副省级城市，"茫茫九派流中国，沉沉一线穿南北"，长江及其最大支流汉江横贯市区。占地面积45万平方米的武汉市塔子湖体育中心，是该市唯一的国家级运动主题公园，当天的放飞活动，就在体育中心前草地广场上举行。

武汉是潍坊风筝万里行活动第二期的第一站。为了迎接远道而来的客人，武汉市风筝协会组织了当地的风筝艺人夹与潍坊的艺人们进行现场交流。早上不到8时，当放飞队员来到放飞地点时，当地的风筝艺人们已经寻早地放起了风筝，

让见惯了大场面的潍坊艺人，一下子提起了兴趣。

前两天刚刚降雨的武汉，温度适宜，风力较稳，虽然放飞地点位于市区内，但较为适合放飞风筝，放飞队员们经过精心准备，首先亮出了潍坊风筝的典型代表——龙头蜈蚣，长度达到80多米的龙头蜈蚣，在草坪上一亮相，就引起了众多江城市民的关注，龙头栩栩如生，色彩艳丽，龙眼一眨一眨、龙须随风飘动，十分逼真动人，"太精彩了，这只风筝不但能飞，还是一件艺术品！"不少市民发出啧啧的惊叹声。

好不容易打发了一拨一拨问这问那的龙头蜈蚣"粉丝"，47岁的褚光亮在王兆瑞的帮助下，瞅准风力较稳的时机，前后配合，稍加用力，这只长80多米的风筝便腾空而起，扶摇直上，在空中摇头摆尾，大展雄姿。随着风筝的升空，远处观众的目光也被吸引过来，一时间，草坪上欢呼声、叫好声响成一片。

江城爱好者踊跃参加

场地上，潍坊龙头蜈蚣风筝夺得了头彩，江城风筝也不甘示弱，来自武汉市风筝协会的风筝爱好者，也亮出了自己的绝活，各色风筝纷纷升空，长达三百余米的串式风筝"小蝌蚪"，灵活多变的盘鹰，引来广大市民驻足观赏。

今年66岁的陈先生是汉阳区汉水队的放飞队员，是一名风筝放飞运动的忠实"粉丝"，"我放了十年盘鹰，随着放飞技艺的越来越精，身体也越来越好。他认为，放风筝是一项非常不错的运动，虽然没有去过潍坊，但是每年一届的潍坊国际风筝会，万鸢飞舞的盛大场面，让他十分神往，"有机会一定去参观一下。"他表示。

武汉市风筝协会副秘书长曾望芬介绍，武汉风筝有独特的地方特色，风筝放飞拥有十分庞大的爱好者群体，所放飞的风筝多以盘鹰、串式等风筝为主。这次活动吸引了武汉市风筝协会的十五六支代表队、200 余名队员前来放飞表演，"听说潍坊风筝放飞队要来武汉放飞风筝后，协会的会员十分踊跃，纷纷表示要前来参加交流、放飞。"曾望芬介绍说，"潍坊风筝世界知名，这次来到武汉，对我们的风筝运动发展将起到极大的推动作用。"

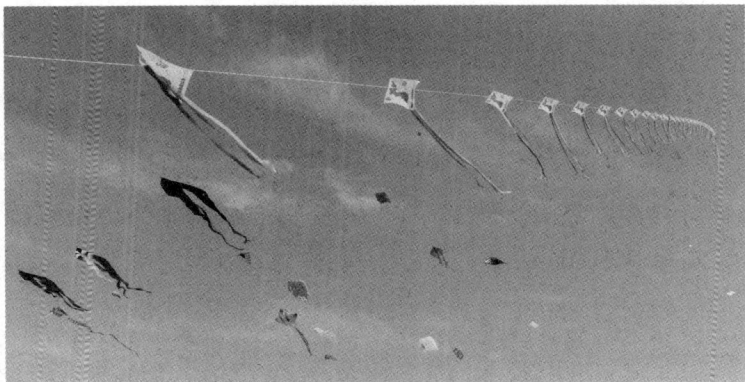

据介绍，今年风筝会实施"走出去"战略，以潍坊风筝、地方文化艺术、景观名胜为主题，扎制装饰独具特色的风筝大篷车，深入到国内重点城市、重要景点，通过进行风筝放飞，风筝及民俗工艺品、潍坊旅游景观名胜图片展演、媒体互动等一系列活动，宣传推介潍坊，展示潍坊风筝的独特魅力。

风筝万里行活动分三个时段进行，计划巡游国内 10 多个重点城市。今年三月，首批出发的风筝艺人们走进南京、上海、杭州、芜湖、济南等城市。第二期 5 月 27 日出发，计划巡游武汉、贵阳、北川等城市，总行程五千余公里。参加万里行的风筝艺人纷纷表示，将会以一流的状态向所到城市展示潍坊风筝的风采，让更多的外地人了解潍坊风筝，喜欢上潍坊风筝。

（作者李中伟，系潍坊晚报记者）

（八）潍坊风筝万里行抵达贵阳

贵阳天无三日晴。在蒙蒙的细雨当中，绿带环绕、风光旖旎的贵州省会贵阳迎来了潍坊风筝万里行放飞队一行。5月31日，由我市知名风筝艺人组成的放飞队在贵阳地标建筑——奥林匹克体育中心前广场上进行潍坊民俗展示与风筝放飞活动，向贵阳市民展示世界风筝都潍坊风筝的魅力。

图片展示精彩潍坊

经过十五六个小时的车程，潍坊风筝万里行成员一行于30日晚近12时才抵达贵阳。贵阳天气多变，晚上下起了细雨，一直持续到第二天仍然是细雨纷飞。

早上8时许，队员们赶到了放飞场地——贵阳奥林匹克体育中心，偌大的空地上，一块

块展示潍坊风筝特色的展板，很快整齐地摆放起来，向贵阳的市民展示世界风筝都的独特魅力。

在展示的展板当中，既有潍坊国际风筝会举办的历史，还有丰富的旅游资源，也有潍坊的民俗文化，更有反映潍坊近年来城市巨大变化的内容。

风筝、年画、民俗，山水、景观、名胜……一张张精美的图片，让贵阳的市民深入了解了潍坊，越来越多的市民被吸引到放飞场地。"以前只听说过潍坊是风筝的故乡，对潍坊并不了解。通过这次展示，可以看出，潍坊还是一个历史文化底蕴深厚的城市。"现场参观的一位市民告诉记者。

展示潍坊、宣传潍坊，是此次万里行活动最重要的目的。潍坊国际风筝会办公室的有关负责人告诉记者，此次活动，就是要通过风筝及民俗工艺品、旅游景观图片展示、媒体互动等活动，宣传推介潍坊，打响城市品牌。

小风筝放飞唱主角

贵阳海拔较高，但是常年风力较小，当天的风力也不例外，潍坊风筝艺人们带来的一些大的风筝便不能如愿放飞，像龙头蜈蚣、巨型水母、喜玛尔图蝴蝶风筝等，这给当地的市民带来了不少的遗憾。

潍坊风筝艺人们做了两手准备，大风筝受风力所限无法放飞，他们精心准备的小风筝也非常具有潍坊特色，潍坊著名风筝艺人谭洪的"五福捧寿"、王兆瑞的"板式蜈蚣"、潍坊国际风筝会办公室统一制作的"三角风筝"等，在艺人们手中，在细雨中轻巧地飞上了天空，和着若隐若现的轻雾，展现出一幅迷人的画面。

在当天的放飞活动中，贵阳市风筝协会的风筝爱好者们也来到了活动现场，他们带来的主要是盘鹰以及一些小型的轻薄风筝，"贵阳常年风力轻小，雨水较多，放飞的风筝也就适应了本地特色，我们的风筝多以轻便、小巧为主，小风、微风的情况都能放飞。"前来参加交流的贵阳市风协秘书长黄云芬告诉记者，"很多材料都是轻便的薄膜，一来是轻了易飞，二是防雨，不容易坏。"

放飞队员带来的印有"中国潍坊"标志的三角风筝，也十分受当地市民的喜爱，一些市民领到了风筝，就在现场放了起来。各式各样的风筝把天空装扮的异常夺目，市民对于潍坊风筝也不吝溢美之词，夸赞潍坊风筝做工精美。几位来参加比赛的风筝选手表示，潍坊风筝世界一流，我们能在家门口看到顶尖的风筝放飞，是一次很好的学习机会。

（作者李中伟，系潍坊晚报记者）

（九）潍坊风筝飞进北川校园

经过几天的长途跋涉，2013 年 6 月 5 日，"喜玛尔图"杯潍坊风筝万里行一行来到第二期活动的目的地——四川省绵阳市北川羌族自治县举行放飞和宣传活动。为了迎接远道而来的客人，北川羌族自治县专门举行了"情系北川、放飞梦想"潍坊风筝北川行活动启动仪式等一系列活动。在永昌小学操场上，两地的风筝艺人及爱好者共同放飞风筝、交流技艺，学校的 1000 余名小学生也在课间时间，兴致勃勃地放飞起了潍坊风筝，欢呼雀跃的孩子们，顿时成为场地上的主角。操场四周，一条条充满真情的横幅，流露出北川对山东、对潍坊深深的感情。

风筝飞进永昌小学　操场成为欢乐海洋

几年前的汶川大地震，对原来的北川县城造成极大的破坏，整个县城几乎成为一片废墟。新的北川县城易地重建，由山东对口援建，位于县城的永昌小学，是山东援建的建筑之一，放飞的场地就在学校的操场上。

6 月 4 日晚上，放飞队一路风尘仆仆来到北川后，第一件事就是看看第二天的天气预报。得知 5 日当天，北川有雨并且是旋转风的消息后，放飞队员心中均是十分着急。

"本来四川风就小，要是再下雨，这风筝可就不好放了。"

一位放飞队队员说。5日8时许，队员们来到永昌小学操场上时，天气预报果然十分准确。细密的雨丝已经下了起来，风不但小，而且风向不稳、时有时无。

好在天公作美。活动的开始时间是上午9时30分，随着活动时间的接近，细密的雨居然停了。雨后的操场上空气清爽、气温宜人，而风虽然还是断断续续，但比刚才要大了不少。放飞队员们顿时提起了精神，赶紧拿出来准备已久的风筝，趁着风力稍大的时机，风筝艺人彭现春的大型软体风筝熊猫，谭洪的风筝老板鱼，李恺的软体风筝太极熊，韩子成的软体风筝凤凰等，一只只风筝便争相飞上了天空。

风筝艺人褚光亮的巨型龙头蜈蚣，也是不甘寂寞，几名放飞队员们干净麻利地摆好，几人托"龙身"，一人牵龙头，轻轻一拉，龙头蜈蚣便摇摇摆摆腾空而起，飞向天空，引来一片啧啧赞叹之声。

风筝放飞，最高兴的还是小学生们。适值学生课间操，千余名学生们纷纷来到操场上。放飞队员从潍坊带来的"三角"风筝成为孩子们的抢手货。队员们有的组装，有的拴线，还有的教着孩子们放飞，很快数以百计的"三角"风筝由孩子们牵着，在操场上欢快地飞了起来，伴着风筝在空中飞舞，还有孩子们一路银铃般的笑声。

天上风筝飞舞，地上欢歌笑语，永昌小学操场上成为欢乐的海洋。

世界风筝都举世闻名 爱好者前来淘金

闻知潍坊风筝放飞队的到来，当地也有大批风筝爱好者来到了放飞场地上，与放飞队队员一起放飞风筝、交流技艺。

今年 74 岁的付明春，是绵阳市风筝俱乐部的主任，这次他带着十几名队员跑了近百里路来到北川，进行放飞交流活动。人物脸谱、国宝熊猫等独具地方特色的风筝，飞舞在空中，与潍坊风筝一道，将天空打扮得十分漂亮。

"我从事风筝放飞活动多年了，借鉴潍坊等地的风筝扎制技巧，设计制作了七条不同的龙头蜈蚣风筝，还获过不少比赛的大奖呢！"他兴冲冲地告诉记者，"不过这次，我们是来学习的，潍坊风筝全国闻名，不论是款式、品种，用料，还是扎制技艺，都大大领先，这么好的机会，可不能放过。"

跟付明春一样，还有不少爱好者来到了放飞场地。借这次放飞活动举办的有利时机，北川县铁牛社区老年风筝俱乐部的队员，还在现场举办了"欢庆'六一'儿童节、邻里放飞中国梦"的放飞活动，"放飞风筝，放飞梦想，祝愿我们早日实现中国梦。"一位老人说。

来自世界风筝都的风筝艺人，那都是顶尖的风筝高手，他们自然是广大风筝爱好者关注的焦点。在放飞之余，不少风筝爱好者会问这问那，咨询一些风筝扎制、放飞中遇到的难题，对于这些，放飞队员毫不藏私，"只有交流才能提高，在交流中他们学到了我们的长处，而他们的一些经验和优点，也对我们扎制风筝大有帮助。"风筝艺人褚光亮告诉记者。他是专门扎制龙头蜈蚣的，在业内他扎制的蜈蚣以易飞、平稳、精巧而闻名，一些扎制上的技巧，他都是毫不保留地告诉了前来咨询的爱好者，"无论是问到什么，我都会一五一十地告诉他们。"

两地携手放飞活动　处处流露真情厚谊

为了配合潍坊的本次活动，北川县做了精心的准备，除了上午举行的"情系北川、放飞梦想"潍坊风筝北川行活动外，下午还举行了两地文化旅游交流座谈会，探讨在文化旅游等方面进行深入合作与交流。

在永昌小学操场风筝放飞活动现场，"潍坊北川携手放飞风筝、鲁川同心促进文化交流"、"大爱无疆、享誉四海、中国羌城、感动全球"、"情系北川、放飞梦想"等一条条标语，分布操场四周。

北川县委宣传部有关人员在介绍情况时表示，潍坊北川情同手足，在灾难面前，潍坊人无私地伸出了援手，帮助北川人民渡过难关，这种情谊弥足珍贵。

记者了解到，潍坊与北川相隔千里，两地在共同抗击地震灾害过程中，结下了深厚友谊。前期北川有关部门专程邀请潍坊到当地举行放飞表演活动，与当地风筝爱好者进行交流，并专程到潍坊学习取经，得到了潍坊市的大力支持，将北川列为潍坊风筝万里行第二期巡游的城市之一。

潍坊风筝万里行引起了当地媒体的高度关注，他们纷纷前来对放飞活动进行宣传报道。北川县委宣传部新闻中心副主任王守雷告诉记者，包括四川日报、华西都市报、新华网、中新社、四川新闻网、绵阳日报、绵阳晚报、绵阳电视台、北川电视台等在内九家媒体参加了当天的活动。

（作者李中伟，系潍坊晚报记者）

（十）古韵流长飞彩鸢
——潍坊风筝万里行第三期首站在安阳启动

魅力安阳，古韵流长，彩鸢飞翔。2013年12月10日至11日，"喜玛尔图"杯潍坊风筝全国万里行活动第三期首站来到具有"殷商故都"、"文字之都"、"中国航空运动之都"美誉之称的河南安阳举行放飞活动。

火凤凰、双飞燕、龙头蜈蚣、魔鬼鱼、花仙子、红青蛙、黄小鸭、花壁虎、长青蛇……12月11日，潍坊市的风筝艺人与当地风筝爱好者来到安阳殷都区商魂广场，把广场上空装扮得五彩缤纷。在放飞现场，潍坊市风筝艺人谭新波还向安阳市民赠送了潍坊风筝。许多市民拿到风筝后立马就加入到了放飞的行列。一根根细细的银线，把潍坊风筝的独特魅力展现在安阳市民面前，也让更多的安阳市民认识了潍坊风筝，也认识了潍坊这座充满活力和生机的世界风筝之都。安阳市风筝运动协会的老艺人薛玉国，他从小就喜欢放风筝，玩风筝已经 30 年了，曾三次到潍坊参加国际风筝会的放飞活动，认为潍坊的风筝品种齐全，应有尽有，本人非常喜爱。今年 65 岁的安阳市民田先生，从 3 岁就开始玩风筝，他得知潍坊风筝万里行到安阳后，当天一大早便到现场，与我市风筝艺人褚光亮成功将龙头蜈蚣风筝送上蓝天。

远在南北朝时，安阳就出现过风筝和风筝载人的故事。从上世纪初，安阳风筝已很活跃。安阳的风筝种类繁多，常见有凤凰、蝙蝠、蝴蝶、螃蟹等多种。放风筝，也成为安阳百姓一项有益有趣的户外活动，成为安阳人的一大爱好。安阳风筝协会会长冯海峰告诉记者，安阳的放飞活动与潍坊的风筝放飞活动一样，主要是群众基础较好，不同的是安阳现在是松散性的，潍坊是产业性的。安阳风筝爱好者非常喜欢潍坊的风筝，每年都要从潍坊采购大量的风筝。当天安阳风筝爱好者还组织了一支特技运动风筝队，为潍坊艺人表演了编队飞行。

内蒙古包头市特技风筝俱乐部会长姜伟从安阳的朋友处得知潍坊风筝万里行要到安阳后，他们提前组织 3 人乘飞机赶到安阳学习、观摩潍坊风筝万里行活动。他们认为，潍坊的风筝已经形成产业，走向世界，很值得学习。

安阳是中华文明的重要发祥地之一，是甲骨文和易经的故乡，自古人杰地灵，历史文化积淀深厚，灿烂的殷商文化给人类留下了历史瑰宝，被誉为"文字之根、文化之根、人祖之根"，期间，放飞团成员还参观了安阳中国古文字博物馆，体会了我国古文字的独特魅力，感受了中华民族丰厚的历史记忆与文化积淀。

（作者侯江宏，系潍坊日报记者 ）

（十一）潍坊风筝万里行活动在安徽合肥举行

淝水上空风和日丽，天鹅湖畔彩鸢飞舞。2013 年 12 月 13 日，"喜玛尔图"杯潍坊风筝全国万里行活动来到安徽省省会合肥市，成功举行放飞活动。

13 日上午，平坦整洁的合肥新市府广场视野开阔，空气清新；旁边的天鹅湖烟波浩渺，风光旖旎；眺望远处的体育场犹如大鹏展翅，在蓝天飞翔。当天一大早，当地市民和风筝爱好者就在此等候着潍坊风筝的到来。不巧的是，合肥当天上午只有微风轻拂，仿佛是在对潍坊风筝能否顺利飞上蓝天进行考验。

虽然风力稍小，不利于放飞，但潍坊风筝艺人们还是克服困难，各显神通，各展绝活。潍坊风筝艺人谭洪凭丰富的放飞经验，先后将彩螺、老板鱼、五福献寿等板式风筝轻松放上蓝天，潍坊风筝艺人李乃增扎制的传统风筝双飞燕，小巧珍珑，做工精细，当天在微风中正好派上用场。只见这对小燕子就像情侣一样，时而顽皮撒娇，时而各奔东西，时而相拥相抱，给观赏的人们增添了无限乐趣。当潍坊风筝大师们让数十种风筝在广场上空轻盈漫舞时，看得观众们畅快淋漓，如醉如痴，不少老人和小孩也加入放飞队伍。合肥"风之缘"俱乐部发起人李奉军已参加潍坊国际风筝会 11 届，他告诉记者："潍坊的风筝是做得最好、玩得最好的，已得到国际风筝爱好者的承认"。

（作者侯江宏，系潍坊日报记者 ）

（十二）英雄城上空彩鸢翱翔

赣江北岸彩鸢竞舞，秋水广场热闹欢腾。2013 年 12 月 14 日，"喜玛尔图"杯潍坊风筝万里行活动来到英雄城南昌市举行放飞活动。

12 月 14 日上午，潍坊风筝全国万里行放飞团成员来到位于赣江北岸红谷滩新区的秋水广场，上演风筝大聚会。当放飞团成员赶到广场时，受到了当地上千南昌市民的热烈欢迎，"热烈欢迎潍坊风筝万里行来昌传经送宝"、"祝潍坊风筝放飞圆满成功"等标语

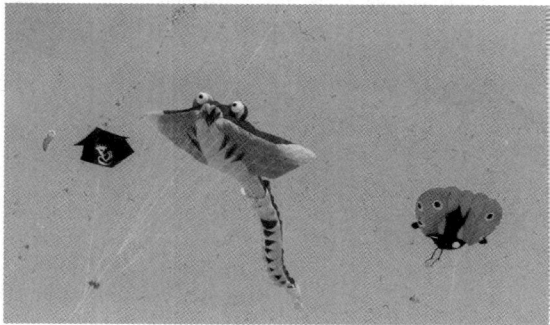

已挂满广场四周，南昌市体育局相关领导也到场表示祝贺。当天，南昌风筝协会组织了 100 余名风筝爱好者加入了放飞队伍，他们纷纷带上了适合在当地放飞的盘鹰、滑翔飞机、十二生生肖等小型特制风筝参加放飞表演，由于秋水广场上空当时风力较小，潍坊放飞团的大型风筝遇到了困难，艺人们只能将一些小型的蝴蝶、燕子、魔幻拇指等板式风筝送上蓝天，与南昌风筝爱好者们的虎、鸡、马、滑翔飞机等风筝共舞，虽然暂时没有达到理想的放飞效果，但潍坊风筝艺人们精湛的放飞表演技术还是让观众们大饱眼福，尤其是所展示出的各式风筝，新颖奇特，做工精细，种类齐全，深受观众们的喜爱。有的观众纷纷围住艺人们讨教风筝的扎制技术和相关知识，有的大胆地与艺人们进行交流和探讨，有的要求预订潍坊风筝，将秋水广场上的活动逐渐推向高潮。

一小时后，秋水广场还是不见风力增大，于是放飞团迅速转

移到秋水广场下赣江北岸的沙滩空地放飞。在适度的风力中，潍坊龙头蜈蚣风筝腾空而起，熊猫、金鱼、魔鬼鱼、长青蛇等大型软体风筝也都大显身手，升空翱翔。在艺人们的表演下，数支潍坊蜜蜂运动风筝就像战机一样轰鸣着，时而左右盘旋，时而上下俯冲，看得观众啧啧称奇。好风凭借力，潍坊艺人与南昌市民将赣江北岸上空装扮五彩缤纷，形态各异、颜色多样的风筝随风劲舞，让驻足观看者都犹如进入了"南鹞北鸢齐亮相"的境界。

（作者侯江宏，系潍坊日报记者 ）

（十三）彩鸢飞进牡丹之乡

国色天香遍地芬芳，五彩风筝漫天飞舞。2013 年 12 月 17 日，"喜玛尔图"杯潍坊风筝万里行走进牡丹之乡菏泽。

12 月 17 日上午，潍坊风筝放飞团来到菏泽市牡丹区第八小学，向 3000 余名小学生们展示了龙头蜈蚣、美丽彩蝶、卡通花仙子、卡通凤凰等潍坊特色风筝。色彩斑斓、造型各异的潍坊风筝，深受学生们的喜爱。在操场上，孩子们团团将风筝艺人围得水泄不通，争先恐后地触摸风筝，好奇地问这问那，艺人们耐心的逐一回答。在现场，风筝艺人王兆瑞向第八小学六年级三班的同学们讲解了潍坊风筝的种类和放飞知识，并以"正"字风筝为例，向孩子们传授了简单风筝的扎制技术。学生们拿着赠送的潍坊三角风筝，喜不自禁，欢呼雀跃，纷纷放飞风筝，围着操场跑起来。当体验到放飞的快乐后，学生们连呼："漂亮！过瘾！"

当天下午，放飞团来到位于曹州牡丹园对面的中国林展馆广场，放飞了小蝌蚪找妈妈、龙头蜈蚣、大章鱼、长青蛇、红金鱼等大小数十种风筝。漫天飞舞的彩鸢，让菏泽市民们大饱眼福，感受到了潍坊风筝的无穷魅力。

本次潍坊风筝万里行第三期活动，主要走进安阳、合肥、南昌、菏泽四城市，途中开展了风筝放飞表演、图片展览、现场讲解宣传、风筝文化进校园等系列活动，传播弘扬了风筝文化，加深了外地人对潍坊的了解，提升了潍坊城市品牌形象。

（作者侯江宏，系潍坊日报记者）

潍坊风筝代表团参加第 35 届澳大利亚邦迪国际风筝会

应澳大利亚韦弗利市委员会和新西兰阿什伯顿风筝协会的邀请，由潍坊国际风筝会办公室主任张崇高任团长的潍坊市风筝代表团，于 2013 年 9 月 6 日，赴澳大利亚参加了第 35 届邦迪国际风筝会。

本次出访的主要任务是，参加第 35 届澳大利亚邦迪国际风筝会，放飞表演潍坊风筝代表作品－龙头蜈蚣风筝；与当地风筝会组织者交流办会经验，互通信息，探讨双方节会合作，建立友好节会事宜；与各国风筝代表队交流，并邀请高水平风筝队参加潍坊国际风筝会。

2013 年 9 月 6 日至 10 日，潍坊代表团在澳大利亚韦弗利市海滩参加了第 35 届澳大利亚邦迪国际风筝会风筝放飞和比赛活动。第 35 届邦迪风筝会规模大、影响大，我市属首次组团参加，

在为期 3 天的放飞比赛中，成功放飞了潍坊风筝代表作——红色的 50 米长的龙头蜈蚣风筝，这一带有中国文化元素的潍坊风筝在当地引起了轰

动，游人纷纷与之合影留念。

第35届澳大利亚邦迪国际风筝会，我市风筝代表团充分展示了高水平风筝制作和放飞技术，展示了世界潍坊风筝都潍坊的风采。期间，经过与韦弗利市政府代表洽谈，双方达成深化风筝文化合作意向，该市风筝协会还就风筝贸易、展览展示与我团达成协议。同时，代表团向韦弗利市市长和议长赠送了精美的潍坊风筝及潍坊风筝会光盘。本次赛事，英国、新西兰等一批风筝高手参加了放飞表演，风筝特色突出，展示了当今国际上风筝新的潮流，代表团拟邀请他们来潍坊参加第31届潍坊国际风筝会，提升风筝会赛事水平和观赏性。澳洲各大媒体对邦迪海滩风筝节盛况进行了报道，中国新华社都在第一时间进行了图文报道，特别对代表团风筝专家刘志平放飞的龙头蜈蚣风筝，作了突出报道。

通过参加邦迪风筝会，潍坊代表团开阔了视野，广交了朋友，收获很大。办好风筝会就要不断追求创新和瞄准国际一流水准。在这方面邦迪风筝会树立了榜样，每届风筝会都有创新标准，要求都很明确。今年突出了海洋环境保护—大批海底动物风筝，如大个头鲸鱼风筝等格外夺人眼球。此外，今年重点邀请了中国潍坊市、英国、新西兰等国高水平、有特色的风筝队，为风筝节增添了光彩。

以人为本，为市民和游客广泛参与创造条件。邦迪风筝会组委会将整个海滩作了科学划分，放飞区域分为大风筝比赛放飞区、中小风筝比赛放飞区、自由表演区。在比赛放飞区，为每位参赛者都投保了巨额人身意外伤害保险。此外，还设立了风筝扎制表演和风筝销售区，文化表演区，美食销售区，工艺品销售区等，吸引了广大市民和游客的广泛参与。

节俭务实办节。邦迪风筝会由该市风筝协会具体组织，市场化运作，经费自筹，不搞铺张浪费。中午放飞队员一律吃盒饭。

高度重视风筝文化传承。在邦迪风筝会上，组委会邀请了一批风筝专家现场进行风筝设计制作，吸引了大批少年儿童现场学习。

（作者张崇高，系国际风筝联合会秘书长 潍坊国际风筝会办公室原主任）

英国班戈大学孔子学院风筝节侧记

2013 年 11 月 15 日，由英国班戈大学孔子学院成功组织了为期两周的风筝节。风筝节包括 19 场活动，超过 1000 人参加了活动。其中 12 场是在班戈、考文湾、坎大风、兰迪诺的中小学进行的风筝绘画工作坊，共有 500 多名学生参加了活动。通过在中小学组织活动，孔子学院与这 12 所学校建立了比较固定的关系。

其中 4 场活动是在班戈、Holyhead、坎大风、兰迪诺的艺术中心进行的，吸引了 450 多名公众参加。在艺术中心或工作室举行的活动，还包括与风筝相关的讲座和室内放飞表演。在班戈大学进行的活动还进行了风筝绘画的比赛。在一所特殊学校的画风筝活动中，学校老师表示，有一位学生平时集中精力 5 分钟都是困难的，而那天画风筝的活动使他集中精力超过了 30 分钟，这是前所未有的。

为了搞好风筝节，在班戈大学孔子学院中方合作院校中国政法大学和潍坊市政府的协助下，孔子学院与世界风筝都潍坊的风筝艺人王永训先生取得了联系。王永训先生曾在潍坊国际风筝大赛中获作品一等奖、被授予"潍坊市工艺美术大师"称号，他也是潍坊风筝非物质文化遗产的传承人。

在班戈大学孔子学院的活动中，王永训先生讲述了关于风筝的历史和文化，大学生们还参与了与风筝相关的猜谜和画风筝比赛活动。在坎大风一艺术工作坊的活动吸引了对风筝感兴趣的当地民众。王永训先生的讲座持续了约 2 小时之久，听众也提出了一些颇为专业的问题，包括风筝在古代有什么用途、如何放飞巨大的"龙"风筝、哪个部位先放飞、风筝的制作、室内放飞风筝的空气动力学问题等。

北爱尔兰孔子学院的中英方院长也应邀前来参加了活动，班戈大学孔子学院的院长们、项目官员、老师们、志愿者、学生大使们通力合作，完成了宣传、原材料的购买、风筝大师的邀请和签证、与各学校及艺术中心的联系、各类法律许可程序（拍照许可、新闻许可、放飞许可、保险等）、活动材料的运输、现场组织等工作。

在最后兰迪诺海滨的放飞活动中，有300人参加了放飞活动，有的人是多次参加孔子学院组织的风筝活动，有一个小姑娘随全家从坎大风追到兰迪诺，参加了3场对公众开放的活动。总之，此次活动对扩大孔子学院的影响力起到了很大的作用。活动结束后，还不断有人询问有关风筝节的活动，如在市长参加的世界文化日活动预备会上，多人提到孔子学院的风筝活动。

英国班戈大学孔子学院由国家汉办、孔子学院总部批准设立，由中国政法大学和英国班戈大学合作共建，于2012年9月举行揭牌仪式。该孔子学院以班戈大学为依托，开设面向全校在校学生的汉语学分课程，支持法学院开设"法律与中文"的LLB学位课程，有关汉语教学与中国文化活动延伸到中小学和社区。

（潍坊天成飞鸢风筝有限公司供稿）

潍坊风筝文化走进福建湄洲岛系列活动

"妈祖故里，放飞希望"潍坊风筝文化走进湄洲岛系列活动于 2014 年 8 月 29 日至 31 日，在福建省莆田市湄洲岛举行。本次活动由国际风筝联合会、莆田市人民政府、潍坊市人民政府主办，湄洲岛国家旅游度假区管委会、潍坊国际风筝会办公室承办。系列活动与"2014 湄洲岛海峡两岸夏季沙滩风筝节"融为一体，内容包括新闻发布会、开幕式、风筝放飞、风筝展览、国际风筝工艺大师现场技艺表演、风筝文化进校园村庄等活动，并以国际风联秘书处名义授予湄洲岛"潍坊国际风筝会放飞基地"铜牌。

8 月 29 日举行了开幕式，并在莲池沙滩设置风筝放飞表演区域和风筝展览展示区域。举行开幕式后，放飞了特制的高 14.35 米的大型妈祖主题风筝，数百只潍坊传统风筝与现代风筝同台放飞表演。同时，组织游客和市民进行一种娱乐性强的"球形"风筝放飞比赛，获胜者将获赠体现妈祖或潍坊风筝文化元素的特制风筝一只。在风筝展览展示区域，主要展示上千只独具特色魅力的风筝，包括潍坊传统与现代精品风筝、体现妈祖文化元素的特制风筝、获得吉尼斯世界纪录的风筝以及大型室外铁艺风筝等。国际风筝工艺大师王永训、谭新

波、杨云胜莅临现场，拿出各自绝活，进行了风筝制作技艺表演，并与游客和市民进行教学互动。此外，组委会在现场向游客和市民赠送了体现风筝文化和妈祖文化元素的特制风筝 2000 余只。除在莲池沙滩举办风筝放飞表演和风筝展览展示外，潍坊风筝专家还深入当地有关学校、自然村，开展了风筝制作技艺的现场讲授和示范表演。

为了确保本次活动圆满成功，潍坊市风筝界的数十名精兵强将，3 名国际风筝工艺大师，以及特邀来自台湾风筝推广协会的 4 名队员为此做了充分筹备，并在现场作了精彩表演和展示，其中为本次活动特制的大型妈祖风筝、软体鲨鱼、海狮戏球、珍珠鱼、螃蟹、龙虾、老鹰、孔雀等各式风筝格外引人注目。

这次潍坊风筝文化走进湄洲岛系列活动，标志着两地友好合作的新开端，将进一步加强潍坊与莆田两市的风筝文化交流，密切两地的友好合作关系，弘扬风筝文化和妈祖文化，促进两市风筝文化产业的合作发展，为今后在更多领域的更广泛深入合作奠定更加深厚的基础。

（作者张崇高，系国际风筝联合会秘书长，潍坊国际风筝会办公室原主任）

潍坊国际风筝会创新设立全国分区选拔赛

潍坊国际风筝会全国风筝分区选拔赛，始创于2014年第31届潍坊国际风筝会之前，先后在山东青岛、四川北川、贵州万山、辽宁沈阳等地设立分赛区，按照国际比赛规则，在全国范围内选拔优秀风筝代表队和特色风筝，符合条件的应邀参加潍坊国际风筝会。从2014年到2017年，4年的分区选拔赛，在全国范围内选拔了一大批优秀代表队和特色风筝，参与潍坊国际风筝会的国际大赛和放飞表演。此举提高了潍坊国际风筝会的放飞比赛档次，促进了风筝运动的普及和提高，弘扬了风筝文化，打造了城市品牌，取得了实效，在国内外产生了广泛影响。

（作者张崇高，系国际风筝联合会秘书长，潍坊国际风筝会办公室原主任）

潍坊风筝展在澳门举行

2016 年 5 月 25 日，为期 30 天的《翱翔银河》风筝展在澳门银河娱乐城举行，风筝《飞龙在天》与《凤凰展翅》交相辉映。此次展出的 60 款风筝来自被誉为"世界风筝都"的潍坊，是多次在潍坊国际风筝会上获奖的作品。这些风筝造型优美、扎工精细、色彩艳丽、

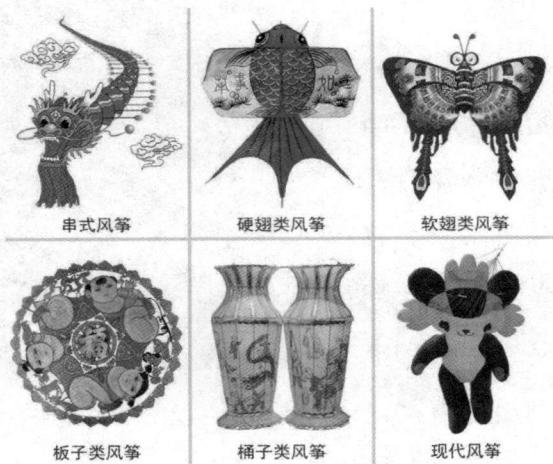

串式风筝　　硬翅类风筝　　软翅类风筝

板子类风筝　　桶子类风筝　　现代风筝

风格独特，不仅为澳门市民和游客带来美的感受，还让人们近距离了解中国传统工艺风筝的文化、技艺及内涵。

澳门银河娱乐集团负责人祁礼敦先生表示，《翱翔银河》风筝展，把潍坊的工艺、色彩与传统带到了澳门。宾客可透过 60 款风筝及别具特色的艺术品，探究中国优秀的传统工艺。

来自山东潍坊天成飞鸢风筝有限公司的李宝全师傅，在接受记者采访时说，作为潍坊市非物质文化遗产传承人，在多年从事风筝扎制技艺的时间里，不断对传统技艺进行挖掘、创新，逐渐形成了自己独特的风格。现在他们制作的风筝已走出国门，先后在数十个国家和地区举办展览和交流活动。

此次《翱翔银河》风筝展中最具震撼力、最具创意的巨型风筝——《飞龙在天》与亮丽夺目、气派万千的《凤凰展翅》，交相辉映地腾空飞翔在澳门银河娱乐城的明珠大堂，给人以强烈的

视觉冲击和美的感受。而以《三国演义》中家喻户晓的历史人物为题材的风筝，更是以丰富的艺术表现形式活灵活现地呈现在人们的眼前。此次展出的部分风筝已有40多年的历史，是风筝中的艺术精品。

中国山东潍坊风筝制作技艺于2006年5月20日，被国务院批准列入第一批国家级非物质文化遗产名录，潍坊风筝是中国风筝中的一个重要流派，它造型优美、绘画艳丽、扎制牢靠、品种繁多、起飞灵活，具有浓郁的乡土气息和民间生活气息，蜚声古今中外。每年一届的潍坊国际风筝会吸引了多个国家和地区的风筝代表队参赛。

（作者王永训，系中国风筝协会副主席，潍坊市风筝产业协会会长）

潍坊风筝展在香港成功举办

2015 年 9 月 12 日至 14 日，由山东省人民政府港澳事务办公室、山东省文化厅、山东省政协港澳台侨和外事委员会、香港中国 21 世纪友好协进会联合主办的"感知传统文化"山东文化交流系列活动在香港南区数码港隆重举行。此次文化交流的重要活动之一"山东风筝艺术导赏——山东潍坊风筝展暨山东风筝同乐日"同期举办。"山东风筝艺术导赏——山东潍坊风筝展暨山东风筝同乐日"活动由潍坊市政协、潍坊国际风筝会办公室赴香港代表团负责承办。

据介绍，"山东风筝艺术导赏——山东潍坊风筝展暨山东风筝同乐日"主要进行了 3 项交流活动。一是在香港南区数码港举办潍坊风筝展览。据悉，现场布展了大型龙头蜈蚣等潍坊精品风筝 200 多只，悬挂了 15 米 ×1.2 米大型壁画《风筝魂》长卷，由风筝大师、年画大师进行现场制作表演，教授少年儿童现场扎制风筝、印刷年画，进行室内无风风筝放飞表演，山东 10 名书画家现场在风筝上示范作画等。二是在附近滨海公园放飞各具特色的风筝。活动期间，代表团成功放飞了各种特制山东名家书画风筝，以及特制大小黄鸭风筝、潍坊龙头蜈蚣风筝以及人物、老虎、章鱼等风筝。各种风筝陆续放飞，使香港市民亲身感受到潍坊风筝带来的欢乐。三是与香港有关团体、企业进行风筝产业合作洽谈。代表团加大沟通力度，与香港中国 21 世纪友好协进会和两家文化企业进行了务实洽谈和交流。

在友好热烈的气氛中，为期3天的"山东风筝艺术导赏——山东潍坊风筝展暨山东风筝同乐日"活动圆满地落下帷幕。"同乐日"活动有力地展示推介了潍坊风筝和年画艺术，通过风筝、年画展演，加强了与香港市民近距离交流，扩大了潍坊风筝和年画的知名度，促进了潍坊风筝、年画所承线的传统文化传播，先后吸引2万余名香港市民到场参观和交流互动。

"同乐日"还突出展现了潍坊风筝运动的魅力。现场放飞的潍坊传统风筝如龙头蜈蚣、蝴蝶、老虎、人物、书画风筝（大的3只、小的10只）、大小黄鸭风等，都给香港市民留下了美好印象。同时，代表团免费向市民赠送了数百只印有潍坊风筝都标志的特色三角风筝，吸引了广大市民参与放飞。

不仅如此，"同乐日"还促成了双方合作发展风筝文化产业的共识。据了解，潍坊国际风筝会办公室赴香港代表团与香港21世纪友好协进会进行了深入洽谈并达成共识，拟从明年开始，此项活动升格为香港风筝节，此举将对推动潍坊风筝、旅游、文化发展起到重要作用。同时，与香港有关企业达成了合作开发风筝旅游纪念品的意向。

此外，"同乐日"活动也提升了潍坊城市美誉度和文化传播。香港《文汇报》等多家媒体先后对活动进行了跟踪报道，代表团准备的1000册潍坊宣传画册，一幅大型壁画《风筝魂》长卷在现场也得到充分展示。LED大屏幕滚动播出潍坊国际风筝会万人放飞的盛况，风筝大师、年画大师现场手把手地进行示范教学，这些举措都有力地传播了以风筝、年画文化为代表的潍坊传统文化，提升了潍坊市的知名度和美誉度。

（作者张崇高，系国际风筝联合会秘书长，潍坊国际风筝会办公室原主任）

潍坊风筝代表团参加美国旧金山风筝会侧记

2015年5月30日至6月3日，应美国旧金山风筝会组委会邀请，潍坊市组成由潍坊国际风筝会办公室副主任李伟带队，王金祥、范梅庆、刘志平、王永训等为队员的潍坊风筝代表团，赴美国进行了风筝文化交流及经济、贸易、文化活动的洽谈，按期圆满地完成了出访任务。

5月31日，在美国旧金山市，代表团参加了旧金山风筝会暨运动风筝比赛活动。该风筝比赛规模大、影响大。运动风筝比赛在我国是正在蓬勃发展的风筝运动项目，在潍坊市举办的世界风筝锦标赛中运动风筝比赛是重要的比赛项目。代表团积极与当地的风筝协会及赛事组织者进行了广泛的交流，互通情况、信息及办会经验；代表团还成功放飞了潍坊传统风筝蝴蝶风筝、金鱼风筝等中国传统风筝。带有中国文化元素的潍坊风筝在当地引起了轰动，游人竞相与之合影留念。

6月1日至2日，在圣拉蒙市，代表团参加了由当地文化协会组织的青少年户外风筝和剪纸艺术文化交流活动。代表团首先向大家介绍了中国及潍坊传统风筝历史、制作工艺和放飞技艺等，大家非常兴奋地见识了工艺精湛的潍坊传统风筝和潍坊剪纸艺术。

大多数孩子都是第一次接触潍坊的剪纸艺术，第一次亲手放飞造型各异五彩缤飞的中国传统风筝，并对潍坊的民间文化艺术表现

出浓厚兴趣，惊叹不已。

代表团实地查看、了解潍坊硅谷高科技孵化器暨潍坊中美技术交流中心的建设、运营情况。与美国怀俄明州 James W. Byrd 议员的代表洽谈在黄石公园举办潍坊风筝放飞表演及展览。深入当地的风筝销售商店，双方在风筝贸易合作方面进行了深入的探讨，业务交流。

本次参加美国旧金山风筝会暨运动风筝比赛，潍坊市风筝代表团充分展示了中国传统风筝制作和放飞技术，以及悠久的历史文化。特别是独具特色的蓝蝶风筝吸引了大批观众。经过与该风筝会组织者及有关成员洽谈，双方达成深化风筝文化合作意向，并初步达成协议：2016 年在美国怀俄明州黄石公园举办潍坊风筝放飞表演及展览。本次赛事，当地一批风筝高手参加了放飞表演，风筝特色突出，展示了当今国际上风筝新的潮流。

通过本次出访，代表团主要有以下收获和体会：

突出创新重点。旧金山风筝节每届都有创新要求。今年突出了运动风筝的潮流，空中芭蕾运动风筝格外夺人眼球。

突出以人为本。旧金山风筝节组委会将整个放飞场地作了科学划分，放飞区域分类大风筝比赛放飞区，中小风筝比赛放飞区；自由表演区。在比赛放飞区，为每位参赛者都投保了巨额人身意外伤害保险。吸引了广大市民和游客的广泛参与和互动。

突出学生动手能力培养和潜移默化教育。美国对学生们的教育，特别注重的是自我能力的培养以及民族文化价值的认同感。

（作者刘志平，系国际风筝联合会执委，潍坊国际风筝办公室业务科科长）

海峡两岸风筝文化交流活动越办越好

　　海峡两岸风筝文化交流活动始于 2007 年，至今已连续成功举办了 11 届。这项活动由潍坊市人民政府主办，潍坊市人民政府台湾事务办公室、潍坊国际风筝会办公室、潍坊市教育局承办。通过开展这项活动，加强了两岸青少年的友谊，使他们加深了对中国历史文化和风筝文化的认知。

　　4 月芳菲，万物生辉，一场春雨的洗礼让风筝的色彩更加鲜亮。2017 年 4 月 17 日上午，第 10 届海峡两岸风筝文化交流活动之"走进风筝故里·感知齐鲁文化"风筝创意绘制比赛活动在坊子区现代风筝文化创意创业园举行，来自台湾海峡两岸交流促进协会、台湾大仁科技大学师生及我市大学师生代表共 100 余人参加了此次活动。

　　活动现场，两岸青少年们参观了风筝制作工艺，合作完成了风筝创意绘制比赛，并共同进行了风筝放飞。活动进一步增强了两岸青少年们对风筝传统文化的认知，拓展了两岸交往交流渠道。

　　据了解，第 10 届海峡两岸风筝文化交流活动将从 4 月 14 日持续至 21 日，其间将进行潍台青年风筝放飞、"印象台湾"手绘墙、两岸青年创业交流等多项活动，不断增进两岸文化、经贸交流与合作。

　　（作者王永训，系中国风筝协会副主席，潍坊市风筝产业协会会长）

赴德国参加冲浪风筝质量标准国际会议侧记

应德国标准化委员会邀请，受中国国家体育总局委派，为了研讨制定统一的国际冲浪风筝质量标准，潍坊国际风筝会办公室组成代表团，由会展科科长石岳带队，业务科科员纪晓强，潍坊国际风筝工艺大师王永训一行 3 人，于 2017 年 2 月 19 日至 2 月 23 日，赴德国慕尼黑市，参加了由 ISO 国际质量标准委员会主办，德国标准化委员会承办的首次国际冲浪风筝质量标准制定国际会议。

会议从 2 月 20 日开始至 21 日，为期两天。会议地点在慕尼黑市奥伯哈兴镇 Keltenring 街 Boards & More 北方风筝冲浪体育用品有限公司一楼会议室。与会人员除潍坊风筝代表团成员外，有 ISO 风筝冲浪质量标准工作小组负责人、德国标准化协会秘书长，法国迪卡侬体育用品有限公司代表，法国国家风帆与水上运动学院代表，德国 Boards & More 北方风筝冲浪体育用品有限公司代表，英国风筝冲浪协会代表，世界风筝冲浪运动协会秘书长、德国风筝冲浪运动员代表等。

此次会议为上述工作小组第一次正式会议，主要议题是冲浪风筝安全释放系统质量标准的制定。此次会议时间紧，议题新，研讨取得实效。

根据会议日程，两天的会议各分为两部分内容。第一天的会议，第一部分内容，是各国代表就本国的冲浪风筝质量标准进行发言，就提纲内容开展讨论，讨论提纲由法国代表提交，内容是就冲浪风筝安全释放系统专业术语的定义开展讨论。

第二部分内容，是潍坊风筝代表团与 ISO 专家 Jens Bauch 进行探讨，回答 Jens Bauch 先生对中国风筝质量标准的技术性提问。

第二天的会议，第一部分内容，是根据第一天的会议进度，就冲浪风筝在设计、安全要求、特定状况、测试方法、仪器、检测状态及风筝的耐受力等技术性指标的术语进行定义与解释。第二部分内容，是潍坊风筝代表团向全体代表推介潍坊国际风筝会，交流节庆开展情况。

潍坊风筝代表团对此次会议十分重视，会前做了充分准备，了解掌握了中国各地近十几年开展风筝冲浪竞赛活动情况，冲浪风筝制造原理及市场营销状况，就冲浪风筝标准制定涉及的关键环节和问题形成了有关思路、方法和对策建议。与会期间，代表团积极发言交流，与各国代表作了认真沟通，传达了潍坊暨中国声音。会期虽短，但代表团不虚此行，有以下收获：

1. 主动发声，就中国冲浪风筝标准进行了专题性发言，提出了有根据的意

见建议，引起会议主办方和与会代表的关注。

2. 助推了冲浪风筝标准化进程，其中标准化术语解释制定进展顺利，已形成了初步草案，上传平台，进一步广泛征求意见。

3. 在首次召开的这一领域重要国际会议上，代表团认真回答了 ISO 专家 Jens Bauch 的技术性提问，并与其充分沟通交流，达成了共识，ISO 专家 Jens Bauch 同意将中国冲浪风筝质量标准作为借鉴和参考的依据；

4. 代表团积极推介潍坊国际风筝会和潍坊风筝文化，同时通过与参会代表交谈，了解了德国、法国、英国及其他欧洲国家运动风筝，以及风筝冲浪运动开展的情况，为有针对性邀请高水平欧洲风筝代表队参加潍坊国际风筝会创造了有力条件。

潍坊风筝代表团完成参会任务并顺利归国后，为扩大会议成果，进一步抓了有关工作落实。

1. 与 ISO 冲浪风筝质量标准工作小组保持了密切联系，随时沟通反馈有关信息，保证标准制定工作按时如期完成。

2. 着手开展了标准化术语的汉语版本翻译工作。

3. 加强遥联，及时发出邀请函，邀请有关国家风筝代表队按期参加了 2017 年第 34 届潍坊国际风筝会。

（作者石岳，国际风筝联合会执委，潍坊国际风筝会办公室会展科科长；作者纪晓强，系潍坊国际风筝会办公室业务科科员）

潍坊风筝代表团出访新西兰和澳大利亚

应新西兰奥克兰发展局、澳大利亚维多利亚对外经济、就业、交通、资源部邀请，为洽谈交流会展领域项目合作，潍坊市组成由潍坊国际风筝会办公室主任张崇高任团长的文化与经贸代表

团，于 2016 年 6 月 30 日至 7 月 7 日，赴新西兰奥克兰市、澳大利亚墨尔本市成功地进行了以风筝文化产业和会展项目交流、合作为主题的出访活动。

在新西兰奥克兰，代表团与新西兰奥克兰市屋仑华侨会所（新西兰亚洲信托基金会）主席李勃等高层人员进行了务实洽谈，就加强风筝文化交流与产业合作，以及明年潍坊国际风筝会期间新西兰毛利风筝文化走进潍坊达成了共识，双方正式签署了书面合作协议。同时，张崇高主任全面介绍了潍坊风筝文化历史、风筝会的创新发展、国际风联等情况，对方负责人李勃、张培军等分别介绍了新西兰的风筝文化及产业情况，会上展示了代表

团带来的潍坊风筝文化及风筝会图片长卷。同时，代表团还向对方赠送了潍坊国际风筝会及潍坊会展业有关宣传资料。

实地察看了奥克兰国际会展中心，就奎文区拟于明年春组织部分外贸企业到奥克兰举办会展事宜，以及现场举行潍坊风筝放飞表演等，与该会展中心进行了友好洽谈，届时拟用该会展中心展厅面积 6000 平方米，展位安排 150 个以上。

与新西兰新溪岛蜂蜜有限公司，就同奎文区山东曜海国际贸易有限公司合作搭建跨境电商平台及海外仓库项目进行了深入探讨和交流，并实际考察了正在建设的海外仓库项目。

在澳大利亚悉尼，代表团与悉尼奥林匹克公园合作，举办了"潍坊风筝文化展演活动"，国际风筝工艺大师王永训作了现场风筝扎制放飞示范表演，代表团成员与现场市民共同放飞了各具特色的潍坊风筝，并向现场部分少年、儿童赠送了印有中英文对照的"世界风筝都——潍坊"欢迎您字样的三角风筝。

代表团与墨尔本市图书馆就建立风筝文化友好合作伙伴进行了友好洽谈，达成了共识。该馆将开辟一个宣传窗口，对潍坊市提供的宣传资料进行宣传展示。在会谈现场，还举行了赠送仪式，代表团向该馆赠送了潍坊国际风筝会宣传图册及风筝放飞视频光盘。

在墨尔本市皇家植物园，代表团按计划成功地开展了潍坊风筝放飞表演活动，现场放飞了 10 多种潍坊风筝，吸引了不少市民观赏。同时，向现场市民赠送了部分潍坊风筝。

与墨尔本山东同乡会及山东恒易投资集团恒易（澳大利亚公司）进行了工作交流。现场查看了恒易（澳大利亚公司）项目进展情况，就奎文区企业走出去，在澳洲投资优惠政策及相关事宜进行了探讨和交流。同时，代表团向该公司赠送了潍坊国际风筝会长卷和潍坊会展业宣传图册。

通过此次出访代表团有以下收获：

潍坊风筝文化在此次国际交流中得到进一步传承、弘扬。此次出访，通过与有关方面洽谈交流和风筝放飞表演，突出展示了潍坊风筝的特色和魅力，有力地宣传推介了潍坊城市品牌，同时，代表团成员也深切感受到了潍坊风筝在国外深受人们喜爱的程度。

潍坊风筝产业拓宽了新的发展平台和空间。依托奥克兰会展中心和奥克兰国家博览馆、屋仑华侨会所，以及与奥克兰风筝工作室、墨尔本图书馆等的合作，潍坊风筝产业发展迎来新的发展机遇，前景更加看好。

潍坊会展业创新转型得到有益借鉴。通过实地考察了解，奥克兰会展中心精心打造的"绿色与生活展"、墨尔本市精心打造的"国际包装展"等展会活动的经验做法，十分值得我市同行学习借鉴。

通过此次出访代表团有以下体会：

主动"走出去"进行拓展，有针对性地传播潍坊风筝文化，开展会展项目合作，是扩大潍坊影响力，促进会展业、风筝产业转型发展的重要举措。

加强与当地华人协会的沟通和联系，沟通信息，增进了解，加深友谊，建立战略合作关系，整合资源，是潍坊会展业、风筝产业走向国际市场的一个有效途径。

发扬"工匠精神"，制作独具特色的精品风筝，唱响"潍坊制造"品牌，不仅有利于弘扬传承潍坊风筝文化，扩大潍坊市的知名度和美誉度，而且有利于促进潍坊风筝产业可持续发展和做强风筝国际贸易。

（作者韩军，系潍坊国际风筝会办公室综合科科长）

潍坊风筝放飞新西兰

2018年9月12日上午11时，新西兰首都百年名校塞缪尔·马斯顿女子学校的六年级女生凯丽·罗斯，兴奋地看着自己亲手制作的风筝飞上了天空。"这还是我第一次放飞自己制作的风筝，太有趣了！"这位12岁的新西兰少女知道即将到来的2019年是"中国－新西兰旅游年"，她相信明年会有很多机会体验到来自中国的有趣民俗，更希望将来有机会去中国潍坊实地体验各式风筝的放飞。

和凯丽·罗斯一样兴奋的，还有来自这所学校的其他60多名新西兰女生。9月7日、12日上午，由新西兰中国文化中心、山东省文化厅共同举办的"非遗进校园——山东潍坊风筝扎制及展演活动"走进维多利亚大学孔子学院旗下塞缪尔·马斯顿学校孔子课堂，特别邀请国家级非物质文化遗产项目风筝代表性传承人郭洪利走进该校园，为该校七年级、六年级女生依次讲述中国传统风筝文化，让更多的新西兰学子了解这一源自中国的古老技艺。这是新西兰中国文化中心常年推进的"非遗进校园"系列文化展示活动之一，旨在为即将到来的2019"中新旅游年"引入富有中国地域特色的民俗文化内容，让有意前往中国旅行的新西兰居民获知更多饶有趣味的中国文化精品。

在塞缪尔·马斯顿学校孔子课堂上，经中文老师刘晶莹、中文助教王圆圆与中国文化中心工作人员文德的翻译协助，60多名女生全神贯注地聆听郭洪利介绍有关中国风筝的传统技艺，认真记录下风筝扎制的"四大窍门"，即扎、糊、绘、放的细节与要领。

自幼喜爱风筝艺术、擅长潍坊传统风筝创制的郭洪利，曾先后参加 2008 年北京奥运会、2011 年上海世博会文化展示活动，前往近 30 个国家和地区进行风筝放飞与扎制展演，其本人创制的龙头蜈蚣风筝更是在首届中国非物质文化遗产博览会上夺得金奖。

"在中国，风筝上往往绘有吉祥寓意的图案，以表达人们对美好生活的向往、追求与憧憬。"郭洪利悉心指导每位学生创制一只专属于自己的"原创风筝"放飞校园上空，勉励她们尽情发挥自己的想象力，在风筝专用砂纸上描绘出自己最心仪的图案。

七年级的伊莎贝尔·佩森尼斯提在风筝上画出了一只栩栩如生的大熊猫，并用工整的中文写下"熊猫"二字。当问及为何选择这一图案时，她兴奋地表示："熊猫是中国的国宝级动物，憨态可掬，十分可爱，真希望有机会去中国实地看一看大熊猫。"

同为七年级的佩奇·马丁则以一只毛利风情十足的猫头鹰画作吸引了大家的目光。她得意地说："希望我制作的这只毛利风格的猫头鹰风筝，可以承载着新西兰毛利部落的各种传说，一直飞到中国去，把这些精彩的故事讲述给中国人听。"

"根据史书记载，一位叫李邺的匠人在宫中制作纸鸢，并在纸鸢的头部系上竹哨，在天空放飞时，风吹入竹哨中，就会发出像'筝'一样的声音。故称之为'风筝'。"课堂上，郭洪利以通俗易懂的语言向塞缪尔·马斯顿学校女生讲解中国风筝的起源、发展史与种类，称以潍坊风筝为代表的中国风筝距今已有两千多年历史，早期的风筝主要承担军事战争中传递信息的角色，随时间推移，其军事用途逐渐被娱乐功能取代，成为一项老少皆宜的运动娱乐方式和中国第一批非物质文化遗产项目。

在塞缪尔·马斯顿学校操场上，郭洪利为女生们重点示范了风筝的放飞过程，强调了放飞风筝的关键技巧："一手持着风筝的线轮，一手拉住风筝的提线，等一股风来临，顺势将风筝放飞，根据风速和风向的变化，不断收缩提线的长度，以更好地控制

风筝的平衡。"在郭洪利的耐心指导下，新西兰女生亲手制作的风筝犹如曼妙的精灵，在空中随风飞舞。

令新西兰女生大开眼界的是，郭洪利针对惠灵顿大风天气居多的特点，带来了适合大风放飞的软体类章鱼、眼镜蛇等造型的巨型风筝放飞体验，眼见 100 米长的蛇形风筝、26 平方米之巨的章鱼造型风筝随风而上，偌大的天空瞬间变得五彩斑斓、灵动有趣，引得新西兰女生个个兴奋不已、欢呼雀跃，直呼这是她们第一次亲眼见证如此巨大的风筝扶摇升空、遨游天际，也让她们对郭洪利口中的"一年一度吸引数万只巨型风筝集体放飞的潍坊国际风筝会"盛况神往不已。以郭洪利多年实践来看，风筝项目不啻文化旅游与体育竞技的完美结合。

新西兰中国文化中心主任郭宗光表示："中新两国旅游合作

发展势头强劲，中国已成为新西兰第二大游客来源国，随着 2019 年中新旅游年到来，两国旅游业发展及文化交流有望进一步加快

步伐，中国文化中心将联合诸多合作方推出精彩纷呈的旅游概念文化精品活动。"为迎接即将到来的 2019 "中新旅游年"，新西兰中国文化中心已着手推进一系列促进中新两国文化、旅游交流互鉴的精彩活动。如 8 月 9 日，惠灵顿市政府、新西兰中国文化中心共同签署 2018-2019 年度面向惠灵顿市政府及文化、旅游机构工作人员的旅游商务中文培训课程合作备忘录，为迎接 2019 "中新旅游年" 并推动两国旅游业可持续发展与文化交流做好基础性服务。

（编译）

全面系统地开发整合风筝文化资源

　　现代社会发展迅速，科技创新一日千里，与风筝有关的事业发展、品牌拓展也随着世界的发展而变化。

　　潍坊国际风筝会是潍坊市非常宝贵的城市品牌，前景广阔。潍坊市从 1984 年创办第 1 届潍坊国际风筝会，至今已连续成功举办了 35 届。潍坊国际风筝会的成功举办，振兴了传统的风筝产业，弘扬了风筝文化，加强了潍坊与世界各国的交流，增进了潍坊人民与世界各国朋友的深情厚谊。它已经成为潍坊对外开放的窗口，让世界各地的朋友认识潍坊、了解潍坊、投资潍坊、发展潍坊、热爱潍坊、情系潍坊，带动了潍坊经济、文化、旅游、商贸、交通、通信、城建、社会等方面的飞速发展，有力地增强和提升了潍坊的知名度和影响力。潍坊国际风筝会已成为潍坊市最有影响力、最有价值、最有代表性的品牌节会和城市品牌，先后获得"中国最具国际影响力的 10 大节庆""改革开放 30 周年最受关注的 30 个节庆""改革开发 40 年中国十佳品牌节会"等荣誉称号。从近几年潍坊国际风筝会总体安排来看，活动内容是很丰富的，有特色、有亮点。如潍坊国际风筝会全国风筝分区选拔赛活动，风筝工艺美术博览会、中国画节等活动，都很有创意，富有文化内涵。潍坊作为中国的一座中小城市，举办以风筝为主题的、内容如此丰富的重大国际节庆会展活动，这在世界上是独一无二的，体现了潍坊人的聪明才智和创新思维，已经取得的成

效是很大的。风筝的内涵十分丰富，风筝文化的资源需要开发整合。展望未来，潍坊国际风筝会和潍坊风筝发展的前途是光明的。

风筝是体育项目。放风筝始于民间，千百年来放风筝不仅愉悦心情，而且有利于强身健体。新中国成立以来，风筝运动得到长足发展。在历届潍坊国际风筝会影响带动下，风筝运动的规则、规程不断完善，风筝运动的种类和样式不断拓展，风筝竞技水平和组织工作等都有了很大提升，风筝运动在国内外的普及也有了质的飞跃。把风筝打造成体育品牌，开展一系列竞赛和展演，对风筝运动的发展以及带动全民健身和经济社会发展具有多方面的意义。

风筝是文化活动。风筝有着鲜明的文化属性，挖掘风筝的文化内涵，开展一系列的文化活动是大有作为的事情。比如，可以开展风筝扎制表演、放飞表演、风筝大师作品展览，风筝的创新创意评比，可以申报世界非物质文化遗产，可以"走出去，请进来"，开展丰富多彩的风筝文化传承、弘扬等活动。

风筝是民生。风筝与老百姓生活息息相关，通过风筝可以拓展利于民生的事项。像潍坊市风筝企业大大小小400多家，解决了数万人就业问题，也有利于社会稳定和发展。在学校开设风筝专业，让孩子们学习风筝的文化和技艺，使孩子们不仅受到了中国文化的熏陶，还掌握了生存的技术，对于改善民生也

有好处。

风筝是产业。风筝是一个集生产、推广、营销、材料、工艺等于一体的产业，蕴含着巨大的商机，经济效益十分可观。制作风筝的几十道工艺，每一个环节都可以有挖掘的潜力，风筝产业链条的设计、培育，围绕产、研、学、销四位一体，统筹谋划，发展壮大风筝产业是风筝拓展的重要方向。

风筝是丰富的文艺宝藏。一项传承千年的技艺一定蕴含着丰富曲折的故事，要深深挖掘。比如，以风筝为题材，创作电视连续剧、动漫作品；以风筝为主线，创作文学作品，培育风筝文学、诗歌、小说、电视文学、电影等。通过时代和社会的变迁，折射出风筝在不同时代与人们息息相关的命运和变化。"年年岁岁花相似，岁岁年年人不同"，丰富的风筝文化激发创作灵感，一定会有精彩的文艺作品出现。

风筝是科技。风筝的制作、生产里都有科技元素，这些元素给风筝插上腾飞的翅膀，使其可以更好地拓展。当代世界风筝的制作和放飞包含的科技含量越来越大，使风筝的可操作性、参与性、观赏性等都大大增强。空气动力学在风筝中的应

用可以大有作为，风筝与飞行原理在学校中的科技知识普及也可以做很多事情。

风筝是教育。风筝制作、风筝文化、风筝科技，可以陶冶人们的情操。围绕风筝可以进行相关的教育和熏陶，无论精神或物质教育，对百姓都是很好的。在大学里开设风筝专业，形成系列人才培养链条，传承中国文化。在精神领域，现代人生活节奏快，通过放风筝慢下来，身心还能得到调节。培育风筝教育事业，挖掘风筝人文故事，用在社会和人们生活当中，使人们受教育，经洗礼，懂科学，提素质，享幸福，是一项很有意义的事情。

风筝是品牌。任何一个项目都有世界一流。风筝品牌的培养、维护，风筝的大小、轻重，飞得高与稳，风筝的系列制作，不同人群的使用，不同天气条件下的放飞，风筝的质量品牌，都值得探讨和研究。

潍坊市抓住风筝大做文章，把风筝会办成了风筝的盛会、文化的盛会、旅游的盛会、经贸招商的盛会，搭建了宽广的合作发展平台，打造提升了城市品牌，促进了经济社会发展进步，值得国内外一些节会学习借鉴。

（作者冯建中，系国家体育总局原副局长，中国奥委会副主席，国际风筝联合会主席）

潍坊国际风筝会让风筝文化发扬光大

因为有悠久风筝文化传统的存在，潍坊有了国际风筝会，反过来，因为有了国际风筝会，潍坊的风筝文化便注入了新的活力，"芝麻开花节节高"。鉴于其影响力和对民间文化的保护与推动，2004 年10 月，潍坊国际风筝会被联合国教科文国际民间艺术组织列入非物质文化遗产及民间艺术保护工程。

在当今中国乃至世界范围内，文化遗产保护已成为一个非常重要的课题。而这一课题的提出，正是因为在现代化过程中，人类许多宝贵的文化遗产正在日渐被边缘化、走向衰退乃至消亡。在我国，随着现代化、城市化的加速发展，许多优秀的民间传统文化的失传乃至衰亡已是一个不争的事实。这一现状的出现，原因固然是多方面的，但其中一个不可忽视的原因，恐怕就是作为这些传统文化的载体——传统节日（当然其本身也是一种传统文化形式）渐渐淡出了人们的日常生活。我们知道，在民俗学上，节日"主要是指与天时、物候的周期相适应，在人们的社会生活中约定俗成的、具有某种风俗活动内容的特定时日"。所以，固定的时间——自然因素，以及在此时间内特定的民俗文化活动——人文因素是节日的两大要素。这就是说，节日是民间民俗文化的载体，具有传承文化的功能。历史表明，我国历史上丰富的民间民俗文化正是借着众多传统节日而得以代代相传的。可是，在我国现代化进程中，由于在社会结构中加入了许多主流的带有纪念意义而缺乏传统民俗文化内涵的节日，加之近些年那些更不具中国传统文化基础和内涵但因商业炒作而流行的如"情人节""感恩节""圣诞节"等洋节的盛行，致使那些以民俗活动为主要内容的我国传统节日受到挤压、被淡化了，结果使传统的民间民俗文化失去了其存在的载体。

潍坊国际风筝会是一个在新的时代背景下产生的新生节日，并集传统性与现代性于一体。所谓传统性，是说它的出现是有其历史文化渊源的，它无论是在节庆时间上还是在节庆活动内容上与我国传统的民俗节日——清明节保持了明显的一致性，是具有民俗传统文化内涵的新生节日。在某种意义上说，国际风筝会对于今天的潍坊人来说，就是新时代的"清明节"。因此，对于风筝文化的传承它也就有着与清明节相同的文化功能。所谓现代性，是指作为一个新生的节日、一个大型的文化节庆活动，潍坊国际风筝会与传统的清明节又有所不同，它的组织化、国际性等特点表现出明显的现代性，隆重的节日气氛或造势所形成的强烈的"在场感"对风筝文化进一步起到了有力的强化和明显的导向作用，尤其是风筝会期间所组织的各项大型风筝放飞或比赛活动，更是直接推动了风筝文化的发扬光大。

"开发式保护"是潍坊国际风筝会对于风筝文化传承与发展所表现出的第二方面的直接意义。所谓"开发式保护"，就是将传统文化资源进行有效整合，并将其作为一种资本加以运用，以推动地方经济发展，同时也实现对传统文化的保护。在当前中国现实生活中，将传统文化与市场经济相嫁接、相结合是一种趋势，而这一种趋势体现的是一种双向的需要：市场经济需要传统文化，传统文化需要在市场经济中找到其存续和发展的新契机。

从潍坊国际风筝会的初衷及其后来的发展看，毋庸讳言，它是有着明确目标的。不管是初期的为了发展旅游业——通过风筝放飞、风筝展览活动，吸引人气，扩大旅游，还是发展期的"一种形式（风筝会），四个结合（旅游、文化、体育、经济）"，都是一个目的，那就是要借助风筝这一具有地方特色和传统优势的民间传统文化，以实现扩大旅游、发展地方经济。客观地讲，这种借题发挥的做法确有"醉翁之意不在酒"之嫌，但从另一方面看，它也确实对风筝文化的保护与发展带来了极大的好处。无论是风筝产业的发展，还是风筝艺术创作水平的提高，甚至包括潍坊人对风筝文化的自信与自觉等，正是得益于国际风筝会的推动作用，这一点是不容否认的。实践证明，潍坊国际风筝会不仅让传统的风筝文化的经济价值得到了充分的释放，为地方经济社会发展提供了动力，同时，也为风筝文化自身在新的历史条件下的保护、传承与发展建立了制度机制，促进了风筝文化保护、发展与地方经济社会发展的互动。正像麦坎（Mckean）对印度尼西亚巴厘岛旅游业的研究所发现的那样，旅游业的发展导致了当地的文化复兴，不仅居民的传统、文化自信心、族群认同感得到增强，而且艺术创造水平也被有意识地保持了下来。

（作者张基振，系博士、教授、博士生导师，山东体育学院体育社会科学学院副院长，山东省风筝协会副主席兼秘书长）

创新办好潍坊国际风筝会

风筝会是潍坊的城市品牌，办好风筝会，使其发挥更大作用，是全市人民的共同心愿。要与时俱进，围绕坚持不懈地创新和提升风筝会作文章，把潍坊国际风筝会做大做强，打造成世界著名的风筝盛会。

突出改革创新，让节会充满活力。创新是节会发展的灵魂。多年来，对每届风筝会的筹备工作，国家体育总局，国际风筝联合会，中国风筝协会，潍坊市委、市政府都高度重视和关心支持，要求不断创新发展，经过潍坊国际风筝会办公室精心策划和组织实施，使每一届风筝会都呈现新亮点、新特色。随着中央八项规定的贯彻执行，风筝会坚持节俭办会、务实办会、创新办会，实现了新的转型和提升。要继续加大创新力度，克服办会疲劳，科学设置活动，扩大风筝会的影响力。

突出风筝主题，整合节会资源。要毫不放松地组织好风筝扎制创新，将其作为风筝大赛的一项重要任务，落实到各有关县市区和市直部门单位，以及有关风筝专家艺人。同时学习借鉴国内外风筝扎制创新方面的新经验、新技术，使潍坊的风筝扎制创新

年年有新突破。要认真组织风筝大赛和放飞表演，推选出能够代表潍坊水平的一流风筝参加风筝会。要积极为风筝企业牵线搭桥，提供优质服务，促进潍坊风筝产业发展。借风筝会平台，加大双招双引工作力度。

突出以人为本，增强参与性。风筝会的各项活动，要始终坚持先进文化的前进方向和以人民为中心的理念，创造广泛参与的氛围条件，降低参与门槛，能不收费就不收费，利用新媒体及时传播风筝会信息，让市民和中外客人实实在在地感受到风筝会浓郁的节庆气氛，让风筝会的办会成果更好地惠及广大市民和所有参与者。

（作者姜连绍，系国际风筝联合会执委，中国风筝协会监事，潍坊国际风筝会办公室原主任）

实施"走出去"战略 放大"风筝会"品牌效应

从 1984 年举办第一届潍坊国际风筝会，至今潍坊市已成功地举办了 35 届国际风筝会。风筝会的举办，使潍坊的知名度、美誉度和竞争力不断提升，经济和社会各项事业发展不断加快，市民的文明素质也不断提高，成为举世闻名的"世界风筝都"和国际风联总部所在地，风筝会也获得了"中国 10 大节庆"和"改革开放30 年最受关注的 30 个节庆""改革开放 40 年中国十佳品牌节庆"和"改革开放 40 年中国会展经济产业贡献奖"等荣誉称号，风筝和风筝会已成为我市最有代表性、最有影响力的城市品牌，成为潍坊市一笔巨大的无形资产。

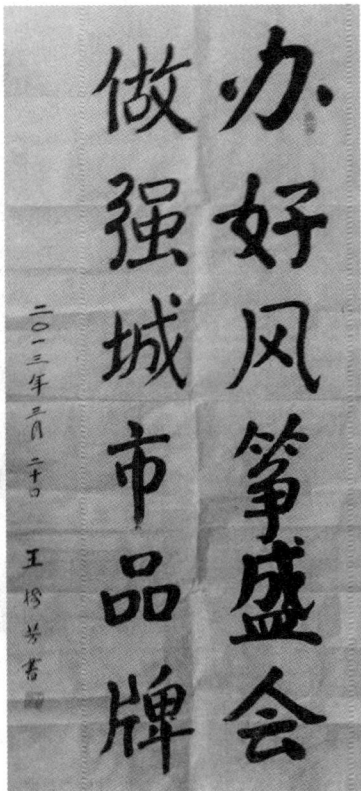

同时，必须清醒地看到，近年来国内不少城市在争办不同层级的风筝会，竞争也越来越激烈，如广东、江苏、贵州以及京、津等省市都在不遗余力地利用风筝这个载体，扩大自己的影响力，这对我市风筝城市品牌建设带来了不小的冲击和挑战。从我市情况看，近几年"走出去"进行风筝文化对外交流的机会偏少，从而直接影响我市风筝文化的影响力。"走出去"是拓展风筝会内涵与外延，弘扬潍坊风筝文化，提升风筝城市品牌的重要举措和途径。笔者认为，在创新办会，开放办会，集全市之力办好风筝盛会的同时，今后围绕实施"走出去"战略，应着重抓好以下 3 个方面：

更新观念，切实增强"走出去"的紧迫感和责任感

一是要树立潍坊风筝品牌持续培育和提升观念。品牌的打造很难，品牌的可持续培育更难。潍坊风筝品牌的打造和提升不会一劳永逸，需要拓展延伸，不断注入新的生机和活力。

二是要树立风筝是潍坊文化之魂观念。这不是一句空话，而是有着丰富的内涵。潍坊所有文明、智慧和艺术的结晶应以风筝文化为核心、为载体、为依托，并发扬光大。

三是要树立做强潍坊世界风筝文化交流中心的观念。这就要求我们以潍坊国际风筝会为平台，发挥好国际风筝联合会作用，采取走出去、引进来的方式，吸收国际、国内的先进经验和做法，在风筝研发、比赛、展览、展示、贸易等各个环节上勇于创新，巩固发展"世界风筝都"的地位。

四是要树立节会之间互相学习的观念。要加大对国内外重要节会、赛事交流合作力度，学他人之长，补己之短，不断研究新情况、解决新问题，切实增强抓好风筝城市品牌建设的紧迫感和责任感。

强化措施，加大潍坊风筝城市品牌宣传推广力度

一是围绕做大做强风筝赛事品牌，加大每年一届的世界风筝

锦标赛的投入力度。多年来，风筝会比赛内容和办会成本在不断增加，但在办会资金投入上偏少，直接影响了风筝大赛品牌的提升。因此，应适当加大资金投入。

二是设立潍坊市风筝文化对外交流发展扶持资金。主要用于风筝产业扶持、发展，对外风筝文化交流，以及风筝文化的研究，等等。

三是充分发挥国际风筝联合会的作用。国际风筝联合会总部设在潍坊，这是含金量很高的"金字招牌"。我们应倍加珍惜，充分发挥其作用，为世界风筝文化发展做出不懈努力和贡献。

四是成立专业化、高水平的风筝放飞和展览队伍，积极参与国内外组织的风筝放飞比赛和展示展览活动。通过专业化队伍的参与，持之以恒地放大潍坊风筝城市品牌效应，提升风筝品牌的影响力，尤其要借鉴（青岛）潍坊周"放飞青岛"，上海世博会"放飞世博"，潍坊风筝万里行，潍坊国际风筝会全国分区选拔赛等

的成功做法，采取多种形式向国内外重点地区、重要城市、重要景点展示我市以风筝为代表的特色文化和产品，加强彼此间的合作，进一步弘扬风筝文化，宣传推介潍坊。

大力协同，为实施"走出去"战略提供有力保障

打造、培育、放大风筝城市品牌，各级部门要树立"一盘棋"思想，通力协作，形成合力。在创新办好风筝盛会的同时，要注意研究和制定好"走出去"的具体规划和措施，积极主动参加国内外的重要风筝赛事，展览和有关会议论坛，讲好潍坊故事，弘扬风筝文化。同时，要积极与新闻宣传、文化、旅游、商务、海关、检验检疫等部门协同动作，互通信息，整合资源，共同参与和主办、承办有关风筝文化交流活动，为风筝企业搞好服务，为弘扬风筝文化，放大风筝城市品牌效益，促进我市经济社会更好更快发展做出新的更大贡献。

（作者张崇高，系国际风筝联合会秘书长，潍坊国际风筝会办公室原主任）

提升潍坊国际风筝会赛事品牌价值

创新是节会发展的灵魂和生命。潍坊国际风筝会是潍坊市精心培育的重大国际性、综合性节会品牌和亮丽的城市名片。潍坊国际风筝会要常办常新，做强做优，就必须与时俱进，不断创新，才能在新的起点上实现科学发展和可持续发展，让风筝会充满生机与活力。为此，建议围绕着力提升风筝会重大风筝赛事品牌价值，突出抓好以下三方面工作：

大力提升风筝会重大风筝赛事组织水平。 积极争取国家体育总局、国际风联，中国风协支持，继续重点办好"世界风筝锦标赛"和"潍坊风筝大赛"，按国际赛事规则，完善有关规则、规程，科学严密组织，严格、公正裁判，加大对获胜选手、团队的奖励力度，增强风筝赛事的权威性和吸引力。继续办好全国风筝分区选拔赛，选出高水平放飞队参加潍坊国际风筝会，同时，要坚持以人为本的理念，增加适合大众参与的风筝文化类项目，让大众积极参与风筝会，支持风筝会，共享风筝会，拉动潍坊的休闲旅游消费。

充分发挥有关权威组织的作用。 今后在创新办会、开放办会，以及弘扬传承风筝文化方面，我们要主动与国际风联、中国风协、中国会展经济研究会、联合国教科文国际民间艺术组织等加强战略合作，整合资源，优势互补，不断提升办会的层次水平，弘扬风筝文化，进一步扩大潍坊国际风筝会的全球影响力。

加强风筝人才培养和放飞队伍建设。制订潍坊市风筝人才培训规划，配套有关人才培养的激励措施。继续搞好国际风筝工艺大师评选。继续开展风筝工艺品设计创意大赛、"风筝文化进校园"和大学生风筝知识竞赛等活动。加强与驻潍坊高校的教育教学合作，有针对性地定期培训风筝企业家、风筝设计技术人员，培养造就一支优秀的风筝文化专家队伍。加强对创新风筝的研发，争取多出代表世界一流水平的风筝精品。要好中选优，组建本市专业放飞队伍，加强训练，积极参加国内外重要赛事活动，为推动风筝运动普及与提高做出积极贡献，为巩固世界风筝都文化传播中心地位做出不懈努力。

（作者颜建海，系国际风筝联合会副秘书长、潍坊国际风筝会办公室副主任；作者刘志平，系国际风筝联合会执委、潍坊国际风筝会办公室业务科科长）

扶持潍坊风筝产业做大做强

近年来，世界各国风筝研发速度非常快，尤其是欧美各国在现代风筝的新品种、新材料、新技术的研发应用方面达到了领先水平，风筝贸易发展势头迅猛。相比之下，我市的风筝产业点多面广，主要依靠作坊式生产，研发创新能力不足，

科技水平和人才培养滞后，产品附加值偏低，对国民经济贡献率较小，同时存在量小质弱、品牌少、贴牌多、无序竞争、效益不高等问题，这与潍坊国际风筝会在全球形成的巨大影响力极不相称。

进一步做大做强潍坊市风筝产业，是巩固提升"世界风筝都"地位的需要，是提升城市品牌价值的需要，是风筝会可持续发展的需要，是广大风筝从业者的迫切愿望。为此，建议从每年风筝会经费预算中拿出专项资金，作为风筝产业扶持资金，支持鼓励风筝产业提速发展。本着以奖代补、突出重点、鼓励先进的原则，对下列情况，视情给予年度奖励补助：

1. 奖励品牌企业。凡是有独立商标、专利或省以上驰名商标，风筝产品在国际国内市场认可度高，年销售额超过 1000 万元以上的企业，给予一定数额的奖励。

2. 奖励风筝企业带头人和国际风筝工艺大师。对当年评出的全市"十佳风筝企业带头人"，国际风筝工艺大师，每年给予本

人一定数额的补助费。

3. 对风筝研发，组织销售和参展成效突出的个人、企业及民间社团组织，给予一定数额的奖励。

4. 对有自营出口权的风筝企业，除享受出口退税外，每年对出口额名列全市前三位的企业，给予一定数额的奖励。

5. 鼓励成立风筝合作社、有关风筝业协会或产业联盟，凡作用发挥好，服务好，得到风筝企业拥护的上述组织，给予一定数额的奖励。

6. 鼓励各种社会组织兴建风筝市场、风筝小镇、风筝销售一条街，以及风筝龙头企业兼并小、散、弱等风筝企业，对上述业绩突出的个人或企业组织，给予一定数额的奖励。

7. 鼓励风筝电商企业发展，对年度网上销售潍坊风筝交易额名列全市前三位的企业，给予一定数额的奖励。

（作者石岳，系国际风筝联合会执委、潍坊国际风筝会办公室会展科科长）

潍坊国际风筝会印象记

风筝会直击，认知精美品质

竞赛现场，分享壮观执裁风筝会，感受运动经典

"世界风筝都"潍坊，自 1984 年 4 月开始至 2012 年 4 月的 29 年里，已经成功地举办了 29 届国际风筝会。作为自幼就非常喜爱亲自动手制作风筝和放飞风筝的我，有幸以观众、运动员和国家级裁判员的不同身份观看、参加和执裁了总共 15 届潍坊国际风筝会，这真是我一生中最大的乐事和幸事！

　　我的青壮年岁月留在了中国酒泉卫星发射中心，其间，也常常在春节放假的时候给自己的孩子和战友的小孩儿做几只风筝放着玩耍；后来我转业到了地方，虽然环境不同了，但制作和放飞风筝，仍旧是我最大的业余爱好和户外活动。

　　从 1993 年到 1997 年的 5 年里，我以观众身份曾 3 次去潍坊国际风筝会放飞现场观看学习；从 1998 年到 2002 年的 5 年里，我以运动员的身份亲自征战了第 15 届、第 17 届和第 19 届潍坊国际风筝会赛场；自 2004 年 4 月开始至 2012 年，我又以国家级裁判员的身份连续 9 年执裁了潍坊国际风筝会的现场比赛。我似乎和潍坊国际风筝会结下了不解之缘——潍坊的风筝，潍坊国际风筝会的比赛场景、比赛形式、比赛规模以及各届国际风筝会上风筝类型的变化、竞赛项目的增添、运动风筝的创新，以及潍坊国际风筝会给潍坊带来的巨大经济效益，城市面貌的变化，无时无刻不在我脑海中萦绕。

风筝会直击，认知精美品质

我虽然自幼喜欢动手扎制和放飞风筝，但真正认识风筝还是从观看了1993年4月第10届潍坊国际风筝会之后。

我从部队转业到地方后，有了更多的时间到处走走看看。当时人们谈到风筝，言必称潍坊，于是我便产生了去潍坊看风筝的想法。1993年4月我第一次来到潍坊，第一次参观了杨家埠。火车站外的街道两旁，风筝商铺内外挂满了五颜六色、各式各样的风筝，杨家埠风筝作坊的师傅们高超的制作技艺和精湛的绘画功底，令我记忆犹新。而浮烟山第10届潍坊国际风筝会放飞赛场上空形状各异、色彩斑斓的风筝、外国朋友放飞的硕大的叫不出名字的风筝，以及一条条几十米长的昂首摇尾的巨龙风筝，让我简直有些目瞪口呆，而那只硕大无比、构思巧妙、制作精良的立体风筝"千手观音"，更是给我留下了很深很深的印象。

1997年4月，我又一次来到潍坊观看第14届潍坊国际风筝会。浮烟山放飞场警戒线外真是人山人海，到处是卖风筝的摊位、放飞风筝的人群，俨然是一片风筝的海洋。警戒线内的赛场上，各种肤色的选手们或在专心组装风筝，或是牵引着自己的风筝向场外观众招手脸上堆满了自豪的微笑。那时香港即将回归祖国，恰逢十五大召开的前夕，"迎接十五大召开""迎香港回归"等各种造型的巨大的各类风筝漫天飘舞，十几条"长龙"更是吞云吐雾，气壮山河，令我和周围的观众情不自禁地不时为其拍手叫好！赛场上空翻翻起舞的色彩艳丽的几千只大小不同、造型各异的风筝，俨然形成了又一个婀娜多姿的风筝海洋！赛场内外遥相呼应，让我犹如进入了梦幻般的风筝世界、风筝王国。

3次直击潍坊国际风筝会、参观潍坊风筝作坊和风筝商铺，使我对风筝有了新的认识——风筝在潍坊已不单单是手中的玩物了，潍坊风筝已形成了大气候，形成了特有的潍坊风筝文化。同时，也让我进一步了解到，潍坊风筝虽然有着不同体系和流派、有着繁多的品种，但它们却有着共同的特点——选材用料考究、扎制造型优美、扎糊技艺精湛、图案形象生动。我既看到了制作风格粗犷、不矫揉造作、乡土气息浓厚的风筝作品，又看到了古老传统色彩浓重、宫廷风格雍容华贵、讲究装饰的风筝工艺品；同时也看到了外国朋友充分利用现代科学技术优势、使用现代制作新工艺，在继承传统风筝的基础上，创造出的现代风筝作品，这些现代风筝作品大多造型简洁明快、色彩对比强烈、图案构思清新巧妙，具有鲜明的时代性和外国风情。所有这些大色块、大体积的板子风筝、立体风筝和软体风筝等，其风格与艺术特色，都令我赞赏不已！

观看浮烟山国际风筝会，我的另一收获是有机会结识了几位外国朋友，进而对外国朋友的风筝作品有了新的感性认识和了解。自此，我对风筝越发喜爱，也越发坚定了我要亲手制作新型风筝和一定要亲自参与潍坊国际风筝会风筝比赛的愿望和决心。

竞赛现场，分享壮观

继三次直击潍坊国际风筝会后，1998年至2002年间，我又以运动员的身份3次参与了潍坊国际风筝会的比赛。

记得1998年4月在第15届潍坊国际风筝赛场上，我虽然把主要精力用在了自己的参赛风筝和赛事上，但还是情不自禁地将一部分精力放在其他运动员（尤其是国外运动员）漂亮的各种类型的风筝上了。参加这一届潍坊国际风筝会的，有21个国家和地区的62支风筝代表队，国内省、市代表队有22支，潍坊本市的代表队有 66 支，参赛的风筝总数少说也有 2000 只。国内代表队的巨型风筝和外国选手软体风筝、立体风筝、板子风筝的造型和精彩放飞，让我手中的相机拍个不停，竟然淡忘了自己的放飞任务。令我更加激动和兴奋的，是来自不同国家和地区的 8 支特技风筝队的放飞表演，不论他们是单人放飞还是多人编队飞行，那犹如真飞机般的呼啸声和上下翻滚的精彩飞行轨迹，不时赢得场外观众阵阵掌声，同时也强烈地震撼了我；而成千上万名小学生和群众集体放飞风筝的宏伟场面更是令我振奋。那天，观看浮烟山国际风筝会风筝放飞的观众，我粗略估计至少有 20 万人。

赛场内，巨型风筝、特技风筝、放飞表演气势宏伟；赛场外，群众一边放飞、一边欢呼，场面热烈又壮观。这宏大壮观的场面是我闻所未闻、见所未见的！

2002 年 4 月 21 日，第 19 届潍坊国际风筝大赛暨全国风筝邀请赛在人山人海的浮烟山国际风筝放飞场举行，我有幸再一次以运动员的身份参与了这一届风筝邀请赛。这一届国际风筝会和风筝邀请赛给我的感受更深、冲击力更强烈。本次国际风筝大赛共有 18 个国家的 73 支代表队参赛；来自全国各地的 25 支代表队参加了全国风筝邀请赛，并评出了"最大风筝""最长风筝""最佳风筝"和"最有创意风筝"四"最"。但是我觉得，比"最大风筝"更大的是这一届国际风筝会的比赛规则，比"最长风筝"更长的是各国运动员之间的情意，比"最佳风筝"更佳的是运动员们的放飞心情，比"最有创意风筝"更有创意的是潍坊国际风筝会的比赛模式。

通过比赛和评比，我进一步认识到，潍坊国际风筝会声势是浩大的、规模是空前的、场面是壮观的、影响是深远的，尤其是"银线连四海，风筝传友谊"的响亮口号，更是深入人心！它成了国内外运动员交往时的标准用语。

参加这一届风筝会让我有幸认识了更多的国内外朋友，这些朋友不仅给了我风筝制作上的技艺帮助，更多的是通过风筝、通过银线，让我们的心贴得更近了，让我们的友谊更深了。

风筝让不同肤色的人们走到了一起，潍坊国际风筝会让潍坊走出了国门、走向了世界！

执裁风筝会，感受运动经典

自 2004 年开始至 2012 年，我以国家级裁判员的身份连续 9 次执裁了第 21 届至第 29 届潍坊国际风筝会的比赛现场。不同的身份，有着不同的感受；不同的身份，看潍坊国际风筝会的视角也有所不同。

（1）风筝运动的经典模式

风筝运动是一项群众性的体育运动。作为"世界风筝都"的潍坊，在过去的 29 年里成功地举办了 29 届国际风筝会，它不仅广交了世界各国的朋友，在展示潍坊特色风筝和风筝文化的同时，也把风筝比赛纳入体育竞赛的轨道。在打造风筝品牌赛事的同时，也在国际上打响了城市知名度，使潍坊国际风筝会成了播撒友谊的使者、闪亮的城市名片。

潍坊是风筝的发祥地之一，是风筝的故乡，原本十分平常的放飞风筝的民俗活动，在潍坊却发展成了一项大型的国际交流活动和国家体育总局正式开展的体育运动项目，这是潍坊人智慧的结晶。为了完善这一体育运动项目，在历届潍坊国际风筝会上，潍坊把风筝放飞表演、全国风筝邀请赛、全国风筝比赛以及世界风筝锦标赛等，均按照体育理念和体育精神去组织实施，进而在风筝表演和风筝比赛中制定出了易于操作、切实可行的比赛规则，从而使潍坊国际风筝会不仅具有观赏性、娱乐性，同时也具备了和其他体育项目一样的竞技性。我们今天在风筝比赛赛场上执行的 2002 年版《风筝竞赛规则与裁判法》，就是以 1986 年潍坊国际风筝会《风筝比赛规则》为蓝本，1990 年经过修改，1993 年又由中国风筝协会组织有关人员修改、完善而成的。潍坊国际风筝会对推动全国风筝运动的开展、世界风筝运动的兴起、全国风筝产业的发展，均做出了突出贡献，功不可没。

潍坊在 1984 年 4 月举办第一届国际风筝会时，只有放飞表演项目。来自 11 个国家和地区的 17 个风筝团队的 185 人参加了放飞表演。当时潍坊市参加表演放飞的，也只有两个风筝队，到了 2010 年，第 27 届国际风筝会时，则有 28 个国家和地区的 58 支风筝代表队和国内 16 个省、市的 29 支风筝代表队的运动员 300 多人参加，参赛风筝近 400 只。这一届风筝会，各国选手同场竞技——参加的比赛项目主要有竞技风筝比赛和特色风筝表演赛两项。其中，竞技风筝比赛包括打斗风筝赛、团体运动风筝规定动作赛和团体运动风筝芭蕾赛三项。特色风筝表演赛包括最长风筝赛、最大风筝赛、最佳软体风筝赛、最佳空中效果赛和优秀传统风筝赛 5 项。由此可以看出，潍坊国际风筝会的规模一年比一年大，参赛项目也一年比一年多，而体育性很强的竞技风筝也成了国际风筝会赛场上的亮点，潍坊国际风筝会把风筝比赛真正纳入了体育竞赛轨道。

2008年，是我国实行改革开放的30周年。鉴于潍坊国际风筝会对全国乃至世界部分国家和地区风筝文化艺术的发展所起的促进作用，潍坊国际风筝会被评选为"改革开放30周年30个最受关注节庆"之一，且荣登金榜，排名第二位。"改革开放30周年最受关注节庆会展评选"，是人民网为纪念改革开放30周年系列活动之一，历时3个月，参与投票的网友多达60万人，共评出最受关注的节庆30个，潍坊国际风筝会能够在参评的众多"节庆"中脱颖而出，这充分显示了潍坊国际风筝会的魅力和影响力。潍坊国际风筝会能够获此殊荣，也是全国广大人民群众对历届潍坊国际风筝会成功举办的最大认可和褒奖，因此，潍坊国际风筝会也就成了国际风筝运动最为经典的成功模式。

（2）系统工程与世界纽带

潍坊国际风筝会是一项浩大的系统工程，它不仅仅是潍坊的风筝盛会、风筝文化交流，而且也是风筝经济、风筝联谊。由于潍坊国际风筝会特别注重、特别强调"风筝牵线，文化搭台，经贸唱戏"的办会宗旨，因此潍坊与国际、国内的文体交往、经济往来愈来愈多、愈来愈频繁，从而让潍坊更快、更坚挺地走向世界。也让世界更多、更全面地了解了潍坊——了解了潍坊的政治秩序和经济发展，了解了潍坊的群众体育和传统文化，了解了潍坊的艺术水平和管理能力，了解了潍坊的创新精神和开拓情怀。这一浩大的系统工程，在展示潍坊特有的传统文化魅力的同时，也让潍坊人民获得了巨大的精神财富、文化财富和无形的社会资产。潍坊国际风筝会从最初单一的放飞表演，到有全国风筝制作艺人、风筝放飞高手参加的邀请赛，到有众多的全国风筝运动员参加的有比赛规程、比赛规则的正式比赛，再到近几年有世界各国和地区更多的运动员参与的世界风筝锦标赛，所有这些赛事，都极大地显示了"世界风筝都"的魅力和影响力。自 1988 年 4 月 1 日第 5 届潍坊国际风筝会主席团一致通过提议，确定潍坊市为"世界风筝都"之后，每年国际风筝联合会的 67 个会员国和地区的风筝代表队都争先恐后地报名，要求来潍坊参加国际风筝会的风筝表演和比赛。是潍坊将一个被称为"雕虫小技"、不能登大雅之堂的民俗活动，提升到国家正式开展的体育竞赛项目，这种功绩是世人看得到的、有口皆碑的。潍坊国际风筝会遵循了国际风筝联合会联络各国和地区风筝爱好者，增进各会员组织的交往与友谊，继承发展各国风筝的传统技艺，推动风筝活动在世界范围内广泛开展的宗旨，不仅推动了国际风筝联合会的规范化、专业化建设，而且为世界风筝运动的普及与发展做了大量的、超前的工作，使得潍坊国际风筝会在世界风筝界的影响日益扩大，成为团结联系世界各地风筝组织和国内广大风筝爱好者的纽带。同时也为世界风筝文化、风筝体育的交流和提高，风筝事业的发展和创新，起到了推波助澜的作用。

（3）经济"助推器"和城市名片

潍坊国际风筝会是潍坊经济发展的"助推器"，它让潍坊风筝成了传播友谊的使者，同时也让潍坊国际风筝会成了潍坊的金字招牌和闪亮的名片。

潍坊国际风筝会连续成功地举办了 29 届，这就使得潍坊国际风筝会不仅仅成了风筝运动最为经典的成功模式，让潍坊国际风筝会荣登有影响力的 30 个"节庆"之首，同时也让潍坊赢得了巨大的商机和经济效益，促使潍坊大踏步地走向了世界。

潍坊国际风筝会的成功举办，扩大了潍坊的开放力度，促进了潍坊与世界各国的文化交流和经贸合作，让潍坊由一座名不见经传的中小城市一跃成为举世闻名的"世界风筝都"和国际风筝联合会的总部所在地。其主要原因，就在于潍坊国际风筝会能够准确地掌握市场化运作的规律，让自己的发展理念和发展机制与国际接轨，走出了一条"政府主办，社会参与，市场运作"的良性循环的路子。潍坊国际风筝会自 1984 年举办以来，先后与 110 多个国家和地区建立了经贸合作关系，与 60 多个国家和地区建立了文化交流关系。"十一五"期间，每届风筝会签约合同项目资金都在 200 亿元上，潍坊国际风筝会已经成了潍坊国际文化、经贸活动的重要平台。因此，潍坊人亲切地把潍坊国际风筝会称作"生产力"，把潍坊国际风筝会看作潍坊经济发展的"助推器"。

潍坊在国际上的影响力不断扩大，潍坊在国内外的知名度越来越高，潍坊国际风筝会也一年比一年办得好，一届比一届办得漂亮。潍坊国际风筝会让风筝飞出了行业、飞出了国界，并让风筝带动了城市经济的腾飞。实际上，潍坊国际风筝会的模式已超越了行业、超越了地域、超越了民族、超越了国界，开创了一条把文化优势转化为市场优势的新路。同时，一年一度的潍坊国际风筝会已经成为传承和发展潍坊风筝文化的重要载体，成为国际文化交流、经贸活动的重要平台；潍坊国际风筝会打响了潍坊城市的知名度，潍坊国际风筝会成了潍坊闪闪发亮的名片和有口皆碑的金字招牌。

我为潍坊国际风筝会欢呼！我为潍坊国际风筝会叫好！

（作者程英华，系河北省石家庄市风筝协会主席）

我在潍坊当解说

风筝放飞我年轻的心
连续几年的主持人
潍坊是世界的

风筝放飞我年轻的心
风筝放飞我年轻的心，
银线牵来了八方的朋友。
放飞希望，
放飞理想。
蓝天白云飞来人间最美的情。
鸢飞人也乐，
国盛民祥和。
风筝啊！风筝！
我永远的梦。
飞翔吧！潍坊！
潍坊！飞翔吧！

连续几年的主持人

每年的 4 月，潍坊就成了风筝的海洋，这时的风筝成了友好的使者，风筝成了天空的主角，我一次次被潍坊感动着，被她的魅力所吸引，被她的精神所感动，被她的巨变所惊叹！

我应潍坊国际风筝会办公室的邀请和国家体育总局的选调，

连续几年担任了潍坊国际风筝会风筝比赛现场的主持人，潍坊人的热情、好客、纯朴、智慧与善良，深深地印在了我的记忆中。每次面对十几万的观众，我身后总有一股巨大的力量支撑着我，让我炽热的话语脱口而出，特别是现场无数条热情的短信，更是文采飞扬，给力无穷。

每次当我拿起话筒，一股巨大的责任感油然而生。2010 年 4 月 21 日的全国哀悼日，天降大雨，全国人民沉浸在玉树地震的悲痛之中，潍坊市委、市政府果断决策，停止了一切娱乐活动，撤掉了第 27 届潍坊国际风筝会和第 6 届世界风筝锦标赛的会标。全市上下包括来自海内外风筝界的朋友们纷纷捐款捐物，一只只支持地震灾区人民重建家园的主题风筝飞翔在浮烟山放飞场上空。我感受着这激动的场面，深深地被潍坊的一切感动着。

第二天，天放晴了，浮烟山放飞场又迎来了新的一天，所有的赛事都低调地进行着。面对这一切，作为一名国家级的风筝裁判员、一名风筝大赛的现场主持人，肩上的担子千斤重，特别是潍坊国际风筝会办公室主任张崇高的一番话，更是让我倍感责任重大。他说："潍坊的风筝连着全世界，你一定要把握全局，掌握局面，发挥你的优势，把党和政府的心声通过你的声音表达出去，完成好这次特殊的国际风筝会比赛的解说任务。"

大赛开始了，我的心也随着风筝一起飞了起来，激情的话语冲口而出。面对数万观众，我给自己下了命令，一定要把大家的兴致完全表达出来，一定要把大赛的节奏把握好，让本届风筝会同样精彩。

为了烘托气氛，现场开通了"青海不倒，玉树常青，玉树在飞翔"的短信互动活动。当我说"4 月的潍坊热情奔放，4 月的潍坊激情飞扬，4 月的潍坊心系玉树，4 月的潍坊大爱无疆"这句话后，全场一片掌声，大家的情绪被充分调动了起来。当我把能够储存 1000 条信息的手机号码"13934117338"告诉了大家，并欢迎大家走进我的短信平台时，马上就涌入了近500条充满爱意的短信。

一位潍坊当地的风筝老艺人，背着一只精美的风筝，来到了我的面前。他向我深深地鞠了一躬，向我提出一个请求，他说："主持人，您好！你能帮我拍卖这只风筝吗？我要把它捐给玉树人民。"老人家眼含热泪，用期盼的眼神望着我。作为一名国家体育总局选派的主持人，在这样一个特殊的日子里，我不能答应他老人家。我拿出一瓶可乐递给他，示意他坐了下来。我在主持的空间，仔细端详着这只风筝，一朵美丽的莲花上，站着招财童子，无论是扎工还是画工，都是风筝中的上品，是典型的潍坊风筝佳作。

老人家深情地看着我说："我是一个风筝世家，孩子当兵那年在唐山抗震救灾中牺牲了，这只风筝是我家祖上传下来的，很多外国友人高价登门收购，我都没舍得出手。他小的时候和我一起放飞过这只风筝，它是我和儿子的情感寄托呀！"老人眼里涌出了泪水，突然，老人把风筝放在玉树方向，慢慢地跪了下去，向玉树方向深深地磕了三个响头，如此的中国大礼，表达了老人家对灾区遇难同胞深深的悼念之情。

我被眼前的这一幕惊呆了，也被深深地震撼了！真正的大爱就在眼前，这是中华民族的根呀！潍坊人再次给了我心灵的震撼，我拿着话筒，激情澎湃的话语像火山一样喷出，把潍坊人民情系灾区的美德和此情此景告诉了现场的观众朋友，一双双的捐款的手，把真情投进了现场的捐款箱内。

一位潍坊籍的企业家，专门来到了老人身边，用5000元要买下这只风筝，老人说："我只要1000元，我要和儿子捐出这份大爱！"

比赛在紧张有序地进行着，一只只五彩缤纷的风筝在浮烟山放飞场演绎着春天的故事。只见老人家把1000元投进了捐款箱，和那位企业家走下了主席台，为玉树人民放飞了这只企盼平安、幸福、吉祥如意的祈福风筝！

从1992年开始走进潍坊，我就和潍坊结下了深深的不解之缘，同时也被潍坊日新月异的巨大变化所吸引。每次在潍坊打车，的哥的姐都会情不自禁地赞美自己的家乡，为家乡的风筝而自豪。

每一次站在潍坊国际风筝会的大舞台上，都会有不同的感受，潍坊的老百姓对风筝的情结是举世公认的，他们把对我的认可和欢迎写在了发来的短信中，让我多喝水，让我保护嗓子，让我别上火；有的为我亲自送来开水，有的为我送来鲜花，有的送来礼物，更多的是走到我身边来聆听我的解说。潍坊学院的十几位大学生，亲自跑到台上来慰问我；一位年过七旬的老艺人竟围着我跳起了舞，我的心被潍坊精神一次次有力地撞击着，我的语言也一次次飞翔在蓝天里。本届风筝会取得了巨大的成功，成了一次展示人间大爱的盛会，也成了历史上最有意义的一次风筝盛会。

潍坊是世界的

潍坊是世界的，风筝是世界的，当所有的风筝一起飞翔时，我的心也飞到了五彩的天空中。激动的话语像喷发的火山，一次次蓄积在我的心中，也一次次喷发着我的情感。我只有把对现场观众、参赛运动员、裁判员、工作人员、政府意志、新闻媒体、知识传播、音准节奏、调节气氛等因素全方位地综合掌握，才算得上一位称职的主持人。是潍坊给了我舞台，给了我施展才华的机会，也让我一次次走进了举世关注的世界风筝大赛，传播光辉灿烂的中国风筝文化。

潍坊作为世界一流的国际风筝大都市，为山东省的经济腾飞做出了重要的贡献。每次来到潍坊，总是被巨大的变化所吸引，改造后的白浪河妩媚动人，亮丽的风筝广场多彩多姿，崭新蝴蝶状的火车站展翅欲飞，宽广的人民广场上空风筝飞翔，整座城市焕发着浓郁的时代气息。我是一只风筝，总想把梦想带给未来。我是一个主持人，更是一名风筝文化的传播者。潍坊的风筝给了全世界和平与希望，给了天空热情与张扬，给了生命快乐与阳光。每年我到潍坊的意愿是强烈的，主持风筝会的感情是真挚的，语言节奏的把握是率真的，因为潍坊成了我生命的一部分，成了我生活中的第二故乡。

银线手中牵，彩鸢飞蓝天。放飞我心中的豪情，放飞我人生的祝愿。放飞一个梦想啊，心也牵动，梦也牵动；放飞一片激情啊，情也牵动，爱也牵动。世界风筝都潍坊正演绎着全世界风筝的精彩。我衷心地祝愿美丽的世界风筝都潍坊，用天空中五彩斑斓的风筝装饰出整个中华民族精彩的天空！

（作者尚兰柱，系太原市著名风筝专家、风筝大赛资深主持人）

风筝文化的传播者——邓华

邓华是潍坊著名文化学者、作家、摄影家。首届潍坊二艺美术协会副会长、山东老摄影家协会副秘书长、潍坊国际风筝会特聘专家、潍坊学院兼职教授、山东科技职业学院客座教授，长期从事历史文化与非物质文化遗产研究。已出版文集、长篇小说、家族研究、诗集、摄影集等 40 多部著作。特别是从 20 世纪 80 年代以来，一直关注潍坊风筝和潍坊国际风筝会，先后编写了《风筝扎制技艺大全》《鸢都潍坊与风筝史话》《潍坊工艺美术大观》等多部有关风筝文化方面的著作，曾荣获潍坊市 10 大文化名人、杰出文化人才、全国书香家庭等称号。

以上是邓华已经出版的三十部著作

设计问道
——我与国际潍坊风筝会的不解之缘

潍坊国际风筝会，是沐浴改革开放的春风，在国内最早冠以"国际"字眼的综合性、国际性重大节会，至今已举办35届，已成为潍坊最有价值的城市品牌、对外开放的窗口、合作发展的平台。

1987年，因缘际会，我设计中标了第四届潍坊国际风筝会入场券。自此之后，开始了对风筝会创意设计的探索与问道，连续为潍坊国际风筝会创意设计30余载。

风筝会一年一度地举办，而每年主题都会有所变化，设计既要注重风格的连续贯通，又要与当年主题相契合；由于风筝会是国际盛会，大会形象设计必须符合国际潮流，又要充分体现中华民族的传统文化和地域特色，让国际友人感受到世界风筝都的文化魅力，从而使风筝会品牌形象成为潍坊的城市名片。

能连续为自己家乡的重大国际节会，创意设计30多载，是我今生之荣幸，这种缘分是可遇而不可求的。在潍坊这个古老而年轻的城市，风筝托起过很多人的梦想，而我个人的设计事业起

飞也与风筝会有着密不可分的关系。

　　1987年第四届潍坊国际风筝会，向国内外征集大会入场券的创意设计。我当时在潍坊市一轻局工作，得到这个消息后喜不自禁，自己暗地查找资料，收集素材，骑着自行车几乎跑遍了大大小小可以给我信息和灵感的角落。开始精心准备自己的参选作品，经过反复构思和创意，绘制了大量的设计草稿，最后决定将风筝会期间的六大主题活动的入场券融为一体，形成一套系列入场券。并以书签的形式呈现，使其具有收藏和实用价值。每张券都以潍坊风筝为主题图案，并将潍坊杨家埠年画的色彩引入其中，使入场券上醒目的风筝图案具有了浓厚的地域特色，会徽、地球和四条彩带，把六张入场券巧妙地串联起来，体现了国际性和当代设计思想。在众多的参选作品中脱颖而出，被最终选中、采用。这套风筝会系列入场券，在1990年全国旅游门券、亚运门券评比中，获得唯一的设计一等奖，我应邀参加了亚运会开幕式。自此，我便与风筝会结下了不解之缘，风筝会年年办，入场券、吉祥物、请柬、招贴画、工作证、纪念品、奖牌、证书等系列设计年年有创新。

　　吉祥物是每届风筝会全套视觉形象设计的核心，以当年生肖为风筝会吉祥物延续着中华民族的传统文化，生肖对中国人来

说，不仅是一个动物形象，更是一个印记，是中国传统文化的象征。而风筝，是潍坊本土文化重要的代表元素，把这两种传统文化符号融合创新，设计出大家喜闻乐见的风筝会视觉形象，向中外来客展现中国传统文化和潍坊地域特色。

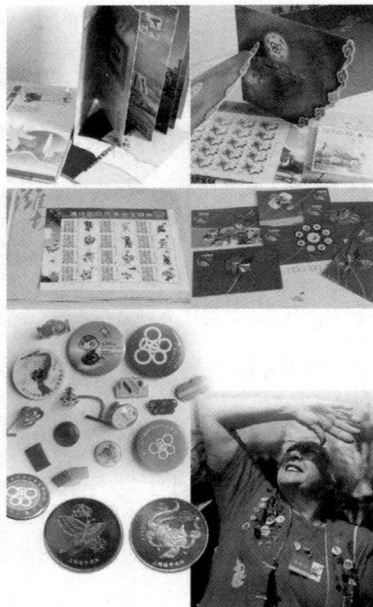

1989 年，我第一次为潍坊国际风筝会设计吉祥物，正逢农历蛇年。生肖蛇作为卡通形象最难设计，因为若将蛇拟人化处理，往往要给它加上手脚之类的东西，这样就无异于画蛇添足。怎么办呢？为了设计好蛇年风筝会吉祥物，我寝食难安。有时为找到一种适合的表现形式苦思冥想，晚上睡着，来了灵感就马上披衣起床，用笔记下想法。为此翻阅了大量的书籍、资料，从姊妹艺术中寻找灵感，从传统民间艺术中得到启迪。我用杨家埠年画中的大胖娃娃，然后在胖娃娃那大大的红肚兜上，设计了一条口含灵芝的花蛇，吉祥喜庆而又有地方特色。十二生肖更替交叠，30 多届风筝会，同一种生肖吉祥物有的我已经设计了三次，每次都要有创新变化。

潍坊因风筝而驰名中外，龙头蜈蚣是潍坊风筝的典型代表。2000 年是生肖龙年，龙又是中华民族的形象和图腾，2000 年是世纪之交的节点，多重因素的巧遇，让我萌生了设计潍坊龙风筝视觉形象的想法。首先想到的是把潍坊龙头蜈蚣风筝的典型符号和美丽元素提炼出来，对不足的部分进行改进提升，如两条龙须和下颚的红胡子在线的造型上使其挺拔有弹性，体现出厚度和力度。龙身平衡杆的羽毛装饰，从造型和色彩都进行了大胆创新，龙头形象设计弱化了凶恶的因素，使其既威武又亲切，色彩运用上喜庆热烈，富有朝气。整个龙头蜈蚣风筝的新形象雅俗共赏，得到了专家和社会各界的一致好评。被收入《中国设计年鉴》，并被官方和社会各界在庆典、影像、印刷品、建筑门面、包装等不同场合广泛使用，成为宣传世界风筝都潍坊的视觉形象代表作品。

回首浸满汗水与泪水的 30 多年设计经历，那难以想象的创作过程和无常变化，让我备尝酸甜苦辣，也曾摔打的"鼻青脸肿"但我依然坚守，从不言败。我已将设计融入生活的方方面面，在一茶一饭一事一物中触发感悟，在一草一木一石一景中获得灵感。面对每项设计委托都亲历其境，切身体会，用心创作。人要想在梦想的道路上保持源源不断的激情和力量，需要的是内心的一种信念，坚定认为自己能行，才会沿着这个信念去努力，再大的梦想也会实现。我设计的风筝会吉祥物，请柬、宣传画、入场券、工作证、奖杯、奖牌、纪念品等都会被中外来宾收藏，也荣获过国内外各种设计大奖。这一件件物品，都代表着潍坊这座城市的文化，更像一张张城市名片，给人留下美好的印象。它体现出的是我们潍坊的整体形象和文化素质。通过对我们风筝会的各种创意设计和视觉形象传播，各界朋友会对我们潍坊这座城市有全新的认识和美好的回忆。

（作者梁文道，系九三学社潍坊市委原副主委，潍坊市体育局原调研员，高级工艺美术师）

后记

POSTSCRIPT

417-418

后 记

编写《世界各国风筝赛会》一书，旨在系统地推介国内外知名风筝赛会及相关节庆会展、场馆设施，总结交流国内外举办风筝赛会及开展风筝文化交流，普及拓展风筝运动，传承弘扬风筝文化，助推风筝产业发展的情况和经验做法，便于风筝界同仁互相交流、学习和借鉴，不断提升风筝赛会的国际性、观赏性、参与性和品牌价值，在更高起点上推动风筝文化事业高质量的发展，更好地满足人们对休闲娱乐和追求美好生活的需求。在本书编写过程中，有幸得到风筝界诸多前辈、同仁的厚爱支持，有的无偿提供了文章、照片等资料，还有的于百忙之中帮助修改校对。尤其知名英文翻译马瑶女士，在时间紧、工作量大，又身怀有孕的情况下，不辞辛苦，加班加点，认真负责地独立完成了本书主体部分的翻译。在此，特别感谢马瑶、孙立荣、姜连绍、刘镇、张基振、张良瑞、邓华、梁文道、程静、张金玉、申燕祥、程英华、尚兰柱、台兰德、窦浩智、李中伟、侯江宏、葛晓鹏、高威、秦杰杰、李林、齐鹏、丁传信、邢顺建、王永训、康朋、李宗成、于灏、张小光、陈永雄、徐远洲、梁耀忠、邓健明等同志的大力支持和无私帮助。同时，山东公远律师事务所为本书提供了法律服务；本书也借鉴吸收了有关媒体的文章资料，一并表示真诚谢意。

本书将作为业务研讨和交流读物，向风筝界同仁、有关博物馆、图书馆、大专院校等提供赠阅。

因时间仓促，水平有限，本书一定还有不尽如人的地方。对本书的错误和疏漏之处，恳请读者批评指正。

编者

Postscript

The book "Kite Festivals and Competitions in the World" was written to systematically introduce famous kites competition, related festivals, exhibitions and venues, to summarize and exchange the kite competitions and kite culture exchange at home and abroad, to popularize kite sports, to carry forward the kite culture, to promote the development of the kite industry and its experience and practice, to facilitate the exchange, learning and reference of the colleagues in the kite field, to continuously enhance the internationalism, ornamental value, participation and brand value of the kite competition, and promote the kite culture career at a higher starting point to meets people's needs for leisure and pursuit of a better life. In the process of writing this book, I was honored to receive the support of many seniors and colleagues in the kite field. Some of them provided articles, photos and other materials free of charge, and others helped to modify the text. Especially well-known English translator Mrs. Ma Yao, being pregnant during the translation of the book, worked hard and completed the translation of the main part of the book independently in a very limit of time. Hereby, I would like to show gratitude to Ma Yao, Sun Lirong, Jiang Lianshao, Liu Zhen, Zhang Jizhen, Zhang Liangrui, Deng Hua, Liang Wencao, Cheng Jing, Zhang Jinyu, Shen Yanxiang, Cheng Yinghua, Shang Lanzhu, Tai Lande, Dou Haozhi, Li Zhongwei, Hou Jianghong, Ge Xiaopeng, Gao Wei, Qin Jiejie, Li Lin, Qi Peng, Ding Chuanxin, Xing Shunjian, Wang Yongxun, Kang Peng, Li Zongcheng, Yu Hao, Zhang Xiaoguang, Chen Yongxiong, Xu Yuanzhou, Liang Yaozhong and Deng Jianming etc. Meanwhile, Shandong Gongyuan Law Firm has provided legal services for this book. In the editing of this book, relevant articles and data were chosen for reference. Hereby, I would like to expresses my sincere gratitude.

This book will serve as reading materials for study and exchange, and will be provided for free to colleagues in the field of kite, related museums, libraries, colleges and universities, etc.

For the errors and omissions of this book due to time limit and other reasons, please don' t hesitate to contact the editor of this book.

Editor